POWERSCORE
TEST PREPARATION

LSAT
LOGIC GAMES
SETUPS
ENCYCLOPEDIA
VOLUME 1: LSAT PREPTESTS 1 THROUGH 20

**Optimal setups for every LSAT
Logic Game from PrepTest 1 through 20!**

Published by
PowerScore Publishing, a division of PowerScore Incorporated
57 Hasell Street
Charleston, SC 29401

Author: David M. Killoran

Manufactured in Canada
April 2011

ISBN: 978-0-9826618-5-7

PowerScore Publications

PowerScore LSAT Logic Games Bible

The ultimate guide for attacking the analytical reasoning section of the LSAT. *The LSAT Logic Games Bible* features a detailed methodology for attacking the games section, extensive drills, and 30 real LSAT logic games with detailed analyses.

Available on the PowerScore website for $51.99.
Website: www.powerscore.com/pubs.htm

PowerScore LSAT Logic Games Bible Workbook

The PowerScore LSAT Logic Games Bible Workbook™ is the ideal companion to the *PowerScore Logic Games Bible™*, providing the opportunity to apply the concepts and approaches presented in the renowned *Games Bible*. *The Logic Games Workbook* contains thirty logic games, reproduced in their entirety from actual released past LSATs, and multiple drills created to reinforce the skills you need to effectively attack the Logic Games section. Each game's answer key presents an ideal setup for the game, with every rule and important logical inference discussed and diagrammed, and all of the questions answered and explained.

Available on the PowerScore website for $29.99.
Website: www.powerscore.com/pubs.htm

PowerScore LSAT Game Type Training

LSAT Game Type Training provides you with the complete text of every LSAT Logic Game from LSAT PrepTests 1 through 20, sorted according to the games classification system created by PowerScore and used in the *PowerScore LSAT Logic Games Bible*.

Containing 80 different games, including hard-to-find games from the early PrepTests, this book is an ideal training tool to increase your LSAT Logic Games score.

Available on the PowerScore website for $29.99.
Website: www.powerscore.com/pubs.htm

PowerScore LSAT Game Type Training II

LSAT Game Type Training II provides you with the complete text of every LSAT Logic Game from LSAT PrepTests 21 through 40, sorted according to the games classification system created by PowerScore and used in the *PowerScore LSAT Logic Games Bible*. Containing 80 different games, this book is an ideal training tool to increase your LSAT Logic Games score.

Available on the PowerScore website for $44.99.
Website: www.powerscore.com/pubs.htm

PowerScore LSAT Logical Reasoning Bible

One of the most highly anticipated publications in LSAT history, the *PowerScore LSAT Logical Reasoning Bible™* is a comprehensive how-to manual for solving every type of Logical Reasoning question. Featuring over 100 real Logical Reasoning questions with detailed explanations, the Bible is the ultimate resource for improving your LSAT Logical Reasoning score.

Available on the PowerScore website for $49.99.
Website: www.powerscore.com/pubs.htm

PowerScore Flashcards

PowerScore Logic Games Bible Flashcards

The Logic Games Bible Flashcards relay and test foundational concepts such as games terminology, game-type recognition, and rule language, as well as advanced conceptual approaches including conditional reasoning, formal logic, and numerical distribution. Mini-challenges allow test takers to develop the skills necessary to create effective diagrams and draw sound logical inferences. Each set includes 140 cards that test the concepts and approaches to logic games taught in the *PowerScore LSAT Logic Games Bible* and in PowerScore LSAT courses.

Available on the PowerScore website for $24.99.
Website: www.powerscore.com/pubs.htm

PowerScore Logical Reasoning Bible Flashcards

The Logical Reasoning Bible Flashcards introduce and test concepts taught in our courses and in PowerScore's LSAT Logical Reasoning Bible. The flashcards cover everything from foundational definitions and question type recognition to more advanced Logical Reasoning skills, including causal reasoning, conditional reasoning, and understanding formal logic. *The Logical Reasoning Bible Flashcards* can be used as a stand-alone study aid, or as an ideal complement to the renowned *Logical Reasoning Bible*.

Available on the PowerScore website for $29.99.
Website: www.powerscore.com/pubs.htm

Tutoring and Admissions Counseling

PowerScore LSAT Private, Virtual, and Telephone Tutoring

PowerScore Private Tutoring gives students the opportunity to work one-on-one with a PowerScore Tutor for the most customized approach to LSAT preparation. Whether you need personalized lesson plans or just want to review a few concepts, PowerScore can create a tutoring plan that suits your specific needs.

Our tutors have all scored in the 99th percentile on an actual LSAT. Aside from having mastered the test themselves, every PowerScore tutor can clearly explain the underlying principles of the LSAT and the most effective approaches to the test.

PowerScore offers hourly tutoring as well as tutoring packages. Please visit www.powerscore.com, or call 1-800-545-1750 for more information.

PowerScore Law School Admissions Counseling

While your LSAT score and GPA will undeniably be major factors during your admissions cycle, to truly separate yourself from the rest of the applicant pool you must assemble the most powerful application folder possible. To do this you must have an outstanding personal statement, top-notch letters of recommendation, and flawless overall presentation.

PowerScore has gathered a team of admissions experts—including former law school admissions board members, top lawyers, and students from top-twenty law schools—to address your admissions counseling and personal statement needs and help you get to where you want to be.

Please visit www.powerscore.com, or call 1-800-545-1750 for more information.

CONTENTS

INTRODUCTION

CHAPTER ONE: JUNE 1991 LSAT GAMES

CHAPTER TWO: OCTOBER 1991 LSAT GAMES

CHAPTER THREE: DECEMBER 1991 LSAT GAMES

CHAPTER FOUR: FEBRUARY 1992 LSAT GAMES

CHAPTER FIVE: JUNE 1992 LSAT GAMES

CHAPTER SIX: OCTOBER 1992 LSAT GAMES

CHAPTER SEVEN: FEBRUARY 1993 LSAT GAMES

CHAPTER EIGHT: JUNE 1993 LSAT GAMES

CHAPTER NINE: OCTOBER 1993 LSAT GAMES

CHAPTER TEN: FEBRUARY 1994 LSAT GAMES

CHAPTER ELEVEN: JUNE 1994 LSAT GAMES

CHAPTER TWELVE: OCTOBER 1994 LSAT GAMES

CHAPTER THIRTEEN: DECEMBER 1994 LSAT GAMES

CHAPTER FOURTEEN: FEBRUARY 1995 LSAT GAMES

CHAPTER FIFTEEN: JUNE 1995 LSAT GAMES

CHAPTER SIXTEEN: SEPTEMBER 1995 LSAT GAMES

CHAPTER SEVENTEEN: DECEMBER 1995 LSAT GAMES

CHAPTER EIGHTEEN: DECEMBER 1992 LSAT GAMES

CHAPTER NINETEEN: JUNE 1996 LSAT GAMES

CHAPTER TWENTY: OCTOBER 1996 LSAT GAMES

ENDNOTES

About PowerScore

PowerScore is one of the nation's fastest growing test preparation companies. Founded in 1997, PowerScore offers LSAT, GMAT, GRE, and SAT preparation classes in over 150 locations in the U.S. and abroad. Offerings include Full-length courses, Weekend courses, Virtual courses, and private tutoring. For more information, please visit our website at www.powerscore.com or call us at (800) 545-1750.

For supplemental information about this book, please visit the *Logic Games Setups Encyclopedia* website at www.powerscore.com/lsatbibles.

About the Author

David M. Killoran is an expert in test preparation with over 20 years of teaching experience and a 99th percentile score on a Law Services-administered LSAT. In addition to having written the renowned *PowerScore LSAT Logic Games Bible*, the *PowerScore LSAT Logical Reasoning Bible*, and many other popular publications, Dave has overseen the preparation of countless students and founded two national LSAT preparation companies.

INTRODUCTION

Introduction

Welcome to the *PowerScore LSAT Logic Games Setups Encyclopedia*. This book provides you with complete setups and explanations for each Logic Game on LSAT PrepTests 1 through 20.

The *Setups Encyclopedia* is intended for anyone studying the LSAT who wishes to improve their Logic Games performance. The book uses the diagramming methodology, approaches, and terminology from the *PowerScore LSAT Logic Games Bible*, and a working knowledge of those techniques will increase the value you derive from the *Setups Encyclopedia*. If you do not currently own a copy of the *PowerScore LSAT Logic Games Bible*, we strongly recommend that you purchase one immediately. If you already own a copy of the *Games Bible*, we recommend that you complete that book prior to using this book.

Each chapter of this book contains setups, notes, and question explanations for each of the four Logic Games that appears on each released LSAT. This book does *not* contain reproductions of the games themselves. This is because many students already have copies of the games, and adding those games would have added prohibitively to the book's cost. If you do not have all of the games in this book, you can purchase PowerScore's *LSAT Logic Games: Game Type Training*, which contains the complete text of every LSAT Logic Game from LSAT PrepTests 1 through 20. If you already have many of the games and are just looking for a few select tests, those can often be purchased directly from PowerScore or Law Services.

The LSATs containing the Logic Games covered in this book can be purchased through our website at powerscore.com.

Because access to accurate and up-to-date information is critical, we have devoted a section of our website to *Setups Encyclopedia* students. This free online resource area provides updates to the book as needed, and contains a cross-reference listing the source location of each game in this book. The exclusive *LSAT Logic Games Setups Encyclopedia* online area can be accessed at:

www.powerscore.com/lsatbibles

You can also visit our LSAT Discussion Forum to ask questions of the author and talk to other students. That site is at:

forum.powerscore.com/lsat

Finally, if you have any questions or comments about the material in this book, please do not hesitate to contact us via email at lsatbibles@powerscore.com. We look forward to hearing from you!

A Brief Overview of the LSAT

The Law School Admission Test is administered four times a year: in February, June, September/October, and December. This standardized test is required for admission to any American Bar Association-approved law school. According to Law Services, the producers of the test, the LSAT is designed "to measure skills that are considered essential for success in law school: the reading and comprehension of complete texts with accuracy and insight; the organization and management of information and the ability to draw reasonable inferences from it; the ability to reason critically; and the analysis and evaluation of the reasoning and argument of others." The LSAT consists of the following five sections:

- 2 Sections of Logical Reasoning (short arguments, 24-26 total questions)
- 1 Section of Reading Comprehension (3 long reading passages, 2 short comparative reading passages, 26-28 total questions)
- 1 Section of Analytical Reasoning (4 logic games, 22-24 total questions)
- 1 Experimental Section of one of the above three section types.

You are given 35 minutes to complete each section. The experimental section is unscored and is not returned to the test taker. A break of 10 to 15 minutes is given between the 3rd and 4th sections.

The five-section test is followed by a 35 minute writing sample.

The Logical Reasoning Section

Each Logical Reasoning Section is composed of approximately 24 to 26 short arguments. Every short argument is followed by a question such as: "Which one of the following weakens the argument?" "Which one of the following parallels the argument?" or "Which one of the following must be true according to the argument?" The key to this section is time management and an understanding of the reasoning types and question types that frequently appear.

Since there are two scored sections of Logical Reasoning on every LSAT, this section accounts for approximately 50% of your score.

The Analytical Reasoning Section

This section, also known as Logic Games, is probably the most difficult for students taking the LSAT for the first time. The section consists of four games or puzzles, each followed by a series of five to eight questions. The questions are designed to test your ability to evaluate a set of relationships and to make inferences about those relationships. To perform well on this section you must understand the major types of games that frequently appear and develop the ability to properly diagram the rules and make inferences.

At the conclusion of the LSAT, and for six calendar days after the LSAT, you have the option to cancel your score. Unfortunately, there is no way to determine exactly what your score would be before cancelling.

The Reading Comprehension Section

This section is composed of three long reading passages, each approximately 450 words in length, and two shorter comparative reading passages. The passage topics are drawn from a variety of subjects, and each passage is followed by a series of five to eight questions that ask you to determine viewpoints in the passage, analyze organizational traits, evaluate specific sections of the passage, or compare facets of two different passages. The key to this section is to read quickly with understanding and to carefully analyze the passage structure.

The Experimental Section

Each LSAT contains one experimental section, and it does not count towards your score. The experimental can be any of the three section types described above, and the purpose of the section is to test and evaluate questions that will be used on *future* LSATs. By pretesting questions before their use in a scored section, the experimental section helps the makers of the test determine the test scale.

The Writing Sample

A 35 minute Writing Sample is given at the conclusion of the LSAT. The Writing Sample is not scored, but a copy is sent to each of the law schools to which you apply.

For many years the Writing Sample was administered before the LSAT.

The format of the Writing Sample is called the Decision Prompt: you are asked to consider two possible courses of action, decide which one is superior, and then write a short essay supporting your choice. Each course of action is described in a short paragraph and you are given two primary criteria to consider in making your decision. Typically the two courses of action each have different strengths and weaknesses, and there is no clearly correct decision.

Do not agonize over the Writing Sample; in law school admissions, the Writing Sample is usually not a primary determining element for three reasons: the admissions committee is aware that the essay is given after a grueling three hour test and is about a subject you have no personal interest in; they already have a better sample of your writing ability in the personal statement; and the committee has a limited amount of time to evaluate applications.

You must attempt the Writing Sample! If you do not, Law Services reserves the right not to score your test.

The LSAT Scoring Scale

Each administered LSAT contains approximately 101 questions, and each LSAT score is based on the total number of questions a test taker correctly answers, a total known as the raw score. After the raw score is determined, a unique Score Conversion Chart is used for each LSAT to convert the raw score into a scaled LSAT score. Since June 1991, the LSAT has utilized a 120 to 180 scoring scale, with 120 being the lowest possible score and 180 being the highest possible score. Notably, this 120 to 180 scale is just a renumbered version of the 200 to 800 scale most test takers are familiar with from the SAT and GMAT. Just drop the "1" and add a "0" to the 120 and 180.

Although the number of questions per test has remained relatively constant over the last eight years, the overall logical difficulty of each test has varied. This is not surprising since the test is made by humans and there is no precise way to completely predetermine logical difficulty. To account for these variances in test "toughness," the test makers adjust the Scoring Conversion Chart for each LSAT in order to make similar LSAT scores from different tests mean the same thing. For example, the LSAT given in June may be logically more difficult than the LSAT given in December, but by making the June LSAT scale "looser" than the December scale, a 160 on each test would represent the same level of performance. This scale adjustment, known as equating, is extremely important to law school admissions offices around the country. Imagine the difficulties that would be posed by unequated tests: admissions officers would have to not only examine individual LSAT scores, but also take into account which LSAT each score came from. This would present an information nightmare.

The LSAT Percentile Table

Since the LSAT has 61 possible scores, why didn't the test makers change the scale to 0 to 60? Probably for merciful reasons. How would you tell your friends that you scored a 3 on the LSAT? 123 sounds so much better.

It is important not to lose sight of what LSAT scaled scores actually represent. The 120 to 180 test scale contains 61 different possible scores. Each score places a student in a certain relative position compared to other test takers. These relative positions are represented through a percentile that correlates to each score. The percentile indicates where the test taker ranks in the overall pool of test takers. For example, a score of 163 represents the 90th percentile, meaning a student with a score of 163 scored better than 90 percent of the people who have taken the test in the last three years. The percentile is critical since it is a true indicator of your positioning relative to other test takers, and thus law school applicants.

Charting out the entire percentage table yields a rough "bell curve." The number of test takers in the 120s and 170s is very low (only 1.6% of all test takers receive a score in the 170s), and most test takers are bunched in the middle, comprising the "top" of the bell. In fact, approximately 40% of all test takers score between 145 and 155 inclusive, and about 70% of all test takers score between 140 and 160 inclusive.

The median score on the LSAT scale is approximately 151. The median, or middle, score is the score at which approximately 50% of test takers have a lower score and 50% of test takers have a higher score. Typically, to achieve a score of 151, you must answer between 56 and 61 questions correctly from a total of 101 questions. In other words, to achieve a score that is perfectly average, you can miss between 40 and 45 questions. Thus, it is important to remember that you don't have to answer every question correctly in order to receive an excellent LSAT score. There is room for error, and accordingly you should never let any single question occupy an inordinate amount of your time.

There is no penalty for answering incorrectly on the LSAT. Therefore, you should guess on any questions you cannot complete.

The Use of the LSAT

The use of the LSAT in law school admissions is not without controversy. It is largely taken for granted that your LSAT score is one of the most important determinants of the type of school you can attend. At many law schools a multiplier made up of your LSAT score and your undergraduate grade point average is used to help determine the relative standing of applicants, and at some schools a sufficiently high multiplier guarantees your admission.

For all the importance of the LSAT, it is not without flaws. As a standardized test currently given in the paper-and-pencil format, there are a number of skills that the LSAT cannot measure, such as listening skills, note-taking ability, perseverance, etc. Law Services is aware of these limitations and as a matter of course they warn all law schools about overemphasizing LSAT results. Still, since the test ultimately returns a number for each student, it is hard to escape the tendency to rank applicants accordingly. Fortunately, once you get to law school the LSAT is forgotten. For the time being consider the test a temporary hurdle you must leap in order to reach the ultimate goal.

For more information on the LSAT, or to register for the test, contact Law Services at (215) 968-1001 or at their website at www.lsac.org.

The Analytical Reasoning Section

As you know, the focus of this book is on the Analytical Reasoning section. Each Analytical Reasoning section contains four games and a total of 22-24 questions. Since you have thirty-five minutes to complete the section, you have an average of eight minutes and forty-five seconds to complete each game. Of course, the amount of time you spend on each game will vary with the difficulty and the number of questions per game. For many students, the time constraint is what makes Logic Games the most difficult section on the LSAT, and as we present the explanations in this book, we will discuss occasional time-saving tips and methods for solving questions more quickly.

Each logic game contains three separate parts: the scenario, the rules, and the questions.

The Scenario

The game scenario introduces sets of variables—people, places, things, or events—involved in an easy to understand activity such as sitting in seats or singing songs. Here is an example of a game scenario:

> Seven comics—Janet, Khan, Leticia, Ming, Neville, Olivia, and Paul—will be scheduled to perform in the finals of a comedy competition. During the evening of the competition, each comic, performing alone, will give exactly one performance.

In the above scenario there are two variable sets: the comics J, K, L, M, N, O, and P, and the seven performance positions, which would be numbered 1 through 7.

In basic terms, the scenario "sets the table" for the game and provides you with a quick picture of the situation to be analyzed. Although many game scenarios simply introduce the variables, on occasion the test makers place numerical information in the scenario, and this information is critical to understanding the possibilities inherent in the game.

Because you cannot afford to misunderstand any of the basics of the game, you must read the game scenario very closely.

On average, you have 8 minutes and 45 seconds to complete each game.

Always write down and keep track of each variable set.

The Rules

The second part of every game is the rules—a set of statements that describe and control the relationships between the variables. Here are the rules that accompany the above game scenario:

> Neville performs either second or sixth.
> Paul performs at some time after Leticia performs.
> Janet performs at some time after Khan performs.
> There is exactly one performance between Neville's performance and Olivia's performance, whether or not Neville performs before Olivia performs.

Each of the initial rules in a game applies to each and every question; however, on occasion a question will explicitly suspend one or more rules for the purposes of that question only. These "suspension" questions always occur at the end of the game.

The initial rules apply to every question unless otherwise indicated.

The third and final part of each logic game is a set of approximately five to eight questions that test your knowledge of the relationships between the variables, the structural features of the game, and the way those relationships and features change as conditions in the game change. More on the questions in a moment.

Approaching the Games

As you begin each game you should carefully and completely read through the entire game scenario and all of the rules *before* you begin writing. This initial reading will help you determine the type of game you are facing, as well as what variable sets exist and what relationships govern their actions. This advice will save you time by allowing you to formulate an exact plan of action, and it will save you from diagramming a rule and then re-diagramming if you find a later rule that alters the situation. At this point in the game you must also fix the rules in your memory. Students who fail to identify strongly with the rules inevitably struggle with the questions. It is also important to identify the most powerful rules in a game and to consider how the rules interact with one another. Of course, we will discuss how to do this throughout our analysis.

Always read through the entire scenario and each rule before you begin diagramming.

In general, these are the initial steps you must take to efficiently move through each game:

1. Read through and fix the rules in your mind.
2. Diagram the scenario and the rules.
3. Make inferences.
4. Use the rules and inferences to attack the questions.

One of the goals of this book is to help you understand the ideal setup for each game you encounter.

Your initial reading of the game will also indicate what setup to use to attack the game. Many students are not aware of the best ways to set up logic games, and waste far too much time during the actual exam wondering what approach to take. Because you must read the rules and set up a diagram quickly and efficiently, the key to succeeding on the Logic Games section is to know the ideal approach to every game type before walking into the exam.

Make a main diagram at the bottom of the page.

You should use the space at the bottom of each game page to diagram your initial setup. This setup should include:

1. A list of the variables and their number. For example: J K L M N O P [7]
2. An identification of any randoms in the game (randoms are variables that do not appear in any rules).
3. A diagrammatic representation of the variable sets.
4. A diagrammatic representation of the rules.
5. A list of inferences. Making inferences involves deducing hidden rules or facts from the given relationships between variables. Inferences almost always follow from a combination of the rules or limiting structural factors within the game.

By following the above list and using the scenario and rules from the previous pages, we can produce this game setup:

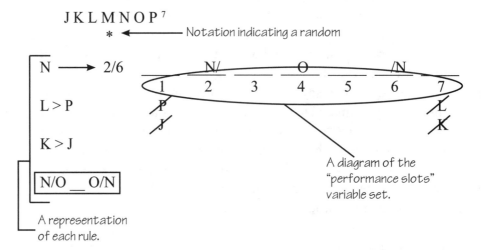

The above setup is linear in nature, on of the most common types of Logic Games.

After making the initial setup, do not write on your main diagram.

Once you have completed your game setup, you should *not* draw or otherwise write on your main diagram again. As you do each question, use the space *next* to the question to reproduce a miniature diagram with the basic structural features of your main diagram. You should *not* use your main diagram for the work of individual questions. For example, if a question introduces the condition that L sits in the third of seven chairs, draw the seven chair spaces next to the question, place L in the third space, make inferences, and then proceed with the question. Refer to your main setup for the details of the relationship between the variables. There are several important benefits that you receive from working next to the question: First, should you need to return to the question later, your work will be readily available and accessible; second, keeping the individual conditions of each question separate from the main setup reduces the possibility that you will mistake a local condition for a global rule; and third, you will be able to more clearly see which conditions produced which results.

Do the work for each question next to that question.

As you complete each question, it is absolutely essential that you *not* erase your previous work. Each question that you complete adds to your repository of game knowledge, and that knowledge can be invaluable when answering other questions. For example, suppose the first question in a game produces a scenario where A is in the first position. Then, the second question asks for a complete and accurate listing of the positions A can occupy. Based on the first question, A can clearly be in the first position, and therefore you can eliminate any answer in the second question which does not contain the first position as a possibility. Thus, the work you do in *some* questions can be used to help answer other questions. This is true as long as the work you are referencing conforms to the conditions in the question you are currently answering. For example, if the third question in the same game states, "If A is in the third position, which of the following can be true?" then you cannot use the information from the first question to help answer the third question because A was in the first position in the first question, and thus does not fit the condition imposed in the third question.

Do not erase unless you make a mistake.

The work done on some questions can be used to help solve other questions.

For students who ignore the above recommendations, the results are often quite negative: confusion, disorganization, constant rereading of the rules, and missed questions. Some students say that they save time by using their main diagram for each question. While they may save a short amount of time, the overall costs always outweigh the benefits, particularly since those same students have a tendency to erase during the game. As we proceed with our analysis of the games section, we will revisit this topic from time to time and further confirm the efficacy of our recommendations.

Once you have completed your diagram and made inferences, you will be ready to answer the questions. Keep in mind that each question has exactly the same value and that there is no penalty for guessing. Thus, if you cannot complete the section you should guess on the questions that remain. If you cannot complete an individual question, do not spend an undue amount of time on the question. Instead, move on and complete the other questions.

Games questions are either global or local. Global questions ask about information derived only from the initial rules, such as "Who can finish first?" or "Which one of the following must be true?" Use the rules and your main diagram to answer global questions. Local questions generally begin with the words "if," "when," or "suppose," and occur when the question imposes a new condition in addition to the initial rules, such as "If Laura sits in the third chair, which one of the following must be true?" The additional conditions imposed by local questions apply to that question only and do not apply to any of the other questions. It is essential that you focus on the implications of the new conditions. Ask yourself how this condition affects the variables and the existing rules. For local questions, reproduce a mini-setup next to the question, apply the local condition, and proceed.

Local questions almost always require you to produce a "mini-setup" next to the question.

Within the global/local designation all questions ultimately ask for one of four things: what must be true, what is not necessarily true, what could be true, and what cannot be true. All questions are a variation of one of these four basic ideas. At all times, you must be aware of the exact nature of the question you are being asked, especially when "except" questions appear. If you find that you are missing questions because you miss words such as "false" or "except" when reading, then take a moment at the beginning of the game to circle the key words in each question, words such as "must," "could," etc.

If you frequently misread questions, circle the key part of each question before you begin the game. You will not forget about a word like "except" if you have it underlined!

The key to quickly answering questions is to identify with the rules and inferences in a game. This involves both properly diagramming the rules and simple memorization. If you often find yourself rereading the rules during a game, you are failing to identify with the rules. And do not forget to constantly apply your inferences to each question!

Attacking the Section

The key to optimal performance on Logic Games is to be focused and organized. This involves a number of factors:

1. Play to your strengths and away from your weaknesses

You are not required to do the games in the order presented on the test, and you should not expect that the test makers will present the games in the best order for you. Students who expect to have difficulty on the games section should attack the games in order of their personal preferences and strengths and weaknesses. You can implement this strategy by quickly previewing each of the four games as you start the section. By doing so you can then select a game that you feel is the best fit for your strengths.

2. Create a strong setup for the game

Often, the key to powerful games performance is to create a good setup. At least 80% of the games on the LSAT are "setup games" wherein the quality of your setup dictates whether or not you are successful in answering the questions. Mastering those elements will help you become an expert in handling any type of game.

3. Look to make inferences

There are always inferences in a game, and the test makers expect you to make at least a few of them. Always check the rules and your setup with an eye towards finding inferences, and then use those inferences relentlessly to attack the questions.

4. Be smart during the game

If necessary, skip over time consuming questions and return to them later. Remember that it is sometimes advisable to do the questions out of order. For example, if the first question in a game asks you for a complete and accurate list of the positions "C" could occupy, because of time considerations it would be advisable to skip that question and complete the remaining questions. Then you could return to the first question and use the knowledge you gained from the other questions to quickly and easily answer the first question.

5. Do not be intimidated by size

A lengthy game scenario and a large number of initial rules do not necessarily equal greater difficulty. Some of the longest games are easy because they contain so many restrictions and limitations.

Although test takers have found the first game on many LSATs to be the easiest, there is no set order of difficulty, and you cannot predict where the easiest or hardest game will appear. On some tests the first game has been the hardest and the last game has been the easiest. That said, for the majority of LSATs, the hardest game usually appears second or third, and the easiest game usually appears first.

6. Keep an awareness of time

As stated previously, you have approximately eight minutes and forty-five seconds to complete each game and bubble in your answers. Use a timer during the LSAT so you always know how much time remains, and do not let one game or question consume so much time that you suffer later on.

7. Maintain a positive attitude and concentrate

Above all, you must attack each game with a positive and energetic attitude. The games themselves are often challenging yet fun, and students who actively involve themselves in the games generally perform better overall.

If you do all four games, you have 8 minutes and 45 seconds to complete each game, inclusive of answer transferring. If you do only three games, you have 11 minutes and 40 seconds to complete each game. If you do just two games, you have 17 minutes and 30 seconds to complete each game.

You can do the games out of order and according to your strengths and weaknesses.

There are three parts to every Logic Game: the scenario, the rules, and the questions.

Always read the scenario and rules once through before you begin diagramming.

Fix the rules in your mind.

Make a main diagram for each game. Include the following:
        List the variables and their exact total number
        Identify Randoms
        Diagram the variable sets
        Diagram the rules
        Make inferences
        Identify the powerful rules and variables

Write neatly.

You can do the questions out of order if it saves time or is more efficient.

For local questions, do your work next to the question.

Always look to use your inferences when answering questions.

Do not erase unless you have made a mistake.

Do not forget that work from one question might be useful on other questions.

Maintain a positive attitude, concentrate, and try to enjoy yourself.

Memorize these points! They are basic principles you must know in order to perform powerfully.

The following pages contain game setups organized by chapter. Each chapter contains the setups for the four games from a single LSAT, and the chapters are presented in order according to PrepTest number. Thus, the setups for PrepTest 1, the June 1991 LSAT, are presented first.

The chapters do not have traditional "chapter divider" headings. Instead, each chapter has a numbered tab along the side of the page with the PrepTest number of the games explained in the chapter. Each game is introduced by a header that indicates the exact source and position of the game, for example, "June 1995 Game #1: Questions 1-6." Finally, at the bottom of each right-hand page is a reference to the month and year of the LSAT games in the chapter, for example, "Chapter Ten: February 1994 Logic Game Setups." In addition, the Table of Contents lists the start page of each chapter. You can quickly find game setups within the book by referring to the side, top, or bottom of each page, or by referring to the Table of Contents.

POWERSCORE®

1

PREPTEST

JUNE 1991 LOGIC GAMES SETUPS

PrepTest 1. June 1991 Game #1: *1. B 2. A 3. B 4. E 5. E 6. C 7. E*

This is a Circular Linearity game.

This is the very first game of the first LSAT of the modern era (marked by the introduction of the 120-180 scoring scale). It is also the last time a Circular Linearity game appeared in a released LSAT section before another Circular game appeared in October 2003. The setup is as follows:

K L M N O P[6]

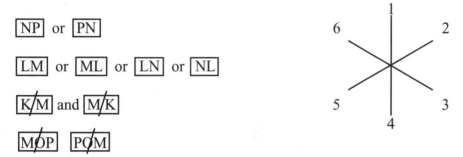

Since there are six chairs and six trade representatives, this is a Balanced game. The chair numbers prove to be relevant only on Question #1. Since the game contains no rules of opposition, the best defined block, PN, should be placed on the diagram:

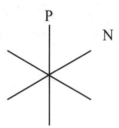

The placement of the PN block is arbitrary. They could be placed at the end of any pair of spokes, and could be in the order PN or NP. Do not assume that P and N are in chairs 1 and 2. Nevertheless, it is important to place the block on the diagram, as it will provide a starting point for adding other variables.

The final rule also bears further analysis. The rule states, "If O sits immediately next to P, O does not sit immediately next to M." Accordingly, every time O and P sit next to each other, then M cannot sit next to O and the configurations MOP and POM are impossible. Even though the rule can be written as a conditional, the representation we have provided is superior since it is easier to apply from a visual standpoint.

Question #1: Global, Cannot Be True, List. The correct answer choice is (B)

Employ the rules in order of ease of application: answer choice (E) can be eliminated since P and N are separated; an application of the KM rule eliminates answer choice (D) (Remember, chairs 1 and 6 are next to each on the circular table!); an application of the LM or LN rule eliminates answer choice (A); and finally, an application of the MOP rule eliminates answer choice (C). Answer choice (B) is correct.

Because none of the rest of the questions include the chair numbers, the rest of the game can be treated as a basic linear exercise.

Question #2: Local, Must Be True. The correct answer choice is (A)

The Local condition in the question stem produces the following mini-diagram:

Since P and N are a block, when L sits next to P, either an LPN or NPL block is formed (the diagram above has LPN). Since L must sit next to N or M, and N is already occupied, it follows that M must sit next to L. There are now only two open spaces. Since K cannot sit next to M, K must sit next to N. O sits in the final chair, next to K and M. Answer choice (A) is correct.

Question #3: Local, Must Be True. The correct answer choice is (B)

The Local condition in the question stem produces the following mini-diagram:

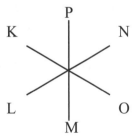

Adding the Local condition to the PN block produces a L-K-P-N sequence. Since L must sit next to M or N, M must sit next to L, and, again, O sits in the final chair. Answer choice (B) is correct.

Question #4: Local, Could Be True. The correct answer choice is (E)

Adding the Local condition to the PN block produces a P-N-M sequence. Since L must sit next to M or N, L must sit next to M. Since there are no restrictions on K or O, they form a dual-option:

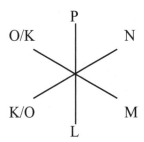

Consequently answer choice (E) is correct.

Question #5: Local, Could Be True, List. The correct answer choice is (E)

The question stem solidifies the second rule to establish that L is sitting next to M. Since this information does not allow a complete diagram to be created, the best approach is to quickly refer to previous questions to see if any meet the criteria that L and M sit next to each other. If so, the work in those questions can be used to attack question #5.

In question #1 L and M are seated next to each other, so the hypothetical created by the correct answer in #1, K-L-M-P-N-O, can be used to prove that L can sit next to K. Accordingly, any answer choice in question #5 that does not contain K must be eliminated. Answer choice (C) can be discarded. Next, consider the work done in question #2. The solution meets the criteria that L and M sit next to each other, and reveals that L can sit next to P. Again, any answer choice that does not contain P must be rejected. Answer choices (A) and (B) can now be discarded. Only answer choices (D) and (E) remain. Question #3 also applies but only reveals that L can sit next to K, a fact established by the analysis of question #1. In question #4 it is shown that O can sit next to L, but since both answer choices (D) and (E) contain O, no progress is made. Since answer choices (D) and (E) are differentiated only by the presence of N, make a quick hypothetical to test N. The following hypothetical proves that N can sit next to L when L and M are seated next to each other:

Answer choice (E) is therefore correct.

Question #6: Local, Cannot Be True. The correct answer choice is (C)

If L sits next to N, a P-N-L sequence is created:

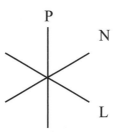

The three remaining variables are K, M, and O. Since K and M cannot sit next to each other, by Hurdling the Uncertainty we can infer that O must separate K and M:

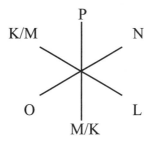

Since O is between K and M, answer choice (C) is correct.

Question #7: Local, Cannot Be True. The correct answer choice is (E)

The question stem creates a KO block. Since no obvious diagramming inferences can be made, reuse information, as was done in question #5.

The hypothetical from Question #1 applies since K and O are next to each other (remember, the first and last variables are next to each other); and this hypothetical proves that L can sit directly between K and M. That is sufficient to eliminate answer choice (A). The work from question #2 also applies and is sufficient to eliminate answer choice (D). Question #3 does not apply. Question #4 does apply and proves that L can sit between M and O (not in the answers) or M and K (already known from question #1). The hypothetical from question #6 must be examined closely. In spite of the fact that M and K rotate in the dual-option, K will always sit next to O, and thus the hypothetical reveals that L can sit between K and N as well as M and N. This information eliminates answer choices (B) and (C). Answer choice (E) is therefore correct via process of elimination.

This question again reveals the power of reusing previous work. With minimal effort all four incorrect answer choices are eliminated. And since the hypotheticals can be visually scanned at a high rate, the question takes less time than a question requiring a new diagram.

Circular Linearity games appear once in a blue moon, and it is not likely that one will appear on your test. Nevertheless, it is worthwhile to be acquainted with the basic principles in case such a game happens to appear.

This is an Advanced Linear: Balanced game.

This Advanced Linear game contains multiple variable sets, and choosing the base can be difficult. The four numbered offices and the three years both have an inherent sense of order, so you must look beyond that element in choosing the base. Ultimately, the four offices are the best base because with the offices as the base, you can show the connection of each computer and printer to that office in an organized fashion. The years can then be used "inside" the diagram:

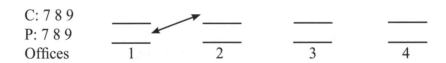

The first rule is a difficult rule to represent, and is ultimately the rule that causes the greatest number of issues in the game.

$$C \geq P$$

This representation captures the idea that the computer in each office was purchased in an earlier year or the same year as the printer in that office.

The second rule should be diagrammed internally, as in on the diagram:

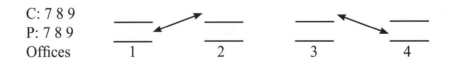

The third rule should also be diagrammed internally:

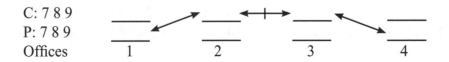

The fourth rule should also be diagrammed internally:

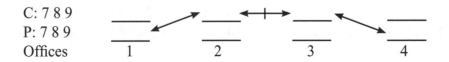

The last rule fixes two of the machines to an exact date:

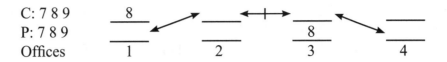

The final rule, in conjunction with first rule, allows us to infer that the printer in office 1 cannot have been purchased in 1987, and therefore must have been purchased in 1988 or 1989. We can also infer that the computer in office 3 cannot have been purchased in 1989, and therefore must have been purchased in 1987 or 1988. Both dual-options should be shown on the diagram:

```
C: 7 8 9      8                 ←——|——→  7/8
P: 7 8 9     8/9 ↖                        8
Offices       1        2          3        4
```

From the second rule, then, we can infer that the computer in office 2 was purchased in 1988 or 1989:

```
C: 7 8 9      8    ↗  8/9  ←——|——→  7/8
P: 7 8 9     8/9 ↖                   8
Offices       1        2        3        4
```

And from the third rule, we can infer that the printer in office 4 was purchased in 1987 or 1988:

```
C: 7 8 9      8    ↗  8/9  ←——|——→  7/8
P: 7 8 9     8/9 ↖                   8     ↘ 7/8
Offices       1        2        3        4
```

Finally, by reapplying the first rule, we can determine that the printer in office 2 cannot have been purchased in 1987, and therefore must have been purchased in 1988 or 1989, and that the computer in office 4 cannot have been purchased in 1989, and must have been purchased in 1987 or 1988. These two inferences lead to the final diagram:

```
C ≥ P     C: 7 8 9      8    ↗  8/9  ←——|——→  7/8         7/8
          P: 7 8 9     8/9 ↖   8/9             8     ↘     7/8
          Offices       1        2        3              4
```

The only considerations remaining are the exact years of each machine (determined in part by the action of the first rule) and the fourth rule about the computers in offices 2 and 3.

Question #8: Local, Could Be True. The correct answer choice is (B)

The question stem indicates that the computer in office 3 was bought in an earlier year than the printer in office 3. Because the printer in office 3 was purchased in 1988, we can infer that the computer in office 3 was purchased in 1987. In addition, from the third rule we can then infer that the printer in office 4 was purchased in 1987. Finally, from the first rule, we can infer that the computer in office 4 was purchased in 1987:

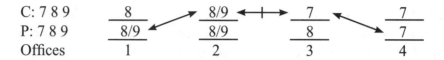

Accordingly, answer choice (B) could be true and is correct.

Question #9: Global, Could Be True. The correct answer choice is (D)

For this question, we need only to refer to the original game diagram, which shows that the printer in office 4 could have been purchased in 1988. Accordingly, only answer choice (D) is possible, and thus (D) is the correct answer.

Question #10: Local, Must Be True, Minimum. The correct answer choice is (A)

The question asks you to identify the minimum number of machines purchased in 1987. To answer this question, you must optimize the setup in a way that avoids 1987 as much as possible. As only the machines in offices 3 and 4 have any possibility of a machine purchased in 1987, start with those two offices and attempt to avoid purchases in 1987. As shown in the hypothetical below, the computer in office 4, the printer in office 4, and the computer in office 3 can all be purchased in 1988, resulting in no machines purchased in 1987:

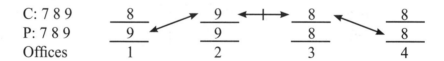

Accordingly, the correct answer is 0, answer choice (A).

Question #11: Local, Must Be True. The correct answer choice is (B)

If the computer in office 4 was bought in 1988, a chain reaction results that forces the printer in office 4 to have been purchased in 1988 (from the first rule), the computer in office 3 to have been purchased in 1988 (from the third rule), the computer in office 2 to have been bought in 1989 (from the fourth rule), the printer in office 2 to have been bought in 1989 (from the first rule), and the printer in office 1 to have been bought in 1989 (from the second rule), resulting in the following solution:

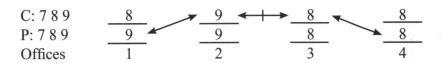

C: 7 8 9	8	9	8	8
P: 7 8 9	9	9	8	8
Offices	1	2	3	4

Accordingly, the correct answer choice is (B).

Note that, interestingly, the hypothetical produced in this answer choice could have been used to answer question #10.

Question #12: Local, Could Be True. The correct answer choice is (D)

If the computer in office 3 was purchased in 1988, then another chain reaction results. First, from the third rule, the printer in office 4 was purchased in 1988, and from the fourth rule, the computer in office 2 was purchased in 1989. And, because the computer in office 2 was purchased in 1989, we can infer from the first rule that the printer in office 2 was bought in 1989, and we can infer from the second rule that the printer in office 1 was bought in 1989. This leaves the purchase date of the computer in office 4 as the only uncertainty:

C: 7 8 9	8	9	8	7/8
P: 7 8 9	9	9	8	8
Offices	1	2	3	4

Because this is a Could Be True question, you should expect the answer to trade on an uncertainty in the game, and as the only uncertainty is the purchase date of the computer in office 4, immediately scan the answer choices for mentions of the computer in office 4. Only answer choice (D) addresses the computer in office 4, and as it is possible that the computer in office 4 was purchased in 1987, answer choice (D) is correct.

Question #13: Local, Could Be True, Suspension. The correct answer choice is (C)

The question stem suspends the fourth rule and replaces it with a rule that states that the computers in offices 2 and 3 were purchased in the same year. Because all of the other conditions remain the same, the only year that the two computers could have been purchased in is 1988 (this occurs because of the interaction of the fifth rule, first rule, and second rule). If the computers in offices 2 and 3 were purchased in 1988, then from the second and third rules, the printers in offices 1 and 4 must have been purchased in 1988. The only uncertainty, then, is whether the printer in office 2 was purchased in 1988 or 1989, and whether the computer in office 4 was purchased in 1987 or 1988:

C: 7 8 9	8	8	8	7/8
P: 7 8 9	8	8/9	8	8
Offices	1	2	3	4

Hence, only the printer in office 2 could have been purchased in 1989, and answer choice (C) is correct.

PrepTest 1. June 1991 Game #3: *14. C 15. E 16. D 17. B 18. D*

This is a Pure Sequencing game.

The rules combine to form the following sequencing diagram:

Variables: G H I J K M N O [8]

The arrows pointing to O and M serve the same purpose as "greater than" signs, and indicate that N joined the firm before O, and that J joined the firm before M. Note that the placement of O and M can appear deceiving if you just visually analyze the diagram. O appears to be "after" K and J, but it does not have to be, and it is possible for O to be hired before K. Similarly, M appears to be "after" H and N, but it does not have to be, and it is possible for M to be hired before H.

As with all sequences, you should analyze the possibilities for the first and last variables. In this case, either H or K is the partner who joined the firm in 1961, and O, I, or M is the partner who joined the firm in 1968.

Question #14: Global, Cannot Be True. The correct answer choice is (C)

Since H, N, K, and J must all have joined the law firm before G, it follows that 1965 is the earliest year in which G could have joined the firm. Therefore, it cannot be true that G joined the law firm in 1964. It follows that answer choice (C) is correct.

Question #15: Local, Cannot Be True. The correct answer choice is (E)

If J joined the law firm in 1962, then K must have joined the law firm in 1961:

$$\frac{K}{1} \quad \frac{J}{2} \quad \frac{\quad}{3} \quad \frac{\quad}{4} \quad \frac{\quad}{5}$$

Thus, if J joined the law firm in 1962, then it cannot be true that O joined the law firm in 1964, because both H and N must have joined the law firm before O. Under these circumstances, 1965 is the earliest year in which O could have joined the firm. Therefore, answer choice (E) is correct.

Question #16: Global, Must Be True, Maximum. The correct answer choice is (D)

Since M, G, and I must all have joined the law firm after J, 1965 is the latest year in which J could have joined the law firm. Therefore, answer choice (D) is correct.

Question #17: Local, Must Be True. The correct answer choice is (B)

If O joined the firm in 1965 and M joined the firm in 1967, then it must be true that I joined the firm in 1968 and that G joined the firm in 1966:

				O	G	M	I
1	2	3	4	5	6	7	8

However, it is still not possible to determine the exact years in which H, N, K, and J each joined the firm. Therefore, if O joined the firm in 1965 and M joined the firm in 1967, one can determine the years in which exactly <u>two</u> of the other partners joined the firm. It follows that answer choice (B) is correct.

Question #18: Local, Must Be True, Minimum. The correct answer choice is (D)

If O joined the law firm before M, then K, J, H, N, and O must all have joined the law firm before M. Under these circumstances, 1966 is the earliest year in which M could have joined the firm. Therefore, answer choice (D) is correct.

PrepTest 1. June 1991 Game #4: *19. E 20. A 21. A 22. B 23. E 24. C*

This is an Advanced Linear: Unbalanced: Underfunded game.

G P Y R [4]

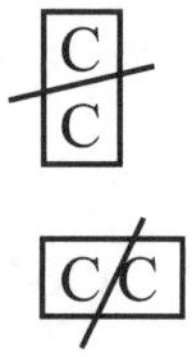

Jan: P R G/Y
Feb: R G Y

	1	2	3
Jan		P	G/
Feb			/G

The CC not blocks are a convenient way of noting that colors (“C”) cannot be identical for months or for lines.

Exactly two of the six sets of tickets must be red, and exactly one of the six sets must be purple.

Question #19: Local, Must Be True. The correct answer choice is (E)

The question stem produces the following setup:

	1	2	3
Jan	G/Y	P	R
Feb			G

If the line 3 tickets for January are R, then from the fifth rule the line 3 tickets for February must be G. Hence, answer choice (E) is correct.

Question #20: Local, Must Be True. The correct answer choice is (A)

The line 2 ticket that must be G is the February ticket. Because no other February ticket can be G, from the fifth rule we know that the January line 3 ticket is G. This forces the January line 1 ticket to be R, and from that inference we can deduce that the February line 1 ticket is not R, and instead must be Y. Because one February ticket must be R, we can deduce that February line 3 is R, leading to the following setup:

	1	2	3
Jan	R	P	G
Feb	Y	G	R

Hence, answer choice (A) is correct.

Question #21: Global, Could Be True. The correct answer choice is (A)

Answer choice (A) can be proven correct by the following hypothetical:

	R	P	Y
Jan	R	P	Y
Feb	Y	R	G
	1	2	3

This hypothetical shows that it could be true that no January ticket is green. Therefore, (A) is correct.

Question #22: Global, Could Be True. The correct answer choice is (B)

Answer choice (B) can be proven correct by the following hypothetical:

	Y	P	R
Jan	Y	P	R
Feb	R	Y	G
	1	2	3

This hypothetical shows that both the line 1 tickets for January and the line 2 tickets for February could be yellow. Therefore, (B) is correct.

Question #23: Local, Must Be True, Except. The correct answer choice is (E)

If the February line 3 tickets are Y, then from the fifth rule the January line 3 tickets must be G. With January filled for line 2 and 3, from the fourth rule we can determine that January line 1 is R. Using the second rule, the February line 1 tickets are then G, and that leaves the February line 2 tickets as R:

	R	P	G
Jan	R	P	G
Feb	G	R	Y
	1	2	3

Therefore, answer choice (E) is correct.

Question #24: Local, Could Be True, Suspension. The correct answer choice is (C)

If no ticket is P, then each month has one R, one G, and one Y. This information immediately eliminates answer choices (A) and (B).

Answer choice (C) can be proven correct by the following hypothetical:

	R	Y	G
Jan	R	Y	G
Feb	G	R	Y
	1	2	3

This hypothetical shows that it could be true that none of the line 2 tickets are green. Therefore, answer choice (C) is correct.

Answer choices (D) and (E) cannot be true because they would leave identical colors on the same line, a violation of the second rule.

POWERSCORE®

PREPTEST 2

OCTOBER 1991 LOGIC GAMES SETUPS

2

PrepTest 2. October 1991 Game #1: *1. D 2. A 3. A 4. E 5. D*

This is a Pure Sequencing: Identify the Possibilities game.

The eight rules of the game can be combined to form the following diagram:

Variables: B C D E F G H I J [9]

$$\begin{matrix} H \\ ------ \\ \boxed{F = I} \end{matrix} > D > E > B > J > \boxed{C = G}$$

This sequence controls the placement of variables over the seven days of hiring. Given the comprehensive nature of the sequence, and the relatively few uncertainties, the game does not appear to be overly difficult. In fact, there are only two possible solutions to this game:

Solution #2:	FI	H	D	E	B	J	CG
Solution #1:	H	FI	D	E	B	J	CG
	1	2	3	4	5	6	7

Although seeing the two solutions drawn out is helpful, it is not necessary because the sequence alone is so powerful that it is sufficient to answer most of the questions.

Question #1: Global, Must Be True. The correct answer choice is (D)

From the diagrams above, the workers hired last were C and G. Accordingly, answer choice (D) is correct.

Question #2: Global, Must Be True. The correct answer choice is (A)

E must have been hired on the fourth day, and consequently answer choice (A) is correct.

Question #3: Global, Must Be True. The correct answer choice is (A)

J must have been hired sixth, leaving six variables—H, F and I, D, E, B—hired before J. Consequently, the correct answer is six. As you might suspect, a number of students incorrectly selected answer choice (B) because they counted just the days before J. The question stem is specific in asking for the number of *workers* hired before J, not the number of *days* before J's hiring. Remember—always read each question stem very closely!

Question #4: Global, Must Be True. The correct answer choice is (E)

The sequence above disproves each of the first four answers. As we know from the discussion that either H or F and I must have been hired on the first day, answer choice (E) is correct.

Question #5: Local, Must Be True, Minimum. The correct answer choice is (D)

If E was hired on a Monday, then Tuesday would be the earliest day on which B could have been hired, and Wednesday would be the earliest day on which J could have been hired. Therefore, Thursday would be the earliest day on which C and G could have been hired. It follows that answer choice (D) is correct.

This is a Basic Linear: Unbalanced: Overloaded game.

Because we have eight apartments that must be distributed over five floors, this is an Unbalanced: Overloaded game. The given rules and restrictions can then be used to create a 2-2-2-1-1 unfixed numerical distribution. Unfortunately, this distribution proves to be of little value in the game. This occurrence should not deter you from seeking numerical distributions in the future. There are many examples of games where the numerical distribution proved to be the key to answering one or more questions.

The game should be set up as follows:

J K L M N O P Q [8]

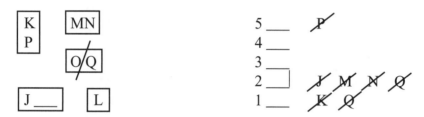

One difficult aspect of this game is the uncertainty over which floors contain two apartments. Since it is certain that there is at least one apartment per floor, we have placed slots on each of the five floors of our diagram. In the case of the second floor, which is known to have only one apartment, a short vertical line has been placed at the end of the slot. This vertical line serves as a visual reminder that the second floor contains one and only one apartment. Also of note in this game is the importance of correctly diagramming each rule. In the case of K, who lives one floor above P, the block must be shown vertically since the main diagram is vertical. On the other hand, the rule involving M and N must be shown horizontally because they live on the same floor. By diagramming these rules correctly, you gain a powerful advantage over the game, and you also eliminate a possible source of confusion. Also note that if this game were set up horizontally, then the diagramming of each rule would shift accordingly. For example, the KP block would be horizontal, whereas the MN block would be vertical. In essence you align the blocks with the diagram in order to make the most visual sense. On a vertical diagram a vertical block suggests one variable on top of another, but on a horizontal diagram a vertical block suggests that the two variables share the same space.

Let us take a moment to examine the Not Laws in the game:

> The occupancy limitation on the second floor produces Not Laws for J, M, and N, each of which is involved in a block rule.

> Because K must live on the floor *directly* above P, P cannot live on the fifth floor and K cannot live on the first floor.

> The last rule creates Q Not Laws on the first two floors. Also note that although Q cannot live on the first and second floors, this does not affect the placement of O. In Linear games, not-blocks tend to be relatively weak rules (this will not be the case when discussing grouping

games), because the not-block cannot be applied until one of the variables in the block is placed. Since Q has not been placed, it has not yet had an effect on O.

One of the keys to doing well on the questions is to remember all of the different rules, each of which is unique in form (this is, of course, why we represent rules visually—doing so makes them easier to remember).

Question #6: Global, Must Be True. The correct answer choice is (D)

This question is tailor-made for a Not Law attack. Since M and N must live on the same floor, and the second floor contains only one apartment, answer choice (D) must be correct.

Question #7: Global, Cannot Be True. The correct answer choice is (E)

This question is also suited for a Not Law attack. Since P must live one floor below K, it follows that P cannot live on the fifth floor, and therefore answer choice (E) must be correct. As you may have noticed, with many Global questions, especially the ones that appear early in a game, the first avenue of attack is to check the existing Not Laws. Make sure you always follow this guideline!

Question #8: Local, Could Be True. The correct answer choice is (A)

After completing the first two questions with relative ease, you should arrive at this question feeling confident. Since this is a Local question, you should always make a mini-diagram next to the question. The "if" statement in the question, in combination with the second rule, produces the following setup:

```
5  K         M̸  N̸
4  P    J |
3  ___
2  ___|
1  ___
```

Several of the answer choices can be eliminated by using the rule that states that each floor has either one or two apartments. Since both J and P live on the fourth floor, no other residents can live on the fourth floor, and answer choices (B) and (D) can be eliminated. Since K lives on the fifth floor, the M and N block cannot live on the fifth floor, and answer choice (C) can be eliminated. Answer choice (E) can be eliminated since P must live on the fourth floor. Accordingly, answer choice (A) is correct.

Question #9: Local, Cannot Be True. The correct answer choice is (E)

This question is more difficult than any of the first three questions in this game, and it is based upon one of the test maker's favorite modes of attack, the use of uncertainty.

If O lives on the second floor, then the second floor is completely occupied, and no other resident can live on the second floor. For some variables, such as the MN block or the J block, this has no effect. For the KP block, however, the placement options are significantly reduced. Since the second floor is now "closed off," the KP block must be placed on the third and fourth floors (3-4) or on the fourth and fifth floors (4-5). At this point, many test takers stop their analysis under the mistaken impression that since the exact position of the block cannot be determined, further examination is worthless. In fact, to get past this situation you must Hurdle the Uncertainties™: in games situations with limited solutions, it is often possible to make inferences in spite of the uncertainty. In this case, since the KP block is always on 3-4 or 4-5, it can be concluded that K or P is *always* on the fourth floor. *So, even though we cannot be certain of the KP block placement, we can deduce that in this question K or P must be on the fourth floor, and we must account for the space taken up by the K/P dual option:*

```
5  __
4  K/P  __|
3  __
2   O  |
1  __
```

Thus, since K or P must always live on the fourth floor, L cannot live on the fourth floor since L must live in the only apartment on her floor. Therefore, answer choice (E) is correct. Note that an answer that attempted to place either M or N on the fourth floor would also have been correct as the presence of K or P on the fourth floor would have eliminated the MN block from the fourth floor.

Essentially, the placement of O builds a "wall" on the second floor. This wall affects the placement of any block which takes up adjoining spaces, such as the KP block. In Linear games where blocks are present, always closely examine the placement of a variable (such as O) into an interior space (such as the second floor). There may be inferences that follow from the reduced placement options of a block (such as either K or P must live on the fourth floor). Opportunities to Hurdle the Uncertainty™ appear in a number of games (including questions #10, #11, and #12 in this game), and the tends to appear in harder questions.

Question #10: Local, Cannot Be True. The correct answer choice is (C)

Do not forget to convert Must Be False into Cannot Be True! This question uses the same Hurdle the Uncertainties™ principle seen in question #9. If M lives on the fourth floor, then the MN block completely occupies the fourth floor, again creating a wall in the interior of the game. This affects the placement of the KP block, which is now limited to floors one and two (1-2) or floors two and three (2-3). Accordingly, either K or P must live on the second floor:

```
5  __
4   M   N|
3  __
2  K/P|
1  __
```

Thus, no other variable can live on the second floor, and answer choice (C) must be correct.

Question #11: Global, Must Be True. The correct answer choice is (B)

If you have difficulty finishing the Logic Games section, or if you find yourself in trouble on a game, this "5 if" question format is one you should avoid. Observe the construction of the question: a Global Must Be True question stem where each of the five answer choices begins with an "if" statement. Essentially, each of the answer choices is a new scenario, and for the most part information cannot be shared among the answer choices in this question. This type of question is designed to consume time! Avoid it if you have time problems in the Logic Games section.

In a possible oversight by the test makers, this question contains an Achilles heel which allows the observant test taker to answer the question quickly. Whenever you encounter a Logic Games question where each answer choice begins with the word "if," always make sure to check your previous work in case some of the information can be reused. In this case, the information from question #9 is duplicated in answer choice (B). Since question #9 proves that, when O lives on the second floor, L cannot live on the fourth floor, and that is what answer choice (B) states in question #11, it must be true that answer choice (B) is correct.

Honestly, it is a stroke of good fortune that the information from question #9 solves this question. Generally, on questions where each answer choice begins with "if," using the information from previous questions would perhaps eliminate one or two answer choices at most. Of course, that would still provide a great advantage. Here, that technique answers a very time-consuming question quite quickly. Always remember to check your previous work to see if it applies to the question you are working on, especially when you know the question is specifically designed to consume time. Should you wish to complete this question, and you fail to refer to previous work, your only choice is to work through each answer until you come to one you can prove correct.

Question #12: Local, Must Be True. The correct answer choice is (C)

The Local conditions in the question stem establish the following partial setup:

```
5  ___
4   O        L̸  Ø  M  N̸
3   K        L̸  M  N̸
2   P ⌐      L̸  M̸  N̸  Ø
1  ___
```

Because L, M, and N cannot live on the second, third, or fourth floors, they must live on either the first or fifth floors, and because the MN block and L each require a floor of its own, it can be inferred that L, M, and N will completely occupy the first and fifth floors, creating a L/MN dual split-option:

```
5  MN / L
4   O
3   K
2   P ⌐
1  L / MN
```

Given this information, you can Hurdle the Uncertainties™ and come to the realization that only floor three and floor four are available for J and Q, and since Q cannot live on the same floor as O, Q must live on the third floor and thus J must live on the fourth floor, resulting in the following setup:

```
5  MN / L
4   O     J
3   K     Q
2   P ⌐
1   L / MN
```

It follows that answer choice (C) is correct. Also of interest is the fact that this is the first question in the game to directly address the OQ not-block. The test makers probably left this rule out of the game until the end in an effort to see whether careless test takers would forget about the rule and then miss the question. You must fix the rules in your mind at the beginning of the game and never forget them!

This is a Grouping: Defined-Moving, Balanced, Numerical Distribution game.

This is a very unusual game, because it is purely numerical. That is, the game setup consists of identifying the distributions of days to cities, and cities to countries. The three named countries—X, Y, and Z—do not play a role until specific questions locally reference the countries. Thus, they play no role in the setup.

14 days
6 cities
3 countries: X, Y, and Z

Days-to-Cities Numerical Distributions:

4-2-2-2-2-2
3-3-2-2-2-2

Cities-to-Countries Numerical Distributions:

4-1-1
3-2-1
2-2-2

Days-to-Countries Numerical Distributions:

10-2-2	7-4-3
9-3-2	6-6-2
8-4-2	6-5-3
8-3-3	6-4-4
7-5-2	5-5-4

The ten possible days-to-countries numerical distributions are not needed to answer the questions in this game.

Question #13: Local, Cannot Be True. The correct answer choice is (A)

If Hannah spends eight days in country X, she must visit either three or four cities in country X. For example, if she visits four cities in X, she would spend two days at each, in a 2-2-2-2 distribution. If she visits three cities, she would spend three days at two of the cities, and two days at the other city, in a 3-3-2 distribution, or she could spend 4 days at one city, and two days at the other two cities, for a 4-2-2 distribution. However, there is no way for her to visit two cities in X because she cannot spend eight days in just two cities and still meet the conditions of the game for visiting the other cities in the days remaining. Therefore, answer choice (A) is the correct answer, because it cannot be true that she visits two cities in country X.

Question #14: Local, Must Be True, Maximum. The correct answer choice is (D)

This question dictates the Cities-to-Countries numerical distribution in this case to be 2-2-2 (two cities in each country), so Hannah will be visiting exactly two cities in country X. To *maximize* her number of days in those two cities, we should consider the Days-to-Cities numerical distributions:

With a 4-2-2-2-2-2 distribution, she could spend 4 days in one X city, and 2 days in another X city, for a total of six days.

With a 3-3-2-2-2-2 distribution, she could spend 3 days in each of two cities in X.

Either way, the most time Hannah could possibly spend in two cities would be six days, so the correct answer choice is (D).

Question #15: Local, Cannot Be True, FTT. The correct answer choice is (D)

Seven days are spent in country Z. As discussed in question #14 above, the most time that could possibly be spent in two cities would be 6 days, so answer choice (D) is the correct answer choice—it cannot be true that only two cities are visited in the seven days spent in country Z.

Approaching the question by using the other information given in the question stem, we can actually determine the number of cities and days visited in each country:

	X	Y	Z
Cities	2	1	3
Days	4	3	7

This again proves answer choice (D), and helps disprove the other answer choices.

Question #16: Local, Must Be True. The correct answer choice is (B)

To answer this question we must again consider the possible Days-to-Cities numerical distribution. The distribution which provides the greatest number of days in one city is the 4-2-2-2-2-2 distribution, which would allow Hannah to spend 4 days in Nomo, and 2 days in each of the other five cities she visits.

Answer choice (B) is the correct answer choice because although Hannah maximizes her time in Nomo, she can still visit the counties in the 4-1-1 Cities-to-Countries distribution, allowing her to visit four cities in Y.

Note also that this question and answer choice is phrased oddly: literally, it must be true that it is possible for her to visit four cities in Y.

Question #17: Local, Must Be True, Maximum. The correct answer choice is (C)

Hannah visits four cities collectively in X and Y; she must minimize her visits in X to maximize her visits in Y. She must visit at least one city in each country, so Hannah should visit one city in X, allowing her to visit three cities in country Y.

We should again consider the Days-to-Cities distributions to determine how much time she can spend in country Y's three cities:

Using the 4-2-2-2-2-2 distribution, she could spend 4 days in a city, 2 days in another city, and 2 days in the third city, for a total of eight days.

Using the 3-3-2-2-2-2 distribution, she could spend 3 days in each of two cities, and 2 days in a third city, for a total of eight days.

With either distribution, the most time Hannah could spend in country Y would be eight days, so choice (C) is the correct answer choice.

PrepTest 2. October 1991 Game #4: *18. E   19. B   20. E   21. A   22. E   23. B   24. D*

This is an Advanced Linear: Defined-Balanced game.

This game is challenging because with seven rules the setup can be tricky, and many students fail to draw the key inference about S.

The game scenario establishes that six dogs are being judged. The six dogs are a variable set, and the ribbons are another variable set. The ribbons make the most sense to choose as a base because there is an inherent sense of order, but there is a catch: only four ribbons are awarded. Thus, the first four spaces will be numbered 1 through 4, but the last two spaces will be listed as "NR" for No Ribbon. These last two spaces are interchangeable in that there is no "fifth" or "sixth" ribbon. We will also place a vertical divided bar after the fourth ribbon in order to emphasize this difference. On top of the ribbon base there will be a row for the six named dogs.

Let us examine each rule:

First and Second Rules

The first rule establishes a variable set wherein each dog is either G or L, but not both. To account for this variable set another row must be added to the diagram.

The second rule establishes a variable set wherein each dog is either M or F. To account for this variable set another row must be added to the diagram.

Neither of the first two rules addresses any specific variable, but they both create a greater number of elements to track. With these new variable sets, the basic game structure appears as follows:

Dog Types: G L						
Sex: M F	___	___	___	___	___	___
Dogs: P Q R S T U	___	___	___	___	___	___
Ribbons:	1	2	3	4	NR	NR

Third Rule

This rule establishes that both female dogs win ribbons, meaning that the two dogs who do not win a ribbon are both male. In addition, exactly one of the female dogs is a labrador, meaning that the other female dog is a greyhound, which creates the following situation:

	Dog Types: G L						
L F	Sex: M F	___	___	___	___	M	M
	Dogs: P Q R S T U						
G F	Ribbons:	1	2	3	4	NR	NR

Fourth Rule

This is a very helpful rule. If only one labrador wins a ribbon, then the other three dogs that win a ribbon are greyhounds. Plus, because from the third rule we know that one of the females who wins a ribbon is a labrador, we can be certain that there are no male labradors that win a ribbon.

Fifth Rule

This rule establishes a powerful sequence:

$$
\begin{array}{ccc}
\text{R} & & \text{Q} \\
\text{----} > \text{S} > \text{----} \\
\text{P} & & \text{T}
\end{array}
$$

Even though U is not addressed in this rule, the sequence still produces several important inferences:

1. Both P and R win ribbons. Because P and R each finish ahead of at least three dogs, P and R must both win ribbons.

2. S wins a ribbon. Because S finishes ahead of at least two dogs, S must win a ribbon.

3. At least one of Q and T does not win a ribbon.

The biggest uncertainty, then, is where U places as that will directly affect Q or T.

Sixth and Seventh Rules

The final two rules connect certain dogs to specific dog types. Using subscripts for greyhound and labrador, let's review the sequence again:

$$
\begin{array}{ccc}
\text{R}_\text{G} & & \text{Q} \\
\text{----} > \text{S}_\text{L} > \text{----} \\
\text{P}_\text{G} & & \text{T}
\end{array}
$$

U is also a labrador.

With this new information, and the fact that exactly one labrador wins a ribbon, we can infer that S is the labrador that wins the ribbon, and that therefore U *cannot* win a ribbon (as U is also a labrador). Thus, U must finish in one of the last two places (and thus behind S), and therefore S must place third. P and R must then place first and second in some order.

Further, because S is the labrador that wins a ribbon, from the third rule S must be female. In addition, from the fourth rule, the other three ribbon-winning dogs are greyhounds, meaning the dogs in places 1, 2, and 4 are greyhounds. The information above leads to the following setup:

Dog Types: G L	G	G	L	G		
Sex: M F			F		M	M
Dogs: P Q R S T U	P/R	R/P	S	Q/T		
Ribbons	1	2	3	4	NR	NR

To complete the setup, we need to examine the last two places. Remember, there is no true order to the last two places; that is, neither is necessarily "fifth" or "sixth." One of the two dogs is U, which is a male labrador. The other is the remainder of Q or T, and will be either a greyhound or a labrador. Applying this information leads to the final setup:

Dog Types: G L	G	G	L	G	L	L/G
Sex: M F			F		M	M
Dogs: P Q R S T U	P/R	R/P	S	Q/T	U	T/Q
Ribbons	1	2	3	4	NR	NR

With the information above, the questions should now be considerably easier.

Question #18: Global, Must Be True, List. The correct answer choice is (E)

As shown in the diagram, P and R (ribbons 1 and 2, not necessarily in that order) and Q and T (ribbon 4) *could* be greyhounds, and so answer choice (E) is correct.

Question #19: Global, Cannot Be True. The correct answer choice is (B)

According to the diagram, the second place ribbon is awarded to a greyhound. Thus, answer choice (B) cannot be true and is therefore correct.

Question #20: Global, Must Be True. The correct answer choice is (E)

As established in the setup discussion, U is a labrador that does not win a ribbon, and thus U must be male. Answer choice (E) is thus correct.

Question #21: Global, Not Necessarily True, FTT. The correct answer choice is (A)

Either P or R could place first, and thus answer choice (A) does not have to be true. Therefore, answer choice (A) is correct.

Question #22: Local, Not Necessarily True, FTT. The correct answer choice is (E)

If Q is a female, then Q wins a ribbon and must place fourth. Dogs P and R then must be male. Dog T does not win a ribbon, and T is a male greyhound or a male labrador. The rest of the information in the main setup remains as-is.

As dog T can be a greyhound or a labrador, answer choice (E) is not necessarily true and thus correct.

Question #23: Local, Must Be True. The correct answer choice is (B)

If dog T wins the fourth place ribbon, then T is a greyhound. Dog Q then finishes with no ribbon and must be a male. Accordingly, answer choice (B) is correct.

Question #24: Global, Could Be True. The correct answer choice is (D)

As shown in the diagram, either dog Q or dog T could win the fourth place ribbon. Thus, dog T could win a ribbon and answer choice (D) is correct.

Interestingly, this answer can also be identified by looking at question #23. The question stem to question #23 indicates that dog T can win a ribbon, and thus, since this is a Global Could Be True question, answer choice (D) is automatically proven correct. Remember, even if you were struggling with this game and hope seemed lost, always check the work in other questions for information. It is unusual for a question stem to provide the answer to another problem, but as this game shows, it is possible.

2

PREPTEST 3

DECEMBER 1991 LOGIC GAMES SETUPS

This is a Advanced Linear: Balanced game.

The variables in this game are easy to identify:

> Men: J L N [3]
> Women: K M O [3]
> Entrees: P R S T V [5]

The setup, however, can be a bit more complicated because the men and women are paired in the first rule, and because there is also a rule about the men not ordering the same entree. So, we need a way to see both connections easily, and the best way to set the game up, then, is as follows:

Women:	K	M	O
Men:	J	L	N

This setup has the advantage of showing each couple (they are each vertical pair) and also showing each gender (in the rows) in a compact, easily visualized manner.

The first rule in the game establishes that the two people in each couple cannot order the same entree as each other. This can be diagrammed as:

$$\boxed{\begin{array}{c} E \\ E \end{array}}\!\!\!/$$

The "E" represents "entree," and the "E" is a shorthand way to express the five not-blocks produced by this rule.

The second rule establishes that none of the men can order the same entree:

$$\boxed{E\!\!/\!E}_{M}$$

These two rules are critical to the game, but we will consider the implications of these two rules after considering the last three rules.

The last three rules of the game place certain variables and establish several Not Laws:

Women: K   S   R
                   M   O

Men: J   L   N
          S̶   S̶
          T̶   T̶

With these rules represented, we can turn to combining the information already provided.

The combination of the first rule and the third rule results in the deduction that L cannot order swordfish, and the combination of the first rule and the fifth rule results in the deduction that N cannot order roast beef:

Women: K   S   R
                   M   O

Men: J   L   N
          S̶   S̶   S̶
          T̶   T̶
                            R̶

As always, examine the most restricted areas in the game. In this case, N is extremely restricted because N cannot order S, T, or R. Thus, there are only two entree choices for N: P or V. This inference is the key to the game, and leads to the final setup:

Men: J L N [3]
Women: K M O [3]
Entrees: P R S T V [5]

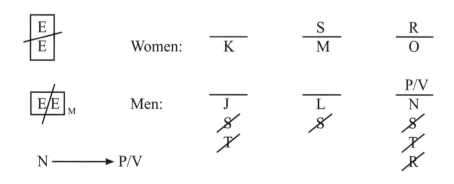

Women: K   S   R
                   M   O

                                     P/V
Men: J   L   N
          S̶   S̶   S̶
          T̶   T̶
                            R̶

N ──────▶ P/V

Question #1: Global, Could Be True, List. The correct answer choice is (D)

From our diagram, we know that L cannot order swordfish, and so answer choices (C) and (E) can be eliminated immediately. There is no restriction on the other entrees L can order, and ultimately the correct answer choice is (D), the answer that includes the other four entrees.

Question #2: Global, Could Be True. The correct answer choice is (B)

Answer choice (A): From the third rule we know that M orders swordfish, but from the fourth rule we know that J cannot order swordfish, and so this answer cannot be true.

Answer choice (B): This is the correct answer choice. N and K can both order pork chops or veal cutlet.

Answer choice (C): L and N are both men, and according to the second rule none of the men order the same kind of entree. Hence, this answer choice cannot be true and is incorrect.

Answer choice (D): From the third rule we know that M orders swordfish and from the fifth rule we know that O orders roast beef. Thus, M and O do not order the same kind of entree and this answer choice is incorrect.

Answer choice (E): N and O are a couple, and according to the first rule the two people in each couple do not order the same kind of entree. Hence, this answer choice cannot be true and is incorrect.

Question #3: Global, Must Be True. The correct answer choice is (A)

From our discussion of the setup, we determined that N orders pork chops or veal cutlet. Hence, answer choice (A) must be true and is correct.

Question #4: Local, Must Be True. The correct answer choice is (E)

The condition in the question stem establishes that J order veal cutlet. If J orders veal cutlet, then from the second rule we can deduce that N cannot order veal cutlet and must then order pork chops:

		S	R
Women:	K	M	O

		R/T	P
Men:	V	L	N
	J		

This is sufficient to prove answer choice (E) correct.

In addition, because the two men order veal cutlet and pork chops, and because M orders swordfish, L can only order roast beef or tilefish.

Question #5: Local, Must Be True. The correct answer choice is (C)

If no one orders pork chops, then from our inference we know that N must order veal cutlet, and neither of the other two men can order veal cutlet:

		S	R
Women:	K	M	O

	J	L	V
Men:	~~S~~	~~S~~	N
	~~T~~	~~P~~	~~S~~
	~~P~~	~~V~~	~~T~~
	~~V~~		~~R~~
			~~P~~

J is extremely restricted, and J must now order roast beef, and from the second rule that entree order eliminates roast beef from L's choices and forces L to order tilefish:

		S	R
Women:	K	M	O
	~~R~~		

	R	T	V
Men:	J	L	N
	~~S~~	~~S~~	~~S~~
	~~T~~	~~P~~	~~T~~
	~~P~~	~~V~~	~~R~~
	~~V~~	~~R~~	~~P~~

Consequently, answer choice (C) is correct.

Question #6: Local, Could Be True, List. The correct answer choice is (A)

If L orders pork chops, then from our major inference N must order veal cutlet, leaving only roast beef available for J to order:

		S	R
Women:	K	M	O

	R	P	V
Men:	J	L	N
	~~S~~		
	~~T~~		
	~~P~~		
	~~V~~		

Accordingly, answer choice (A) is correct.

Question #7: Local, Could Be True, Suspension. The correct answer choice is (D)

This question stem suspends the first rule and replaces it with a rule that states that each couple orders the same entree. From the third rule, we then know that L and M both order swordfish, and from the fifth rule we know that N and O both order roast beef. From the second rule, J cannot then order roast beef. Consequently, J must order pork chops or veal cutlet, and K must also order pork chops or veal cutlet:

	P/V	S	R
Women:	K	M	O

	P/V	S	R
Men:	J	L	N
	S̶		
	L̶		
	R̶		

Because both J and K could order pork chops, answer choice (D) could be true and is correct.

This is a Basic Linear: Balanced game.

The variables and basic setup to this game can be diagrammed as follows:

Variables: K L M N O P R [7]

W $\underline{\quad}$ $\underline{\quad}$ $\underline{\quad}$ $\underline{\quad}$ $\underline{\quad}$ $\underline{\quad}$ $\underline{\quad}$ E
   1   2   3   4   5   6   7

The first rule establishes R Not Laws on the first and last houses on the street, and the second rule establishes that K is the fourth house on the street:

W $\underline{\quad}$ $\underline{\quad}$ $\underline{\quad}$ $\underline{K}$ $\underline{\quad}$ $\underline{\quad}$ $\underline{\quad}$ E
   1   2   3   4   5   6   7
   R̸   R̸

The third rule establishes a MK or KM block. Because there are two options for this block but K is already fixed, this is shown as a dual-option for M. In addition, because M is not completely fixed, we will show the M Not Laws on houses 1, 2, 6, and 7:

MK or KM

W $\underline{\quad}$ $\underline{\quad}$ $\underline{M/}$ $\underline{K}$ $\underline{/M}$ $\underline{\quad}$ $\underline{\quad}$ E
   1   2   3   4   5   6   7
   R̸ M̸   M̸ R̸
   M̸   M̸

Finally, the last rule produces a sequence that appears as follows:

K
---- > P > L
M

This sequence produces a number of Not Laws for P and L, in particular that P and L cannot occupy any of the first three houses, and that L cannot be fifth and that P cannot be last (because P > L):

MK or KM

K
---- > P > L
M

W $\underline{\quad}$ $\underline{\quad}$ $\underline{M/}$ $\underline{K}$ $\underline{/M}$ $\underline{\quad}$ $\underline{\quad}$ E
   1   2   3   4   5   6   7
   R̸ M̸ P̸   L̸ M̸ R̸
   M̸ P̸ L̸   M̸
   P̸ L̸   P̸
   L̸

3

As always, before moving on to the questions make sure to check the restrictions within the game. The first house has the greatest number of Not Laws, so take a moment to examine the possibilities for the first house. The first house cannot be occupied by K because K is already placed, and also cannot be occupied by R, M, P, and L due to Not Laws. Thus, only N or O remain to occupy the first house, an inference that plays a significant role within the game. Adding this information to the game leads to the final setup:

Variables: K L M N O P R [7]

Notes:

N and O are randoms (despite the fact that they appear on the diagram; this is a result of the actions of the other rules, not from a specific rule involving N or O), and are noted with asterisks.

As a result of the combination of the second, third, and fourth rules, we can infer that P must live in either the fifth house or the sixth house, and L must be in either the sixth house or the seventh house. This occurs because the P > L sequence must be to the east of the MK block, leaving P > L to fit into the fifth, sixth, and seventh houses. Although P and L options could be added to the diagram, doing so could be confusing because a P/M dual-option would appear on house 5, when it is also possible that others could occupy the house.

Also, if M lives in the fifth house, then P lives in the sixth house and L lives in the seventh house.

Question #8: Global, Could Be True. The correct answer choice is (C)

The second rule eliminates answer choice (A). The Not Laws eliminate answer choices (B), (D), and (E). Thus, answer choice (C) is correct.

Question #9: Global, Cannot Be True. The correct answer choice is (A)

As shown on the diagram, L cannot occupy houses 3 or 5, meaning that L can never live next door to K. Thus, answer choice (A) is correct.

Question #10: Local, Cannot Be True. The correct answer choice is (C)

This can be a difficult question. The question stem stipulates that M lives west of K, and so M must live in the third house. The most logical place to look for an answer then, would be with variables that are forcibly separated. P and L must both live east of K, and so a combination of M and P or M and L would be correct.

Specifically, when M lives in the third house, and we know already that P must live in the fifth or sixth house, we can infer that R cannot live next to both M and P because K will serve to separate the houses. Thus, answer choice (C) is correct.

Question #11: Local, Cannot Be True, FTT. The correct answer choice is (A)

If N lives in the third house, then M must live in the fifth house. When M lives in the fifth house, P and L must live in houses six and seven, respectively. From the first rule R cannot live in the first house and must then live in the second house. O is the only family remaining, and O must live in the first house:

$$\frac{O}{1} \quad \frac{R}{2} \quad \frac{N}{3} \quad \frac{K}{4} \quad \frac{M}{5} \quad \frac{P}{6} \quad \frac{L}{7}$$

Accordingly, answer choice (A) cannot be true and is correct.

Questions #12 (Local, Must Be True) and #13 (Local, Must Be True).

The question stems in these two questions each establish that O must live east of the MK block. For this to occur, O must live in houses 5, 6, or 7. Consequently, O, P, and L must occupy the fifth, sixth, and seventh houses in some order, and M must live in the third house:

$$\frac{}{1} \quad \frac{}{2} \quad \frac{M}{3} \quad \frac{K}{4} \quad \frac{(O, P > L)}{5 \quad 6 \quad 7}$$

Only N and R remain unplaced, and we can infer from the first rule that R must live in the second house and that therefore N must live in the first house. Thus, the scenario for both questions turns out to be identical:

$$\frac{N}{1} \quad \frac{R}{2} \quad \frac{M}{3} \quad \frac{K}{4} \quad \frac{(O, P > L)}{5 \quad 6 \quad 7}$$

The scenario above proves answer choice (A) correct in #12, and proves answer choice (D) correct in #13.

This is a Balanced Advanced Linear game.

F S N U P R [6]

```
S                        3  ____  __U__  __P__
v
F                        2  ____  ____  ____

U ◄——┼——► R              1  ____  __N__  ____
R ◄——┼——► S                 F/S   N/U   P/R
```

The three floors are chosen as a vertical base, and then slots for each car choice are provided. Because there are three choices—F or S, N or U, and P or R—there are three slots for each floor.

The second and third rules are negative conditional rules that establish that U and R cannot be on the same floor, and that R and S cannot be on the same floor. This leads to several key deductions:

U ——► P   R ——► N   R ——► F   S ——► P

The key deductions above follow from the two-value system that exists for each of the three choices for cars on each floor. For example, since the cars on each floor must be either family cars or sports cars, and cannot be both, if family cars are not included on a floor then that floor must include sports cars. The same holds true for the new or used car choice and for the production or research model choice. This simple fact yields some powerful inferences when combined with the second and third rules. For example, the second rule states that the exhibition includes no used research models. Thus if the cars on a floor are used, they are not research models. This can be represented as:

U ——► R̸

However, if a car is not a research model then it must be a production model and thus the rule can be more effectively diagrammed as:

U ——► P

From this inference it follows that since the third floor of the exhibition has used cars, the third floor must also have production models, and this inference is shown on the main diagram.

Continuing on, the contrapositive of U ——► P is:

P̸ ——► U̸

But, again applying the two-value system, if a car is not a production model, then it must be a research model which cannot be used, and if it is not used, then it must be new, which can be diagrammed as:

$$R \longrightarrow N$$

The same type of reasoning can also be applied to the third rule which involves research models and sports cars.

This set of inferences, which follow from the two negative conditional rules and the two-value system, are critical to solving this game quickly.

Question #14: Local, Could Be True. The correct answer choice is (A)

If S is on *exactly* two floors, then from the first rule, S must be on floors 2 and 3, and F must be on floor 1. Applying the key inferences, we can then deduce that P is on the second and third floors as well:

3	S	U	P
2	S	N/U	P
1	F	N	P/R

As this is a Could Be True question, you should immediately seek an answer that addresses the two uncertainties in the diagram: N or U on floor 2, and P or R on floor 1. Answer choice (A) addresses the uncertainty on floor 1, and is correct.

Question #15: Global, Could Be True. The correct answer choice is (D)

Answer choices (A), (B), and (C) can be eliminated by referring to the second and third rules. Answer choice (E) can be eliminated by the deduction made during the setup that placed P on floor 3. Answer choice (D) is thus correct. Answer choice (D) can also be confirmed very quickly by referring to the hypothetical created in question #14.

Question #16: Global, Must Be True. The correct answer choice is (D)

This question is answered by the inference made during the setup that placed P on floor 3. Answer choice (D) is thus correct.

Question #17: Local, Not Necessarily True, FTT. The correct answer choice is (E)

If R is on two floors, those must be floors 1 and 2. Applying the R $\longrightarrow$ N and R $\longrightarrow$ F inferences then produces the following diagram:

3	F/S	U	P
2	F	N	R
1	F	N	R

As this is a Not Necessarily True question, you should look for any uncertainty in the question, and in this case the only uncertainty is the choice of F or S on floor 3. Not surprisingly, answer choice (E), the only answer to address floor 3, is correct.

Question #18: Local, Must Be True. The correct answer choice is (D)

This question forces you to link together the condition in the question stem with one of the key deductions. The question stem condition can be diagrammed as:

$$N \longrightarrow R$$

Combining this with the R $\longrightarrow$ F deduction yields:

$$N \longrightarrow R \longrightarrow F$$

Using linkage, we can then conclude that:

$$N \longrightarrow F$$

Thus, answer choice (D) is correct.

Question #19: Local, Must Be True. The correct answer choice is (A)

The question stem, in combination with one of the key deductions, establishes a double arrow where:

$$P \longleftrightarrow U$$

Of course, if U and P must always be together, then via the contrapositive, R and N must also always be together:

$$R \longleftrightarrow N$$

From this we can conclude that floor 1 includes R cars, and adding another of the key deductions, we can conclude that floor 1 includes F cars:

3   ____   U   P

2   ____   ____   ____

1   F   N   R

Consequently, answer choice (A) is correct.

This is a Grouping: Partially Defined game.

The game sets up a scenario wherein three pilots and three co-pilots are all aboard planes in an air show. This creates a basic setup as follows:

Pilots: A B C ^{3}
Copilots: D E F ^{3}

____ ____ ____ ____
 1   2   3   4

Since there are only three pilots available to fly in the air show, the maximum number of planes that can fly is three. Since Dave and Anna must fly in separate planes, the minimum number of planes that must fly is two. Thus, it is possible for a plane to fly with more than one pilot or copilot. It is also possible for a plane to fly without a copilot. Understanding this confusing point makes the questions much easier.

The third rule establishes that for a plane to fly, a pilot must be on board. Thus, a copilot must have a pilot on board as well, which can be indicated by the rule CP ———→ P.

The last two rules establish Not Laws for A and D, and corresponding split options for A and D:

Pilots: A B C ^{3}
Copilots: D E F ^{3}

A/   D/   /D   /A
 1   2   3   4
D̶   A̶   A̶   D̶

By combining the last two rules, the additional deduction D ◄——► A can be made.

Since D cannot fly with A, and since a copilot needs a pilot in order to fly on a plane, D must fly with either B or C or both. Therefore, if B does not fly with D, C must fly with D, and if C does not fly with D, B must fly with D. *This deduction is the key to the entire game.* This final inference leads to the setup for the game:

Pilots: A B C ^{3}
Copilots: D E F ^{3}

A/   D/   /D   /A
 1   2   3   4
D̶   A̶   A̶   D̶

CP ———→ P
D ◄——► A
D ———→ B/C

Incidentally, this game is a repeat of a Logic Game that originally appeared in the 1980s.

Question #20: Local, Must Be True. The correct answer choice is (B)

The question stem sets up the following situation:

$$\underline{\hspace{1cm}} \quad \underset{2}{\underline{\text{D}}} \quad \underline{\hspace{1cm}} \quad \underset{4}{\underline{\text{A}}}$$
$$\phantom{\underline{\hspace{1cm}}}_{1}$$

Since Dave must fly with Bob or Cindy, if Cindy flies on plane 3, then Bob must fly with Dave in plane 2. It follows that answer choice (B) is correct.

Answer choice (E) is incorrect since once it is established that Cindy flies with Dave on plane 2, Bob would then be free to fly on any plane.

Question #21: Local, Must Be True. The correct answer choice is (C)

If Bob and Anna fly on the same plane, we can infer that Dave is not on that plane because D ◄───┼───► A. Hence, Dave must fly with Cindy (because he must fly with Bob or Cindy, and Bob is on a plane that Dave cannot be on), and it follows that answer choice (C) is correct.

Answer choice (D) is incorrect because Ed and Fran do not have to fly with Dave and Cindy. The same type of reasoning can be used to eliminate answer choice (A).

Question #22: Local, Must Be True. The correct answer choice is (D)

If Cindy and Fran are the *only* two people on one of the planes, it follows that Dave cannot fly with Cindy, and thus Dave must fly with Bob. Accordingly answer choice (D) is correct.

Question #23: Global, Could Be True. The correct answer choice is (B)

The crew of plane 1 could consist of everyone except Dave and either Bob or Cindy. Answer choices (D) and (E), each of which contain Dave, are thus incorrect.

Answer choices (A) and (C), which each contain *both* Bob and Cindy, are also incorrect because if both Bob and Cindy fly on plane 1, then Dave would not have a qualified pilot to fly with.

Accordingly, as all of the other answer choices have been eliminated, it follows that answer choice (B) is correct.

Question #24: Local, Must Be True. The correct answer choice is (C)

Since plane 1 is functionally identical to plane 4 in this game, and question #23 established that at least four people could fly in plane 1, we can quickly establish that plane 4 can fly with at least four people. Consequently, answer choices (A) and (B) can be eliminated.

Because either Bob or Cindy must always fly with Dave in plane 2 or 3, it is impossible for 5 people to fly in plane 4, and thus answer choice (D) is incorrect. Selecting answer choice (E), which adds up to exactly five people, would be functionally identical to selecting answer choice (D) and thus it too is incorrect.

The only remaining answer choice is (C), which is the correct answer. Plane 4 could consist of A-B-E-F or A-C-E-F. The other plane in the show (plane 2 or plane 3) would contain D and either B or C.

POWERSCORE®

PREPTEST

FEBRUARY 1992 LOGIC GAMES SETUPS

PrepTest 4. February 1992 Game #1: *1. D 2. C 3. D 4. D 5. C 6. D*

This is a Pure Sequencing game.

The seven rules combine to form the following diagram:

Variables: F G H I J K L M N [9]

$$I > F > M > G > J > H$$
$$K > \text{- - - - - - - - - - - - - - - -}$$
$$L > N$$

The relationships are not overly complex, and in analyzing the diagram two important facts are clear:

> *K must have the highest salary.
> *Either H or N or both must have the lowest salary.

Given the simplicity of the diagram, you should make a quick analysis of the relationships, and then swiftly move to the questions.

Question #1: Global, Cannot Be True. The correct answer choice is (D)

Since K, I, and F must all have higher salaries than M, it follows that M cannot have the third highest salary. Therefore, answer choice (D) is correct.

Note that a variable such as L could have the third highest salary under a hypothetical such as the following: K-I-L-N-F-M-G-J-H. Similarly, I could be third using the following hypothetical: K-L-I-N-F-M-G-J-H.

Question #2: Local, Must Be True, Minimum. The correct answer choice is (C)

If M and N earn the same salary, then N, M, G, J, and H must all have lower salaries than L. Therefore, if M and N earn the same salary, then at least *five* of the partners must have lower salaries than L. It follows that answer choice (C) is correct.

Question #3: Global, Justify. The correct answer choice is (D)

The question stem asks you to add a statement to the rules that will result in a single solution. The easiest way to achieve this goal is to take the two separate chains in the Double-Branched Vertical (the I-H chain and the L > N chain) and place one ahead of the other (these two chains contain the only uncertain variables in the game). Thus, an answer stating that H > L or that N > I would quickly achieve the desired result.

Answer choice (D) contains the N > I statement mentioned above. If it were true that N's salary was greater than I's salary, then the following single chain sequence would result:

$$K > L > N > I > F > M > G > J > H$$

Therefore, if it were true that N's salary was greater than I's salary, then the salary rankings of each of the nine partners would be completely determined. K's salary would be the highest, L's salary would be the second highest, N's salary would be the third highest, and so forth. It follows that answer choice (D) is correct.

Question #4: Local, Cannot Be True. The correct answer choice is (D)

If N's salary is the same as that of one other partner, then L's salary cannot possibly be less than H's salary. If L's salary were in fact less than H's salary, then the following single chain sequence would result:

$$K > I > F > M > G > J > H > L > N$$

Under these circumstances, however, N's salary would be the lowest and could not be the same as that of any other partner. Thus, if N's salary is the same as that of one other partner, then it must be false that L's salary is less than H's salary. It follows that answer choice (D) is correct.

Question #5: Global, Must Be True, Minimum. The correct answer choice is (C)

K, and all the members of the top chain in the Branched Vertical (K, I, F, M, G, J, and H) must all earn different salaries from each other. It is possible, however, that some of these partners could earn the same salaries as L and N. For example, I could earn the same salary as L, and F could earn the same salary as N. Therefore, the minimum number of different salaries is *seven*. It follows that answer choice (C) is correct.

Question #6: Local, Could Be True, List. The correct answer choice is (D)

Quickly glancing at the initial diagram shows that G can be ranked as low as seventh (with only J and H behind G), and as high as fifth (with L, N, J, and H behind G, now necessarily in that order). Given the latitude of L and N, it is reasonable to expect that G could sixth as well, and that the correct answer is fifth, sixth, or seventh (which is answer choice (D)).

However, for further, incontrovertible proof, consider the following three hypothetical sequences:

$$1. K > I > F > M > \mathbf{G} > J > H > L > N$$

$$2. K > L > N > I > F > M > \mathbf{G} > J > H$$

$$3. K > L > I > F > M > \mathbf{G} > J > H > N$$

The first sequence proves that G could possibly be ranked fifth, the second sequence proves that G could possibly be ranked seventh, and the third sequence proves that G could possibly be ranked sixth. Since "fifth," "sixth," and "seventh" must all be in the complete and accurate list of G's possible ranks, answer choices (A), (B), and (C) can all be eliminated. G cannot possibly be ranked eighth since G's salary must be higher than both J's salary and H's salary. Hence, answer choice (E) can be eliminated. Answer choice (D) is thus proven correct by process of elimination.

This is a Grouping: Defined-Fixed, Unbalanced: Underfunded, Numerical Distribution game.

The scenario establishes two variable sets:

Illnesses: J K L M N [5]
Symptoms: F H S [3]

Either of these sets could be the base for this game, but a quick glance at the rules indicates that the illnesses are connected to each other by numbers, and that many of the illnesses have their symptoms specified. Thus, the illnesses are the superior choice for the base:

___ ___ ___ ___ ___
J   K   L   M   N

The rules establish both the exact numbers and the exact types of symptoms that characterize illnesses J, K, and M. The rules also establish the exact numbers—but not the exact types—of symptoms that characterize illnesses L and N. Thus, from the rules we can determine that the distribution is fixed at 2-1-2-3-1, and we also have a significant amount of information about the symptoms of each illness:

Illnesses: J K L M N [5]
Symptoms: F H S [3]

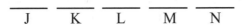

② ① ② ③ ①

J ←——→ K
L ←——→ N
J ←——→ L
   at lst 1

                         S
                         H
   S   F
   H   F   H/S   F   ___
   J ←→ K   L   M   N
     at lst 1

Interestingly, the third rule, which states that "illnesses J and L have at least one symptom in common," is superfluous since it can be deduced from the other rules.

Question #7: Global, Cannot Be True, FTT. The correct answer choice is (E)

Illness N only has one symptom, so answer choice (E) cannot be true.

Question #8: Global, Could Be True. The correct answer choice is (C)

There are only two possible pairs that fit the numerical criterion in this question: J and L, and K and N. J and L are not one of the pairs in the answer choices, so the answer choice must be K and N. Illnesses K and N both have only one symptom, and both could have symptom F (K must have F; N could have F). Thus answer choice (C) is correct.

Question #9: Local, Must Be True. The correct answer choice is (A)

Since L has two symptoms, and L must be different than the other two-symptom illness—which is J—L cannot have H and S. That means that L must have F and either H or S. Since L must have F, answer choice (A) is correct.

Question #10: Global, Must Be True. The correct answer choice is (E)

This type of question would normally be time consuming in the typical game. However, because we have all of the numerical information about the illnesses, and a significant amount of information about the symptoms of each illness, it is easier than would normally be expected. Some of the answers—such as (B)—can be eliminated with a quick glance at the original diagram.

However, there is a better way to think about this problem, and that is from an abstract standpoint. One way to force two illnesses to have exactly one symptom in common is to choose an illness with all three symptoms, and then pair it with and illness with exactly one symptom. This ensures that the two illnesses have exactly one symptom in common. Because M has all three symptoms, M must have *at least* one symptom in common with all other illnesses. Thus, it automatically has *exactly one* symptom in common with both K and N (although not necessarily the same symptom). M and K do not appear as one of the answer choices, but M and N do appear in answer choice (E). Because N only has one symptom it must be one of the symptoms that M has. Thus M and N have exactly one symptom in common and answer choice (E) is correct.

Question #11: Local, Cannot Be True. The correct answer choice is (E)

If Walter has *exactly* two of the three symptoms, then he cannot have illness M (which is characterized by all three symptoms). Unfortunately, M does not appear in any of the answer choices. However, even though M does not appear in this question, it is always worth taking a chance to quickly check the answers for the presence of such a "question solving" variable.

The next step is to check pairs of variables that would, in combination, exhibit all three symptoms (you could also seek a pair of illnesses that conceivably exhibit just one symptom, but L and N—the only such pair—do not have to have the same symptom). There are two pairs that must exhibit all three symptoms when combined: J and K, and L and N (each pair contains three symptoms, but none of the symptoms can be the same). J and K do not appear in the answer choice, so let's examine L and N, which appear in answer choice (E).

L and N together exhibit all three symptoms, since L has two symptoms and N has one symptom, and from the fifth rule they cannot have any symptoms in common. So, if Walter had L and N, he would have all three symptoms (although we cannot determine exactly which symptoms come from L and exactly which symptoms come from N). Because Walter has exactly, two symptoms, he cannot have both L and N, and answer choice (E) is correct.

This is an Advanced Linear: Unbalanced: Underfunded game.

1 2 3 4 5 6 7 8 ^{8} X X ^{10}
* *

8 > 4 > 6

PM	8		X			
AM	1/3	4			7	X
	M	T	W	Th	F	

~~6~~ ~~8~~ ~~2~~ ~~8~~ ~~8~~
                ~~5~~
                ~~8~~

~~2~~ ~~5~~ ~~8~~

The days are chosen as the base because they have an inherent order. The streets, although numbered from 1 to 8, can be cleaned in any order and thus make an inferior choice for the base. The morning and afternoon variable sets are then stacked above the days (either can be on top), and the street numbers fill in the spaces.

The five days with two time slots create 10 available spaces. Because there are only 8 streets, two "empty" variables are created, in this case represented by "X" (however, any variable would suffice, such as "E"). The addition of these two empty slot variables negates the Underfunded aspect of this game (the game becomes ten variables into ten spaces). Also, the assignment of the two empty slots to Friday morning and Wednesday afternoon makes handling the two X variables a non-issue. The further assignment of streets 4 and 7 reduces this game to six variables being placed in six spaces, a very manageable situation.

The combination of the last two rules forces 8th street to be cleaned on Monday afternoon. 8th street must be cleaned before 4th street, so it must be cleaned on Monday, but the last rule indicates that 8th street cannot be cleaned in the morning, so 8th street must be cleaned on Monday afternoon. Note also that street cannot be cleaned on Monday, but that it could be cleaned Tuesday afternoon since that is after street 4 is cleaned.

Finally, the combination of the Not Laws in the last rule, the previously placed streets, and the sequence leaves only a limited number of streets available for cleaning on Monday morning. The key inference in this game is that only streets 1 and 3 are available for cleaning on Monday morning. Question #15 is a great example of how the LSAT makers test your ability to see inferences.

Question #12: Local, Must Be True. The correct answer choice is (B)

If 2nd street is cleaned earlier than 7th street, then 2nd street must be cleaned on Monday, Tuesday, or Wednesday. However, Monday is off-limits because Monday afternoon is already occupied by 8th street. Wednesday is also prohibited because the only available slot is in the morning, and from the last rule we know that 2nd street must be cleaned in the afternoon. That leaves only Tuesday afternoon available for 2nd street, and answer choice (B) is correct.

Question #13: Local, Must Be True, Maximum. The correct answer choice is (C)

If 6th street is cleaned in the morning, then 6th street must be cleaned on Wednesday morning, the only available slot. If 2nd street is cleaned before 7th, then 2nd street must be cleaned on Tuesday afternoon, leaving only streets 1, 3, and 5 unassigned:

$$\begin{array}{ccccc} 8 & 2 & X & (\,5\, , \, 3/1\,) \\ \hline 1/3 & 4 & 6 & 7 & X \\ \hline M & T & W & Th & F \end{array}$$

Hence, answer choice (C) is correct.

Question #14: Global, Must Be True, Maximum. The correct answer choice is (E)

Any street except 8, 4, and 7 can be cleaned on Friday afternoon, and thus the correct answer is (E).

Question #15: Local, Cannot Be True, FTT. The correct answer choice is (A)

This question asks for what must be false. Remember, always convert the question in terms of false into terms of true (false-to-true, or FTT). In this case, the condition in the question stem indicates that 1st street is cleaned earlier than 3rd street, and applying the inference we made in the setup yields that 1st street must be cleaned on Monday morning. Hence, answer choice (A), which asserts that 1st street is cleaned on Tuesday afternoon, cannot be true and is thus correct.

Question #16: Local, Must Be True, Maximum. The correct answer choice is (D)

If 5, 6, and 7 are cleaned in numerical order, the following setup is produced:

$$\begin{array}{ccccc} 8 & 5 & X & (\,2\, , \, 3/1\,) \\ \hline 1/3 & 4 & 6 & 7 & X \\ \hline M & T & W & Th & F \end{array}$$

Because there are two solutions when 2 is cleaned on Thursday, and two solutions when 2 is cleaned on Friday, there are four total solutions, and answer choice (D) is correct.

Question #17: Local, Not Necessarily True, FTT, Suspension. The correct answer choice is (B)

This question suspends and then replaces the third rule, forcing you to re-create the initial setup with a new rule. This is the resulting setup:

$$\begin{array}{ccccc} 8 & 4 & X & 2/5 & 5/2 \\ \hline 1/3 & 3/1 & 6 & 7 & X \\ \hline M & T & W & Th & F \end{array}$$

Because the question stem asks for what is not necessarily true, you should immediately look for answers that include 1 and 3 or 2 and 5 because those are the only uncertainties in the diagram above. Answer choice (B) neatly plays on the uncertainty surrounding 2 and 5, and (B) is the correct answer.

This is a Mapping—Supplied Diagram, Identify the Possibilities game.

This game might seem somewhat intimidating, but in reality it is just an exercise in connecting the dots. While at first there may appear to be a large number of solutions, two factors combine to limit the number of solutions to six total: the limited number of segments, and the limited ways those segments can connect the chalets. Let's examine both factors in more detail.

There are only five total segments (or paths) that must be shown. Because two of the five line segments are already given (J-N and K-L), only three more remain to be drawn. With only three segments left, there are a limited number of possible combinations of those segments.

The three segments are also limited in the way they can be drawn because of the rule that disallows the paths to cross, and the rule that maximizes the number of connections to a chalet to two. Those two rules further reduce the number of possible solutions, and should suggest to you that one way to solve this game would be to Identify the Possibilities.

Let's look at the initial setup to the game:

J K L M N O [6]

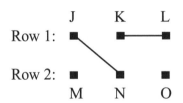

The first thing that should be apparent to you is that M is limited in the chalets it can connect to. Because of the actions of the first and fourth rules, M cannot connect to K, L, or O. Thus, M must be directly connected to either J or N, but it cannot be connected to both or that would be a violation of the third rule. At the same time, from the second rule M must connect to another chalet, so M must be connected to J, or M must be connected to N, but not both. This limitation is one of the keys to the game.

With the that limitation in mind, let's examine the various solutions to the game:

Scenario Set 1: J and M connected

When J and M are connected, three segments are used, and two remain to be placed:

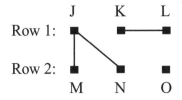

In this configuration, M is now "closed" to further connections, as is J (J is connected to two other chalets, and thus from the third rule J can not connect to any more chalets). Thus, only K, L, N, and O are available to connect the remaining two segments. From here, only four possible connections exist: K-N, L-O, N-O, and K-O. Any viable solution will use exactly two of these connections, so examine those possibilities and make sure they meet the rules.

1. K-N connections

When K and N are connected, N and K are then closed off to further connection (from the third rule), and so the only remaining possible connection is L-O:

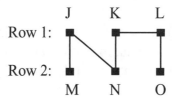

2. L-O connections

When L and O are connected, L is then closed off to further connection (from the third rule), and so the only remaining possible connection is K-N (which we just covered above) or N-O:

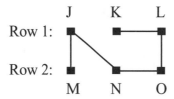

3. N-O connections

When N and O are connected, N is then closed off to further connection (from the third rule), and so the only remaining possible connection is L-O (which we just covered above) or K-O:

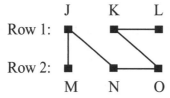

4. K-O connections

When K and O are connected, K is then closed off to further connection (from the third rule), and so the only remaining possible connection is N-O, which was in the prior discussion.

Let's now examine the next set of possibilities, the ones that occur when M and N are connected.

Scenario Set 2: M and N connected

When M and N are connected, three segments are used, and two remain to be placed:

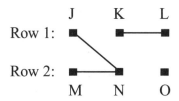

In this configuration, M is now "closed" to further connections, as is N (N is connected to two other chalets, and thus from the third rule N can not connect to any more chalets). Thus, only J, K, L, and O are available to connect the remaining two segments. From here, only four possible connections exist: J-K, J-O, L-O, and K-O. Any viable solution will use exactly two of these connections, so examine those possibilities and make sure they meet the rules.

1. J-K connections

When J and K are connected, J and K are then closed off to further connection (from the third rule), and so the only remaining possible connection is L-O:

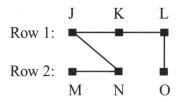

2. J-O connections

When J and O are connected, J is then closed off to further connection (from the third rule), and so the only remaining possible connection is K-O or L-O:

    J-O and K-O

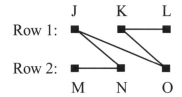

<u>J-O and L-O</u>

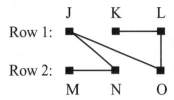

3. L-O connections

When L and O are connected, L is then closed off to further connection (from the third rule), and so the only remaining possible connection is J-O, which we just covered above. K-O is not a viable connection because then all six chalets would not be connected in a single, continuous path as specified in the scenario.

4. K-O connections

When K and O are connected, K is then closed off to further connection (from the third rule), and so the only remaining possible connection is J-O, which was covered in an earlier discussion.

So, there are only six possible solutions to the game:

Solution #1:   Solution #2:

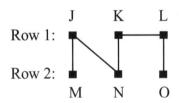   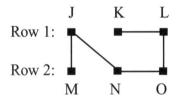

Solution #3:   Solution #4:

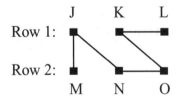   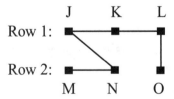

Solution #5:   Solution #6:

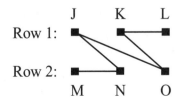   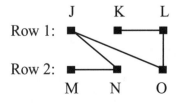

Question #18: Global, Could Be True. The correct answer choice is (E)

As shown in Solution #2, answer choice (E) can be true, and is therefore correct.

Question #19: Local, Must Be True. The correct answer choice is (C)

Only Solution #1 features a K-N connection, and in that solution L and O are also connected. Thus, answer choice (C) must be true and is correct.

Question #20: Local, Must Be True. The correct answer choice is (D)

Only Solution #4 features a J-K connection, and in that solution L and O are also connected. Thus, answer choice (D) must be true and is correct.

Question #21: Local, Could Be True. The correct answer choice is (A)

A K-O connection is featured in Solutions #3 and #5. Solution #3 also includes a J-M connection, and so answer choice (A) could be true, and is the correct answer.

Question #22: Global, Justify. The correct answer choice is (A)

From our analysis of the game, we know that M must connect to either J or N, but not both. The easiest way to force M to connect to N is to eliminate J as a possible connecting chalet. The easiest way to eliminate J from contention is to connect it so another chalet, thus connecting it to two chalets, thereby closing it off to further connections. Answer choice (A), which connects K and J, would maximize the number of connections J has, and would thus force M to connect to N. Answer choice (A) is correct.

Note that, once you determine that closing off J is the correct way to achieve the result desired in the question stem, you should immediately scan the answer choices for J. Only answer choice (A) contains J.

Question #23: Global, Cannot Be True. The correct answer choice is (C)

From our discussion of the setup, we determined that M had to be connected to one and only one other chalet (and a glance at the six solutions confirms that fact). Thus, answer choice (C) is correct.

Question #24: Local, Must Be True, Except. The correct answer choice is (B)

The question stem requires that you find a solution that has no "vertical" connector. Only Solution #5 does not contain a vertical connector. Answer choices (A), (C), (D), and (E) all describe connections contained within Solution #5, and so answer choice (B) is not necessarily true (in fact, (B) cannot be true), and is therefore the correct answer.

4

POWERSCORE®

PREPTEST

JUNE 1992 LOGIC GAMES SETUPS

This is a Basic Linear: Unbalanced: Overloaded game.

E G H I P R⁶

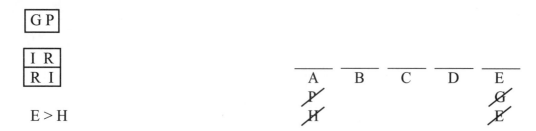

The A-E grades are chosen for the base in this game because they have an inherent sense of order (note that "E" was likely chosen by the test makers instead of the traditional "F" grade in order to make this linear order more obvious). However, this base has a unique, flexible nature where some of the grades do not necessarily have to be assigned. If, for example, John receives all A's and B's, then no grades of C, D, or E will be assigned. There are many other options as well, for example John could receive grades A through D, but no E grade. Or, in a different order, there might be no B grade, or no C grade. This flexibility in grade assignment makes the game much harder, especially because there are already more courses (six) than grades (five). Thus, we have at least a six-courses-into-five-grades relationship, but the five grades can be fewer depending on the circumstance.

A few notes about the rules:

• The first and last rules combine to form a GP block. This block yields a P Not Law on A, and a G Not Law on E.

• The second rule forms a rotating I R block, but because I or R could have the higher grade, no Not Laws can be drawn.

• The third rule creates an E > H sequence, and this creates an H Not Law on A, and an E Not Law on E.

The three rule formations are wholly separate, and at the outset can overlap. Thus, all the grades could be A's and B's, or all the grades could be C's and D's, etc. Because of the nature of the flexible grading, the Not Laws could also move if certain grades are removed from consideration. For example, if No A's are received, the P and H Not Laws on A would "slide" over to B. In short, while the setup to this game is quite easy, the questions can be made quite tricky because of all the options for grades and courses.

Question #1: Local, Must Be True. The correct answer choice is (C)

If John fails Russian, he must receive a D in Italian. Since the question stem specifies that John receives the same grade in economics and Italian, he must then receive a D in economics. From the third rule we know that his economics grade is higher than his history grade, so it follows that John must receive an E in history. Thus, answer choice (C) is correct.

Question #2: Local, Must Be True. The correct answer choice is (D)

If John passes all of his courses, then he does not receive an E in any course, and his grade possibilities are only A, B, C, or D.

Because his geology grade is higher than language block (G > IR or G > RI), at a minimum the geology, Italian, and Russian grades must be three separate grades. This could be A-B-C, A-C-D, or B-C-D. However, since his geology grade is one grade higher than his physics grade, at a minimum the geology, physics, Italian, and Russian grades must be either A-B-C, B-C-D, or A-B-C-D:

$$
\begin{array}{lccccc}
& & & \underline{\text{I/R}} & & \\
\text{Option \#3: B-C-D} & \underline{} & \underline{\text{G}} & \underline{\text{P}} & \underline{\text{R/I}} & \\
\\
& & \underline{\text{I/R}} & & & \\
\text{Option \#2: A-B-C} & \underline{\text{G}} & \underline{\text{P}} & \underline{\text{R/I}} & \underline{} & \\
\\
\text{Option \#1: A-B-C-D} & \underline{\text{G}} & \underline{\text{P}} & \underline{\text{I/R}} & \underline{\text{R/I}} & \\
& \text{A} & \text{B} & \text{C} & \text{D} &
\end{array}
$$

In each instance, at least one B and one C must be assigned, and so answer choice (D) is correct.

Question #3: Local, Justify. The correct answer choice is (E)

The rules in the question stem set up the following sequence:

$$\boxed{\text{G P}} > \text{E} > \boxed{\text{I/R \quad R/I}}$$

Take a moment to examine the sequence. Because of the way the variables are linked, we need at least five *separate* grades for the five courses in the sequence (one for G, a different one for P, a different one for E, a different one for R, and a different one for I). Of course, we only have a total of five separate grades and thus each of the five courses in the sequence must be assigned to a different grade. Hence, geology, which has the highest grade, must be an A, physics must be a B, and economics must be a C. Italian and Russian are the D and E grades, but not necessarily in that order.

The question stem asks us to provide a piece of information that will allow us to determine the grades for each of the six courses. Geology, physics, and economics are all assigned by the sequence above. Thus, only history, Italian, and Russian are yet to be determined. Because history is the only grade not in the sequence, we need an answer that includes history. And, because Italian and Russian have yet to be fully determined, we need an answer that will also allow us to determine the placement of Italian and Russian. Looking at the answer choices, only answer choices (C), (D), and (E) connect history to either Italian or Russian. One of these three answers is thus much more likely to be correct than answer choice (A) or (B), which only address part of what we need.

Answer choices (C) and (D) both fail to indicate whether history is a D or E and thus they do not determine all of the grades. In answer choice (C), history and Italian could both be assigned to D, or both could be assigned to E. Similarly, in answer choice (D), history and Russian could both be assigned to D, or both could be assigned to E. Both answers are functionally identical, and on the LSAT functionally identical answer choices are always incorrect (remember, the correct answer to an LSAT question is always unique; thus, if two answers are basically identical, neither can be correct, and they must both be incorrect).

Answer choice (E) is the correct answer. If the history grade is higher than the Russian grade, then history must be a D, Russian must then be an E, and Italian must be a D. Thus, all six grades are determined by answer choice (E).

Question #4: Local, Must Be True. The correct answer choice is (E)

If John receives a higher grade in physics than in economics, and a higher grade in history than Italian, the following sequence results:

$$\boxed{G\ P} > E > H > I$$

The sequence above includes five courses, and due to the nature of the sequence, all five courses much have a different grade. Thus, each of the five courses above must be assigned from A to E. The only remaining course, Russian, has to be assigned to a grade consecutive with Italian, and since Italian is assigned to E, Russian must be assigned to D. Accordingly, all six courses are determined:

$$
\begin{array}{ccccc}
 & & & R & \\
\underline{G} & \underline{P} & \underline{E} & \underline{H} & \underline{I} \\
A & B & C & D & E
\end{array}
$$

Consequently, answer choice (E) is correct.

Question #5: Local, Must Be True. The correct answer choice is (C)

The question stem states that John's grade in physics is higher that his grade in Italian, but consecutive with it. This creates a GPI block. The question stem also indicates that John's Russian grade is not the same as his physics grade, and this information creates a GPIR block. Because this GPIR block occupies four consecutive spaces, it must take up grades A-B-C-D or grades B-C-D-E. Accordingly, answer choice (C) is correct.

Question #6: Local, Justify. The correct answer choice is (E)

The question stem creates a GP > E > H sequence, and then asks for a piece of information that will force a grade of E to be assigned. Thus, either the sequence has to be pushed to start at grade B (which would force history to receive an E), or one of the languages has to be added to the beginning or end of the sequence in order to force all five grades to be assigned. Answer choice (E) forces all five grades to be assigned by adding Russian to the end of the sequence, creating the sequence GP > E > H > R.

This is a Grouping: Defined-Fixed, Unbalanced: Overloaded game.

There are initially nine possible shirt options: the three sizes in each of the three colors. The rules that indicate that no small red shirts and no large blue shirts are available leave only seven shirt types for Casey to choose from:

L ◄———┼———► S

~~SR~~ MR LR
SY MY LY
SB MB ~~LB~~

Thus, this Grouping game is reduced to selecting three shirts from a pool of seven total shirts. Because Casey cannot purchase both a large and small shirt, and there are not three small shirts or three large shirts available, it follows that Casey must *always* purchase at least one medium shirt:

$$\underline{\quad M \quad} \underline{\quad\quad} \underline{\quad\quad}$$
$$\text{3 shirts}$$

This inference is one of the keys to the game, and is the only significant inference that most people draw based on the game scenario and rules.

In a game such as this one, where there are very few inferences but not apparently a large number of possible solutions, an excellent approach is to make a few hypotheticals before attacking the questions. That can help you discover the medium shirt inference above.

Question #7: Local, Cannot Be True, FTT. The correct answer choice is (A)

This can be a tough starting question, since all of the answers combine colors and sizes in a general manner. However, one of the two "missing" shirts is critical to this question. Because no small red shirt is available, Casey can never buy two shirts that are small and two shirts that are red. For example, if Casey buys two small shirts, they would be blue and yellow, allowing him to buy just one red shirt, the medium red shirt. On the other hand, if he buys two red shirts, they would be medium and large, and then he could not buy even one small shirt (because of the third rule). It follows that answer choice (A) is correct.

Question #8: Local, Cannot Be True, FTT. The correct answer choice is (B)

In several respects, this question trades on the same concept as question #7. If Casey buys a small blue shirt, then he cannot buy any large shirts, and the maximum number of red shirts he can buy is one (a medium red shirt; remember, there are no small red shirts). Thus, answer choice (B) is correct.

Question #9: Local, Must Be True. The correct answer choice is (B)

Because Casey must always buy at least one medium shirt, if he does not buy a medium yellow shirt then he must buy either a medium red shirt or a medium blue shirt. Accordingly, answer choice (B) is correct.

Question #10: Local, Cannot Be True. The correct answer choice is (B)

If Casey buys exactly one medium shirt, and all three shirts are different colors, only two possible solutions exist:

$$\text{1. MR, SY, SB} \qquad \text{2. MB, LY, LR}$$

In neither case does Casey buy a medium yellow shirt, and thus answer choice (B) is correct.

Question #11: Local, Must Be True. The correct answer choice is (D)

The restriction in the question stem leaves Casey with only five shirt types to choose from:

$$
\begin{array}{ccc}
\cancel{SR} & MR & \cancel{LR} \\
SY & MY & LY \\
\cancel{SB} & MB & \cancel{LB}
\end{array}
$$

or

$$SY \quad MR \quad MY \quad MB \quad LY$$

There are a limited number of solutions at this point, and since Casey cannot purchase both a large shirt and a small shirt, each solution involves purchasing either two medium shirts, or all three medium shirts. If Casey must buy at least two medium shirts, then he must buy at least one from the group of the medium red shirt and medium blue shirt. Thus, answer choice (D) is correct.

If you are uncertain about answer choice (D), attempt to remove both the medium red shirt and medium blue shirt from consideration; at that point a viable group cannot be selected as only one shirt of each size remains.

This is a Grouping: Defined-Fixed, Unbalanced: Overloaded game.

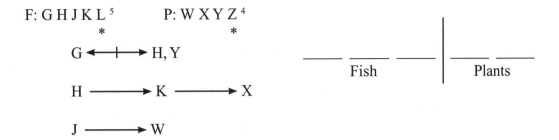

- L is the only random fish in the game, and Z is the only random plant in the game.

- Exactly three of the five fish must be selected. This means that *only two* of the five fish will not be selected. And, because exactly two plant species will be selected, exactly two will not.

- Because X is a necessary condition for two other variables, you should examine the effects of the contrapositive. If X is *not* selected, neither H nor K can be selected. Therefore, if X is not selected, G, J, and L must be the three fish selected. When J is selected, then W is selected, and when G is selected Y cannot be selected, leaving Z to be selected. Hence, when X is not selected, only one solution to the game exists:

$$\cancel{X} \longrightarrow G, J, L, W, Z$$

- A very tricky inference involves Y and X. When Y is selected, G cannot be selected. This leaves only four fish in the selection pool (no pun intended). Because there must be exactly three fish selected, we cannot eliminate X from the selection list because removing X would remove H and K as well, which would leave an insufficient number of fish. Thus, if Y is selected, the other plant that *must* be selected is X. Consequently, if Y is selected, J cannot be selected, since J requires W, and from the first rule G cannot be selected, meaning that when Y is selected there is only one possible solution to the game.

$$Y \longrightarrow H, K, L, X$$

This inference is tested on questions #16 and #17.

Question #12: Local, Could Be True, List. The correct answer choice is (B)

Answer choice (A) is incorrect because G and H cannot be selected together.

Answer choice (C) is incorrect because J requires W.

Answer choices (D) and (E) are both incorrect because H requires X.

Answer choice (B) is thus correct.

Question #13: Local, Must Be True. The correct answer choice is (B)

This question tests the straight linkage inference that when H is selected, then K is selected, and when K is selected then X is selected. Hence, when H is selected, then X is selected, and answer choice (B) is correct.

Question #14: Local, Could Be True, List. The correct answer choice is (C)

If X and Z are selected as the two plants, it follows that W and Y are not selected (because only two of the four plants are selected). If W is not selected, then J cannot be selected. Thus, any answer choice which contains J must be incorrect. Accordingly, answer choices (B), (D), and (E) can be eliminated. Answer choice (A) can be eliminated since it contains both G and H, a violation of the first rule. Thus, answer choice (C) is correct.

Question #15: Global, Could Be True, List, Except. The correct answer choice is (C)

Since the question asks you to find an *unacceptable* grouping of fish, and answer choice (C) contains H but not K, answer choice (C) is correct.

Question #16: Local, Must Be True, List. The correct answer choice is (D)

From the first rule, when Y is selected, G cannot be selected, and therefore answer choice (A) is incorrect. As discussed in the game setup, when Y is selected, J cannot be selected, and thus answer choices (B), (C), and (E) can be eliminated. Answer choice (D) is thereby correct.

Question #17: Global, Could Be True, Except. The correct answer choice is (B)

The correct answer choice is (B), W and Y. If a W and a Y were both selected, then G, H, and K would all be precluded from selection, since G cannot go with a Y, and H and K both need an X. This would leave only J and L as possible fish selections, which is unacceptable, because exactly three fish must be selected.

One effective method of attack on this question is to use the information from other questions and answer choices. For example, the information from question #12 can be used to instantly eliminate answer choice (A), and the information from question #14 can be used to instantly eliminate answer choice (E).

This is an Advanced Linear: Balanced game.

In this game, the ranking of the towns is the base, with a stack for each criterion: climate, location, and friendliness. Then, the towns are placed in each stack, and the set of five towns is repeated for each criterion:

P Q R S T ^{5}

	1	2	3	4	5
C:	___	___	___	___	___
L:	___	___	___	___	___
F:	___	___	___	___	___

The second, third, and fourth rules assign exact rankings to specific towns:

P Q R S T ^{5}

	1	2	3	4	5
C:	___	___	T	S	___
L:	___	Q	R	P	___
F:	___	___	___	Q	S

Thus, in the location rankings, S and T rotate between first and fifth:

P Q R S T ^{5}

	1	2	3	4	5
C:	___	___	T	S	___
L:	S/T	Q	R	P	T/S
F:	___	___	___	Q	S

The fourth, fifth, and sixth rules allow for a number of inferences:

- The fourth and fifth rules reveal that neither P nor R can be ranked first in friendliness. Thus, T must be ranked first in friendliness.

- The fifth rule involving the relationship between Riverdale's climate and friendliness rankings leads to the following inferences:

    If R is ranked second in climate, then R is ranked third in friendliness.

    If R is ranked second in friendliness, then R is ranked first in climate.

- Because Q must have three different rankings per the sixth rule, and Q is second in location, Q cannot be ranked second in climate.

- In climate, R must be ranked first or second, and Q must be ranked first or fifth, but P could be ranked first, second, or fifth.

This information can be combined to form the final diagram for the game:

P Q R S T⁵

$T_F > P_F$

$R_C > R_F$

C:	____	R/P	T	S	P/Q
		~~Q~~			~~R~~

L:	S/T	Q	R	P	T/S

F:	T	P/R	R/P	Q	S
	1	2	3	4	5
	~~P~~		~~T~~		
	~~R~~				

Question #18: Global, Could Be True, List. The correct answer choice is (B)

From the second to last rule, R can never be ranked fifth in climate, and thus answer choices (C), (D), and (E) can be eliminated. R could be ranked first or second on climate, and thus the correct answer is (B).

Question #19: Global, Cannot Be True. The correct answer choice is (C)

The diagram reveals that R can never be ranked fifth in any criteria, and thus answer choice (C) is correct.

Question #20: Global, Could Be True. The correct answer choice is (C)

Note that this game starts off with three Global questions. This is likely due to the fact that the setup contains so much information. After providing a sizable number of rules and inferences, the test makers want to check to see whether you have made all the proper deductions. The diagram reveals that each of the incorrect answers violates either the placement of a variable or a Not Law:

Answer choice (A): P can never be first in friendliness.

Answer choice (B): From the last rule, Q must have three different rankings.

Answer choice (D): S must be first or fifth in location.

Answer choice (E): T must be first in friendliness.

Hence, answer choice (C) is correct.

Question #21: Local, Must Be True. The correct answer choice is (D)

If Q is first in climate, then R must be second in climate. And, in the discussion of inferences, we noted that, "If R is ranked second in climate, then R is ranked third in friendliness." Thus, answer choice (D) is correct.

Question #22: Local, Could Be True. The correct answer choice is (A)

If P is ranked second in climate, then R must be ranked first in climate. This information eliminates answer choices (B) and (D).

Answer choice (C) can be eliminated because R can never be first in friendliness.

Answer choice (E) can be eliminated because T must be ranked first in friendliness. Thus, answer choice (A) is correct.

Question #23: Local, Must Be True. The correct answer choice is (E)

The additional conditions in the question stem establish the exact placement of all of the variables:

C:	R	P	T	S	Q

L:	T	Q	R	P	S

F:	T	R	P	Q	S
	1	2	3	4	5

Consequently, answer choice (E) is correct.

Question #24: Global, Cannot Be True. The correct answer choice is (E)

One of the key inferences of the game established that T must be ranked first in friendliness, and thus answer choice (E) cannot be true and is correct.

POWERSCORE®

6 PREPTEST

OCTOBER 1992 LOGIC GAMES SETUPS

PrepTest 6. October 1992 Game #1: *1. A 2. D 3. C 4. D 5. E 6. D*

This is a Grouping: Defined-Moving, Balanced, Numerical Distribution game.

This opening game on the October 1992 LSAT presented a difficult start for test takers. Upon reading that there are 14 variables in play, you have to expect that the test makers will limit the number of options involving the 14 variables because otherwise the game would be too difficult. Not surprisingly, the first rule limits the number of numerical options, and the next two rules effectively transforms the 14 variables into 7 variable "pairs." The game then becomes a "7 into 4" grouping game, which is considerably more manageable. The rules also create the following inferences:

1. Because at least one gerbil must always be with a hamster, and cages Y and Z cannot contain a gerbil, cages W and X must contain all of the gerbils and hamsters.

2. Because at least one lizard must always be with a snake, and cages W and X cannot contain a lizard, cages Y and Z must contain all of the lizards and snakes.

3. Because no cage can be empty, cages W and X *must* each contain at least one gerbil-hamster pair, and cages Y and Z *must* each contain at least one lizard-snake pair. This deduction is the key to the game.

4. Placing the pairs in inference 3 into each cage places 8 of the 14 animals. Only one gerbil and one hamster remain, and they act as a block that must be placed in W or X. Three snakes and one lizard remain, and they act as two separate blocks: one LS block and one SS block.

5. With inferences 3 and 4 above, only two numerical distributions exist for W and X: 4-2 and 2-4, and only three numerical distributions exist for Y and Z: 6-2, 4-4, and 2-6.

Combining all of the information above leads to the following setup:

Animals: G G G H H H L L L S S S S S ^{14}
Cages: W X Y Z ^{4}

Not yet placed: $\boxed{GH}$ (must go in either W or X) $\boxed{LS}$ (must go in either Y or Z)
$\boxed{SS}$ (must go in either Y or Z)

Placed: $\dfrac{GH}{W}$ $\dfrac{GH}{X}$ | $\dfrac{LS}{Y}$ $\dfrac{LS}{Z}$

Possible Numerical Distributions for W and X: Possible Numerical Distributions for Y and Z:

W	X	Y	Z
4	2	6	2
2	4	4	4
		2	6

Question #1: Global, Could Be True, List. The correct answer choice is (A)

Answer choice (A) is the correct answer choice.

Answer choice (B) is incorrect because cage W has three animals, which is impossible according to the first rule.

Answer choice (C) is incorrect because Y has five animals, which is impossible according to the first rule.

Answer choice (D) is incorrect because in the scenario presented there are four remaining snakes to be placed, but no more lizards to put with the snakes.

Answer choice (E) is incorrect because cages with gerbils must have hamsters.

Question #2: Local, Must Be True. The correct answer choice is (D)

If there are two hamsters in W then there must be two gerbils in W as well (to make an even number of animals). That means the last gerbil must be in X, leaving just one gerbil in cage X. According to the question stem, if there is one gerbil in X, then there is only one snake in Y, and the four remaining snakes must be in Z. Thus, answer choice (D) is correct.

Question #3: Local, Could Be True. The correct answer choice is (C)

If there are twice as many lizards in Z as in Y, then Z contains two lizards and Y has one. So there must be either two or four snakes in Z to make an even number (a total of four or six animals), and there must be either one or three snakes in Y (a total of two or four animals).

Answer choice (A) is incorrect because Y contains one lizard.

Answer choice (B) is incorrect because Y contains either one or three snakes.

Answer choice (C) is the correct answer choice.

Answer choice (D) is incorrect because Z contains either two or four snakes.

Answer choice (E) is incorrect because Z contains a total of either four or six animals.

Question #4: Local, Could Be True. The correct answer choice is (D)

If the number of animals in W equals the number of animals in Z, the cages could either both have two animals or both have four animals, and these are the only two distributions possible:

	W	X	Y	Z
W, Z = 2 animals:	2	4	6	2
W, Z = 4 animals:	4	2	4	4

Answer choices (A) and (B) can be immediately eliminated because they are each numerically impossible.

Answer choice (C) can be eliminated as there are not enough lizards to match with a single snake in order to meet the numerical requirements above.

The correct answer choice, (D), is the only answer that allows these distributions to be possible: If there are three snakes in Y then there are two snakes in Z, which means there are two lizards in Z for a total of four animals in Z. This works with the distribution possibilities so answer choice (D) could be true, and is thus correct.

Answer choice (E) is incorrect because if there were four snakes in Z, then there would have to two lizards as well, combining for a total of six animals, which is more than either distribution allows for.

Question #5: Local, Must Be True. The correct answer choice is (E)

If Y has six animals, then it must contain four snakes and two lizards (six total). That means that Z contains one snake and one lizard (two total). Answer choice (E) is correct because the number of snakes in Z (one) is equal to the number of lizards in Z (one).

Answer choices (A) and (B) are incorrect because W and X are unaffected by the animals in Y, and so although both of these answer can be true, neither of these answer *must* be true.

Answer choice (C) is incorrect because under the scenario in the question stem Z would contain one snake, not two snakes.

Answer choice (D) is incorrect because Y must contain four snakes and two lizards, not an equal amount of snakes and lizards.

Question #6: Local, Could Be True, Maximum. The correct answer choice is (D)

As we saw in the with the previous question, cage Y can contain four snakes at one time, which immediately eliminates answer choices (A), (B), and (C).

Y cannot contain five snakes because then there would be no remaining snakes to go with the gerbils in cage Z. So four is the maximum and (D) is the correct answer.

This is a Pure Sequencing game.

The five rules collectively address all seven of the variables (no randoms), and create the following chain relationship:

Variables: J K L M N O P [7]

N is circled because N cannot be last, and thus there is a special consideration for N that must be tracked at all times. Because N did not receive the fewest votes, it follows that M must have received the fewest votes.

Either L or J must have received the most votes, leading to the following linear diagram:

J/L						M
1	2	3	4	5	6	7

Note that the chain sequence can also be diagrammed as follows:

This diagram, although superficially different than the one above, conforms perfectly to the rules of the game. Regardless of how you diagram this chain sequence, you must have the relationships properly represented.

Question #7: Global, Could Be True, List. The correct answer choice is (C)

The best strategy on List questions is to use the individual rules of the game to eliminate incorrect answer choices:

Because O received more votes than K, answer choice (A) can be eliminated.

Because N did not receive the fewest votes, answer choice (B) can be eliminated.

Because J received more votes than O, answer choice (D) can be eliminated.

Because P received fewer votes that L, answer choice (E) can be eliminated.

Answer choice (C) is thus proven correct by process of elimination.

Question #8: Global, Must Be True. The correct answer choice is (E)

Because P received more votes than O, and because O received more votes than K, we can infer that P received more votes than K. Therefore, answer choice (E) is correct.

Although all of the other answer choices could be true, none of them must be true.

Question #9: Local, Cannot Be True, FTT. The correct answer choice is (C)

If the ranks of P, O, and K were consecutive, a POK block would be created. Consequently, J's rank would be higher than the ranks of P, O, and K because J received more votes than O. L's rank would also be higher than the POK block. N's rank would be lower than the ranks of P, O, and K because N received fewer votes than P. The overall ranking of the seven names would be as follows:

1. L or J
2. J or L
3. P
4. O
5. K
6. N
7. M

Since O would be ranked fourth and N would be ranked sixth, it follows that the statement "N received more votes than O" would have to be false. Therefore, answer choice (C) is correct.

Question #10: Global, Must Be True. The correct answer choice is (A)

Because M received the fewest votes, it can be deduced that M's exact rank is seventh. However, it is impossible to deduce the *exact* ranks of any of the other six names without additional information. Therefore, *one* is the total number of the soft drink names whose exact ranks can be deduced, and answer choice (A) is correct.

Question #11: Global, Must Be True, Maximum. The correct answer choice is (B)

The question asks you to determine the number of different soft drink names that can rank among the top three. Thus, you can configure the results in any fashion that accords with the rules in an attempt to determine the various names.

From our diagram, we can immediately eliminate M from consideration as M must always rank seventh. In addition, O must always have at least three names ranked ahead of it (L, P, and J in some order), and so O can be eliminated. With O eliminated from contention, K can also be eliminated as O receives more votes than K.

The remaining names are L, P, J, and N, and each of these could be (or must be, in some cases) ranked among the three most popular. Therefore, *four* is the maximum possible number of soft drink names any one of which could be among the three most popular, and answer choice (B) is correct.

Question #12: Local, Must Be True. The correct answer choice is (B)

If P received more votes than J, then L must be ranked first (only J or L can rank first, and with J eliminated from first, only L remains). P must then rank second as P has a higher rank than all remaining names. M, whose exact rank is always seventh, would be the only other name whose exact rank could be determined. Therefore, if P received more votes than J, then *three* would be the maximum possible number of names whose ranks could be determined. It follows that answer choice (B) is correct.

PrepTest 6. October 1992 Game #3: *13. E 14. A 15. D 16. A 17. D 18. B 19. C*

This is a Mapping—Supplied Diagram game.

The game scenario provides a diagram of the park benches that you should use for your main diagram.

The fourth rules states that no green bench stands next to a pink bench. Because there are only three bench colors—green, pink, and red—and the green and pink benches each form contiguous blocks that cannot be next to each other, the red benches must separate the two blocks. Further, because the green and pink bench blocks are both three blocks each, we can infer that the two red benches are exactly opposite of each other on the perimeter of the park. Thus, when the fifth rule establishes that T—a red bench—is on the southeast corner, we can infer that U is on the northwest corner:

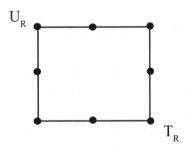

This must be the case otherwise there would not be sufficient room for both of the blocks to conform to the rules.

The sixth rule, which establishes that J—a green bench—is the center bench on the north side, allows us to infer that green benches occupy the three northeast benches and that pink benches occupy the three southeast benches:

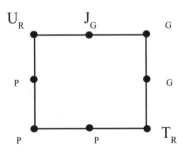

Of course, with J already placed, the remaining two green benches must rotate between K and L. The three pink benches are uncertain, although we know from the final rule that if X is the center south bench then L cannot be the center east bench, forcing K to be the center east bench and L to be the northeast corner bench. Note that the final rule is the only "active" rule in the game at this point, as all the other rules are accounted for and captured within the diagram.

These inferences combine to form the main diagram to the game:

Benches: J K L T U X Y Z ^{8}
Colors: G P R ^{3}

G: J K L ^{3}
P: X Y Z ^{3}
R: T U ^{2}

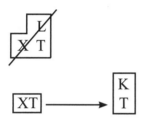

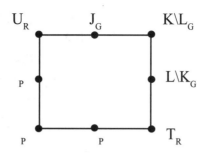

Question #13: Global, Could Be True. The correct answer choice is (E)

From our discussion in the setup, we know that K or L must be the bench on the northeast corner. Accordingly, answer choice (E) is correct.

Question #14: Global, Must Be True, Except. The correct answer choice is (A)

From our discussion in the setup, we know that U—a red bench—must be the bench on the northwest corner. Accordingly, answer choice (A) cannot be true and is correct.

Question #15: Global, Must Be True. The correct answer choice is (D)

From the sixth rule, J is the bench at the center of the park's north side. U is the bench on the northwest corner, and thus U must stand next to J. Answer choice (D) is thus correct.

Note that K or L *could* stand next to J, but neither *must* stand next to J.

Question #16: Global, Must Be True. The correct answer choice is (A)

K and L are both limited to two possible locations. Answer choice (A), which lists K, is thus correct.

Question #17: Local, Must Be True. The correct answer choice is (D)

If Z—a pink bench—is *directly* north of Y—another pink bench—then Z must be the bench in the center of the park's west side and Y must be the bench on the southwest corner. Consequently, the remaining pink bench—X—must be in the center of the south side. With X on the center of the south side, the last rule comes into play, forcing L to the northeast corner and K into the center of the east side:

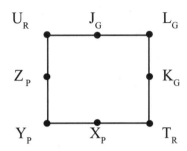

The diagram fills in every available space, and reveals that X is directly south of J. Thus, answer choice (D) is correct. Note that in this question, the word *directly* plays an important role in placing the variables and determining the correct answer.

Question #18: Local, Cannot Be True. The correct answer choice is (B)

The question stem places Y is in the middle of the west side of the park and then asks for what cannot occur. This placement leaves the following scenario:

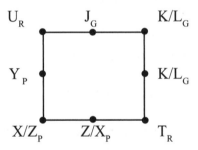

The question asks for what pair of benches cannot be on the corners. U and T are already placed at two of the corners, so focus on the other "open" corners. As mentioned before, the only "active" rule is the final one, so logic suggests that this rule will play a role in this question. What pairing of corner benches would force a violation of that rule? If K and Z are placed in the "open" corners, that would force an XTL block, which cannot occur according to the final rule. Thus, answer choice (B) would create a violation and is therefore the correct answer.

Question #19: Local, Must Be True, Except. The correct answer choice is (C)

If Y is farther south than L but farther north than T, then Y must be at the center of the west side and L must be on the northeast corner. K must then be at the center of the east side, leaving X and Z to rotate on the south side:

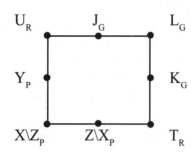

As X and Z are the only two benches that are not fixed, one of them must be in the correct answer. A scan of the answers indicates that only answer choices (C) and (E) contain X or Z or both. Answer choice (E) cannot be the correct answer because X and Z always are next to each other. In answer choice (C), X does not have to be next to T (Z can be next to T instead), and so answer choice (C) is correct.

This is a Mapping—Spatial Relations game.

A superficial reading of this game suggests that it is a Mapping—Spatial Relations game. The five islands are connected by bridges, and the entire scenario and rule set has the feel of a game that must be drawn out. However, a key consideration is missing from the rules: none of the bridges has to be straight. This fact completely changes this game, and makes virtually any configuration of bridges possible. Thus, the game turns from a Mapping game and becomes a Grouping game, where the connection possibilities are paramount. Remember: in games that appear to be based on mapping or connections, *always* determine whether the connections must be straight or not. If they are, then the game is about drawing; if they are not, the game is about grouping.

With the straightness of the bridges a non-factor, we can ignore the rule about intersecting bridges and focus on the connections between the islands. In fact, in our diagram we won't be concerned with any intersections—we just will focus on the connections.

Initially, we know there are five islands: J K L M O⁵.

The fourth rule divides the islands into two groups: J, K, and L, which are each connected to M or O or both. Thus, our initial diagram will show those islands in two separate columns:

J K L M O⁵

J   O

K   M

L

Of course, the last rule establishes that J is connected to O, and O is connected to M:

J K L M O⁵

Note that the connections have no direction, so there are no arrows at the end of each line. This means that once an island is connected to another, the connection goes "both" ways.

Note that O now has two connections, and from the third rule we can infer that O can connect to at most one more island. Because K and L must connect to M or O (or both), we can infer that if K connects to O, then L must connect to M. Alternatively, if L connects to O, then K must connect to M. These two inferences can be shown as:

$$(L — O) \longrightarrow (K — M)$$

$$(K — O) \longrightarrow (L — M)$$

The parentheses are not necessary, but they are used here for the sake of clarity.

The last point of analysis is to analyze the fifth and sixth rules. The sixth rules states that K is connected to exactly one other island. From the third rule, we know that island must be O or M:

$$K \longrightarrow O/M$$

The fifth rule states that J is connected to exactly two islands. From the seventh rule we already know that J is connected to O, so O must be one of the two islands. The other three choices are K, L, and M, but because K can only connect to O or M, J cannot connect to K, leaving J with the choice of one of L or M (J cannot connect to both L and M because that would connect J to three island—O, L, M—a violation of the fifth rule). Thus, J connects to O and either L or M:

$$J \longrightarrow O, L/M$$

With this information, we arrive at the final setup to the game:

J K L M O [5]

$$J \longrightarrow O, L/M$$

$$K \longrightarrow O/M$$

$$(L — O) \longrightarrow (K — M)$$

$$(K — O) \longrightarrow (L — M)$$

```
J — O
      |
K     M

L
```

Question #20: Global, Could Be True, List. The correct answer choice is (D)

In our analysis of the game, we did not directly discuss the possibilities for L, but we did so indirectly. L cannot connect to K (because K can connect to only O or M), but we discussed possibilities for L to connect to J, M, and O. Thus, answer choice (D) is correct.

Question #21: Global, Could Be True. The correct answer choice is (C)

Answer choice (A) is incorrect because if J were connected to L and M, that would violate the fifth rule that states that J is connected to exactly two bridges (remember, J is also connected to O).

Answer choice (B) is incorrect because it violates the sixth rule that states that K connects to exactly one other island.

Answer choice (C) is the correct answer. If L connect to both J and M, then K could connect to M or O.

Answer choice (D) is incorrect because M would be connected to four islands (O, J, K, and L), a violation of the third rule.

Answer choice (E) is incorrect because O would be connected to four islands (J, M, K, and L), a violation of the third rule.

Question #22: Local, Could Be True. The correct answer choice is (B)

From our discussion of the connection possibilities, if K is O, then L is connected to M:

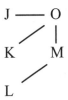

Answer choice (A) is false, and so it can be eliminated.

O is now closed to further connections, eliminating answer choices (C) and (E).

Answer choice (D) can be eliminated because L is connected to M, but it cannot connect to K or O, leaving only J as a possible connection. Thus, L can connect to at most two other islands, not three.

Answer choice (B) is the correct answer because J could connect to L or to M.

Question #23: Local, Must Be True. The correct answer choice is (B)

If L is connected to M and O, the following connections result:

With L connected to O, O is closed and thus from our inference discussion K *must* connect to M:

```
        J ——— O
         /    |
       K——— M
        //
       L
```

Remember, because the bridges can curve as much as needed, we are not worried about the apparent intersection above. We would easily overcome that problem by looping a bridge from K to M around the other islands, but that is a waste of time.

Accordingly, answer choice (B) is correct.

Note that we can also infer that J must connect to L, because J must connect to exactly two bridges, and K, M, and O all have the maximum number of connections allowed by the rules. This information eliminates answer choices (A) and (D).

Question #24: Local, Must Be True. The correct answer choice is (A)

The condition in this question stem immediately affects J. From the fifth and seventh rules, J must connect to O and exactly one other island, namely L or M. If any island connected to M cannot also connect to O, and J is already connected to O, then J cannot connect to M and consequently J must connect to L. Accordingly, answer choice (A) is correct.

6

POWERSCORE

7

PREPTEST

FEBRUARY 1993 LOGIC GAMES SETUPS

This is a Basic Linear: Balanced game.

G H L O P S N[7]
  *   *

LO > N	
P/G _____ _____ G/P	

	1	2	3	4	5	6	7
	N̸	N̸				L̸	L̸
	Ø						Ø

This game, from the February 1993 LSAT, is one of the easiest LSAT games of the modern era. As we will see in the remainder of the explanations for this exam, some of the other games on this particular test were considerably harder.

Given that there are only three rules, which combine into two rule formations, you have to conclude that the key to the game comes from the interaction between the PG split-block and the LON block-sequence.

Question #1: Local, Must Be True. The correct answer choice is (C)

If G is played second, then P must be played fifth. The only placement option then remaining for the LO block is third and fourth:

	G	L	O	P	N/	/N
1	2	3	4	5	6	7

Accordingly, answer choice (C) is correct.

Question #2: Global, Could Be True, Except. The correct answer choice is (A)

The Not Laws establish that N cannot be played first or second, and thus answer choice (A) is correct.

Question #3: Local, Could Be True, Maximum, List. The correct answer choice is (C)

This is a maximum question, wherein you are asked to separate two variables by the maximum number of spaces. Interestingly, H and S are the two randoms in this game, and so to schedule them as far apart as possible would be to place them in the first and last slots, assuming that the two rule formations in play could fit in slots 2-6. As we know from the diagram in question #1, the two rules can occupy slots 2-6, and thus we can place H and S in the first and last slots in some order:

H/S	G	L	O	P	N	H/S
1	2	3	4	5	6	7

Consequently, answer choice (C) is correct.

Question #4: Local, Must Be True. The correct answer choice is (C)

This is an odd question stem because it is identical in function to question #1. Consequently, we can use the same diagram as question #1, and conclude that answer choice (C) is correct.

Question #5: Global, Could Be True, Maximum. The correct answer choice is (E)

As in question #3, this question asks us to maximize the number of spaces between two variables, in this case, N and S. S, as we know, is a random, whereas N is involved in one of the two rule formations. However, N can be moved to the last tape without creating a rule violation, and so it makes sense to examine what occurs when S is first and N is last:

$$\frac{S}{1} \quad \frac{}{2} \quad \frac{}{3} \quad \frac{}{4} \quad \frac{}{5} \quad \frac{}{6} \quad \frac{N}{7}$$

Again, we are left with P and G, and LO to manipulate, plus H, a random. Why not try P and G in 2-5, just as in questions #1, #3, and #4? Not surprisingly, we can create a workable solution:

$$\frac{S}{1} \quad \frac{P}{2} \quad \frac{L}{3} \quad \frac{O}{4} \quad \frac{G}{5} \quad \frac{H}{6} \quad \frac{N}{7}$$

Although P and G could also be placed in 3-6, all we need is one hypothetical that proves that S and N can be separated by the maximum spaces possible to prove answer choice (E) correct.

Question #6: Global, Must Be True. The correct answer choice is (C)

The Not Laws help prove answer choice (C) correct. To prove that N can be played fifth, use a simple hypothetical, such as this one:

$$\frac{P}{1} \quad \frac{H}{2} \quad \frac{S}{3} \quad \frac{G}{4} \quad \frac{L}{5} \quad \frac{O}{6} \quad \frac{N}{7}$$

Question #7: Global, Must Be True, Justify. The correct answer choice is (D)

As we know from questions #1 and #4, assigning P and G into the second and fifth slots forces L and O into the second and third slots. Hence, answer choice (D) is correct.

This game is considered easy for two reasons: there are only three rules (and two of them perfectly link together), and many of the question reuse the same configuration where P and G are placed into 2-5. Because of these two factors, most students move through the questions quickly and with confidence.

This is an Advanced Linear: Balanced game.

This Defined, Balanced game is one of our favorites of all time. The game contains four variable sets: days of the week, morning activities, afternoon activities, and the four different activities. In setting up the game most students make a crucial mistake: they fail to show Thursday on the diagram. At first, this would not seem to be a big issue since the game scenario does not identify Thursday as a day on which Doctor Yamata works. But, because of the rule that states that "she lectures on exactly *two consecutive calendar days*," the issue of consecutive days is critical, and a diagram without Thursday gives the false impression that Wednesday and Friday are consecutive. Once this mistake is made, the options for the LL block appear greater than they actually are, and making inferences becomes difficult. Fortunately, the first question of the game reveals that there is a major inference involving one of the lectures. Answering this question is critical to your success on the game. Remember, if you are faced with a Global question that indicates that one (or more) of the variables *must* be placed in a certain position (as with questions #8 and #12 of this game), you must answer the question. If you do not, you will miss a critical piece of information that will likely affect your performance on all other questions. In the case of question #8, if you do not have the answer when you arrive at the question, it is a fairly clear signal that you have missed something big in the setup.

When representing Thursday, mark each slot with an "X" in order to indicate that no work is done:

Afternoon:	__	__	__	X	__	__
Morning:	__	__	__	X	__	__
	M	Tu	W	Th	F	Sa

Note that you could show Sunday but it too would have an X in both slots. With this basic diagram the rules can now be applied:

L O T R [4]

[L L]	Afternoon:	__	__	__	X	__	__	←	T T T [L L]
[O_M / O_Tu]	Morning:	__	__	__	X	__	__	←	O O O T R
		M	Tu	W	Th	F	Sa		

Listing which activities occur in the morning and afternoon takes a considerable amount of time, and these activities have been placed on the right side of the diagram. The rules indicate that in the afternoon there will be three T's and two L's, and in the morning there will be three O's, one R, and one T. This is extremely valuable information since it defines the composition of each row. Now that the rules have been added, we can begin to make inferences.

The first inference involves Saturday afternoon. According to the rules, Doctor Yamata can only lecture or treat patients in the afternoon. But on Saturday she cannot lecture, so it follows that she must treat patients, and a "T" can be placed on Saturday afternoon:

	M	Tu	W	Th	F	Sa	
Afternoon:				X		T	T T T L L
Morning:				X			O O O T R
						~~L~~ ~~O~~	

Once T is established on Saturday afternoon, it becomes apparent that the LL block can only be placed on Monday-Tuesday or Tuesday-Wednesday:

	M	Tu	W	Th	F	Sa	
Afternoon:	L/	L	/L	X		T	T T T L L
Morning:				X			O O O T R
						~~L~~ ~~O~~	

Note that Tuesday must always have a lecture and the other lecture will be placed on Monday or Wednesday, as shown by the split-option. Thus, in the afternoon, only two treatments remain to be assigned. One treatment will be placed on Friday afternoon (since it cannot be a lecture it must be a treatment), and the other treatment will fill in the Monday-Wednesday option:

	M	Tu	W	Th	F	Sa	
Afternoon:	L/T	L	T/L	X	T	T	T T T L L
Morning:				X			O O O T R
						~~L~~ ~~O~~	

Consequently the afternoon spaces are filled, and it is revealed that only two solutions to the afternoon set exist:

	M	Tu	W	Th	F	Sa
Afternoon option #1:	L	L	T	X	T	T
Afternoon option #2:	T	L	L	X	T	T

When seen in this light, it becomes obvious that the answer to question #8 is (B).

With the afternoon completed, we can now turn to an analysis of the morning row. Since Doctor Yamata cannot operate on Saturdays, on Saturday morning she is left with the choice of treating patients or conducting research. This is shown with a dual-option on Saturday morning:

Afternoon:	L/T	L	T/L	X	T	T		T T T L L
Morning:	__	__	__	X	__	R/T		O O O T R
	M	Tu	W	Th	F	Sa		

(with S̶u̶ and ∅̶ crossed out below Sa)

This leaves four morning spaces to be filled by three O's and the remainder of the T/R dual-option. At first glance it may seem that no inferences can be drawn regarding the placement of these variables. However, the rule involving operations on Monday and Tuesday has a powerful effect on the possible placement of the three O's: because only one operation can be performed on the Monday-Tuesday pair, this forces the other two operations to be performed on Wednesday and Friday:

Afternoon:	L/T	L	T/L	X	T	T		T T T L L
Morning:	__	__	O	X	O	R/T		O O O T R
	M	Tu	W	Th	F	Sa		

(with S̶u̶ and ∅̶ crossed out below Sa)

In summary, when an operation is performed on Monday, the operations rule prevents Doctor Yamata from operating on Tuesday; therefore, the remaining two operations must be performed on Wednesday and Friday. When an operation is performed on Tuesday, Doctor Yamata cannot operate on Monday, and the remaining two operations must again be performed on Wednesday and Friday. Hence, we can infer that operations are always performed on Wednesday and Friday.

The diagram is not yet complete. The final operation must be performed on Monday or Tuesday morning, next to the remainder of the T/R dual-option. This can be somewhat difficult to diagram, and we use a special parenthetical notation:

Morning:	(O , T/R)	
	M Tu	

The parentheses indicate that one of the two enclosed spaces must be an operation and the other space must be a treatment or research; it also indicates that the order is unknown. In this way the notation efficiently captures the four possibilities for Monday and Tuesday morning: OT, OR, TO, and RO. With this final piece the diagram for the game is complete:

L O T P [4]

L L	Afternoon:	T/L	L	L/T	X	T	T	⟵ T T T	L L
O_M /O_Tu	Morning:	(O , T/R)		O	X	O	R/T	⟵ O O O T R	
		M Tu		W	Th	F	Sa		

(with S̶u̶ and ∅̶ crossed out below Sa)

Question #8: Global, Must Be True. The correct answer choice is (B)

As discussed in the setup to the game, the inference regarding the placement of the LL block in the afternoons proves answer choice (B) correct.

Question #9: Global, Could Be True. The correct answer choice is (C)

According to the final diagram, on Wednesday morning Doctor Yamata can only be scheduled to perform an operation. Thus, answer choices (A), (B), and (E) can be eliminated. On Wednesday afternoon she can only treat patients or lecture, and so answer choice (D) can be eliminated. Thus, answer choice (C) must be correct.

Question #10: Global, Must Be True. The correct answer choice is (E)

This is the most difficult question of the game. Each of the answers seem vague—in direct contrast to the final diagram, which is quite specific. The correct answer choice, (E), uses the Overlap Principle.

In answer choice (E) the Overlap Principle applies to the lectures and operations on Monday, Tuesday and Wednesday. Two operations and two lectures must be assigned within this three day period and consequently there must be an overlap between the two groups. Consider all the possible permutations of the lectures and operations for those days:

Afternoon:	L	L	_		Afternoon:	_	L	L
Morning:	_	O	O		Morning:	_	O	O
	M	Tu	W			M	Tu	W

Afternoon:	L	L	_		Afternoon:	_	L	L
Morning:	O	_	O		Morning:	O	_	O
	M	Tu	W			M	Tu	W

In each case at least one lecture is given on a day the doctor operates, and sometimes it occurs twice.

Question #11: Local, Could Be True. The correct answer choice is (E)

According to the rules, Doctor Yamata must treat patients once in the mornings and three times in the afternoons. Answer choices (A) and (B) are both incorrect because they feature two mornings and two afternoons. We have also determined that Doctor Yamata must operate on Wednesday morning, and therefore she cannot treat patients in that slot. Since answer choices (C) and (D) both include Wednesday morning, they are incorrect. Accordingly, answer choice (E) is correct. Note that there are a number of ways to attack this question. For example, it is known that Doctor Yamata must treat patients on both Friday and Saturday afternoon. That fact eliminates answer choices (A) and (C).

Question #12: Global, Must Be True. The correct answer choice is (E)

The first set of inferences proved that Doctor Yamata must treat patients on both Friday afternoon and Saturday afternoon. It follows that answer choice (E) is correct. In a sense, both question #8 and #12 are part of a pair: if you get one correct, you will likely get the other correct. That shows the powerful nature of the inferences, and the necessity of identifying those inferences.

It is also interesting to note that in this game four of the five questions are Global. When a game has a majority of Global questions, that often indicates that the game contains deep and challenging inferences. That is certainly the case here.

This is a Grouping: Defined-Moving, Balanced, Numerical Distribution game.

One popular approach to this game is to use the seven judges as the base. While this approach can work, separating the judges into the For and Against groups is more effective, in part because it turns the game into a two-value system, which has a dramatic effect on the contrapositive of several rules, and in part because it better captures the fact that there are at least two judges in each group. Remember, always look to first establish the composition of the groups in any game. In this case, because each group has at least two votes, there are two unfixed numerical distributions in operation: 5-2 and 4-3.

The only way to track the variables in the rules is to use subscripts indicating which way each judge voted.

The key inference to this game is that at least one L must vote for Datalog because all three cannot vote against Datalog. If all three L's attempted to vote against Datalog, then both C's would have to vote for Datalog, which is impossible according to the given rules.

Once it has been established that at least one L must vote for Datalog, this information can be applied to the other rules and it can be inferred that when the CCL block occurs it must occur on the Against side, and also that when the LLL block occurs it must occur on the For side. This understanding helps eliminate some of the uncertainty that initially appears to be present in this difficult game.

The LLL rule yields an interesting inference via the contrapositive, that if one C votes for Datalog, then at least one L votes against Datalog. This inference is largely useless in the game.

$CCMMLLL^7$

Question #13: Local, Could Be True. The correct answer choice is (B)

Answer choices (D) and (E) can be eliminated because the maximum number of conservatives voting for Datalog is one. Answer choice (C) can be eliminated because if all three liberals vote for Datalog then the two conservatives must vote against Datalog. Answer choice (A) is incorrect because this scenario would mean that two conservatives and a liberal voted against Datalog, and it would then follow that the two moderates voted against Datalog, a violation of the question stem. Thus, answer choice (B) is correct.

Question #14: Global, Must Be True. The correct answer choice is (C)

Answer choice (C) reflects the major inference of the game.

Question #15: Local, Must Be True. The correct answer choice is (E)

Answer choice (E) follows from an understanding of the answer to question #14, and the reasoning behind this inference was discussed in the setup.

Question #16: Local, Must Be True. The correct answer choice is (A)

The condition in the question stem sets up a fixed 5-2 distribution. As nothing may immediately jump out at you from an inference standpoint, try using hypotheticals to solve this problem. The following two hypotheticals effectively attack this problem:

```
   M                        M
   M                        M
   L                        C
   L      C                 L      L
   L      C                 L      C
   F      A                 F      A
```

The two hypotheticals eliminate every answer choice except answer choice (A), the correct answer.

Question #17: Global, Could Be True, Except. The correct answer choice is (E)

Answer choice (E) contains six judges, an impossibility under the numerical constraints of the game. Again, numbers are always important, and games with distributions almost always have answer choices that play upon the numbers.

Question #18: Local, Must Be True, Except. The correct answer choice is (B)

The question stem invokes the "CCL Against" rule discussed in the setup. Accordingly, answer choice (B) is correct.

This is an Advanced Linear: Balanced, Identify the Templates game.

This game contains three variable sets: lanes, runners, and charities. The lanes should be chosen as the base since they have an inherent sense of order, and then the other two variable sets should be stacked above the lanes. This creates an Advanced Linear setup:

Charities: F G H J K ^{5}
Runners: L N O P S ^{5}
Lanes: 1   2   3   4   5

The first rule is easy to address:

Charities: F G H J K ^{5} ____ ____ ____ K ____
Runners: L N O P S ^{5} ____ ____ ____ ____ ____
Lanes: 1   2   3   4   5

The second rule creates a sizable block:

| F/G ___ G/F |
| ___ P ___ |

Because K is already fourth, this block can only be assigned to lanes 1-3 or 3-5. Note that this placement automatically limits P to lane 2 or lane 4, and that lane 3 must be F or G (at this point).

The third rule creates another block, which has two possibilities that must be shown separately:

| G ___ ___ ___ |
| ___ ___ ___ O |

or

| ___ ___ ___ G |
| O ___ ___ ___ |

Because K is already fourth, this block can only be assigned to lanes 1-4 (with G in lane 1) or 2-5.

The fourth rule is a simple sequential rule:

N > S

While we could take a moment and draw out the numerous Not Laws that follow from the rules above, a better approach is to examine the two blocks because they share a common variable: G. In fact, the two blocks can only be combined in two ways, creating two super-blocks that ultimately control the game:

G	_	F	_
_	P	_	O

or

_	F	_	G
O	_	P	_

These two blocks represent the only possible combinations of the second and third rules (other combinations initially appear possible, but could not fit within the five-lane constraint imposed by the game). These two blocks are difficult to place, and with the additional rules that K is fourth and N > S, there can only be a limited number of solutions to the game. The best decision, then, is to diagram the templates that result from placing each block. In this case, the interaction of the blocks is so limiting that it produces only two basic solution paths for the game:

Template #1:

In this template, the super-block is placed in lanes 1-4. In the charities stack, only J and H are uncertain, and they rotate between lanes 2 and 5. In the runners stack, P and O are placed, and L, N, and S are unplaced. However, due to the fourth rule, S cannot be first, leaving a N/L dual-option, and N cannot be fifth, leaving a S/L dual-option. The only rule to track is the N > S rule.

N > S

G	H/J	F	K	J/H
N/L	P		O	S/L
1	2	3	4	5

Template #2:

In this template, the super-block is placed in lanes 2-5. In the charities stack, only J and H are uncertain, and they rotate between lanes 1 and 2. In the runners stack, P and O are placed, and L, N, and S are unplaced. However, due to the fourth rule, S cannot be first, leaving a N/L dual-option, and N cannot be fifth, leaving a S/L dual-option. The only rule to track is the N > S rule.

N > S

J/H	H/J	F	K	G
N/L	O		P	S/L
1	2	3	4	5

By identifying these two templates during the setup, the questions can be answered easily.

Question #19: Global, Could Be True, List. The correct answer choice is (E)

This question asks for a possible assignment of charities to lanes. Answer choice (C) can be eliminated because from the first rule K is always in lane 4. You may have noticed that both templates place F in lane 3, and so any answer choice without F in 3 must be incorrect. That eliminates answer choices (A), (B), and (D) from contention. Answer choice (E) is thus proven correct by process of elimination, and answer choice (E) conforms to Template #2.

Question #20: Global, Must Be True. The correct answer choice is (D)

From the two templates, P must be assigned to lane 2 or lane 4, but that specific answer is not listed. However, we can see that O alternates with P in lanes 2 and 4, and so P is always separated from O by exactly one lane. Hence, answer choice (D) is correct.

Note how easy this question is to solve with the template approach, and think for a moment how difficult this question would be if you did not have the templates.

Question #21: Local, Must Be True. The correct answer choice is (B)

If O is assigned to lane 2, Template #2 is in effect. In that template G must be assigned to lane 5, and so answer choice (B) is correct.

Answer choice (C) could be true, but the question asks for what must be true, so (C) is incorrect.

In contrast to the prior question, this question does not require the templates, and could have been answered easily by applying the third rule.

Question #22: Global, Could Be True, List. The correct answer choice is (D)

We know from the two templates and question #19 that F is always in lane 3. O and P must always occupy lanes 2 and 4, and so any answer containing O or P can be eliminated. This removes answer choices (B), (C), and (E) from contention. The only difference between answer choices (A) and (D) is S, and S can be assigned to lane 3 (N would be assigned to lane 1, and L would be assigned to lane 5). Thus, answer choice (D) is correct.

Question #23: Local, Must Be True. The correct answer choice is (B)

N can represent J only under Template #2, and once J and N are assigned, then H must be assigned to lane 2, leaving L and S rotating between lanes 3 and 5:

N > S		J	H	F	K	G
		N	O	L/S	P	S/L
		1	2	3	4	5

Accordingly, answer choice (B) is correct.

Question #24: Local, Could Be True. The correct answer choice is (A)

L can represent J under either template. In Template #1, L would have to be assigned to lane 5, and in Template #2, L would have to be assigned to lane 1. This immediately eliminates answer choice (D) since L is assigned to lane 3 in that answer.

In the two templates, O or P is assigned to lane 2, and this fact eliminates answer choices (B), (C), and (E). Thus, only answer choice (A) remains, and, accordingly, answer choice (A) is correct. Under Template #2, the runners can be assigned in an L-O-N-P-S order.

PrepTest 8

June 1993 Logic Games Setups

This is a Basic Linear: Unbalanced: Overloaded game.

HIKOUZ[6]

```
              *              M ___ |  Z̸
H        ┌───┬───┐           Tu ___
         │ O │ K │           W ___ |
V        ├───┼───┤           Th _I_
         │ K │ O │           F ___
Z        └───┴───┘
```

This setup has been created vertically to make it easier to show that Monday and Wednesday have only one student. The bar at the end of the slots on each of those days signifies that only one student can be assigned to each day.

This game is Unbalanced: Overloaded because there are six students but only five available days. The game scenario establishes that all five days are used and that all students are tutored, and that one of the days receives two students. Thus, there is a 2-1-1-1-1 numerical distribution of students to the days, where the instructor coaches one student every day, except for one of the days where the instructor coaches two students. Although this distribution is in general quite manageable, this game turns out to be difficult.

The fourth rule establishes that neither Monday nor Wednesday can be the day with two students, and thus either Tuesday, Thursday, or Friday has two students. Within this group of three, Thursday is the most restricted because the addition of one more variable satisfies the two students-on-one-day rule. Thus, Monday, Wednesday, and Thursday should be scrutinized closely in this game because the assignment of any available student to one of those days "closes off" that day to further students.

Note that one approach to this game would be to quickly sketch out all three scenarios—one where Tuesday is assigned two students, one where Thursday is assigned two students, and one where Friday is assigned two students.

The first rule creates an H > Z sequence. Because Monday can be assigned only one student, a Z Not Law is created on Monday. However, because Friday can be assigned two students, no Not for H can be created on Friday, although Friday is the only day on which both H and Z could possibly be coached by the instructor.

The third rule creates a rotating block between K and O. While this block initially appears unimportant, note that the block action in combination with the limitation of only one day having two students creates certain inferences involving K and O. For example, if two students are assigned to Tuesday, that pair must include either K or O (if Tuesday did not have K or O, then K or O would have to go on Thursday, but this would violate the rule about exactly one day being assigned two students).

Question #1: Global, Could Be True, List. The correct answer choice is (D)

Answer choices (A), (B), and (E) would force two students to be assigned to both Tuesday and Thursday, a violation of the rules (if this is not apparent, try hypotheticals for each answer; the violation will become apparent when you attempt to place all the variables). Answer choice (C) is incorrect because K and O must be scheduled for consecutive days. Thus, answer choice (D) is proven correct by process of elimination. Overall, this is a very difficult List question—much harder than average.

Question #2: Local, Must Be True, Minimum. The correct answer choice is (B)

The easiest method of solving this question involves making a quick hypothetical with Z placed as early as possible, on Tuesday (not Monday because we already know from our discussion that Z cannot be assigned to Monday):

$$
\begin{array}{lll}
\text{M} & \underline{\text{H}} \,\rfloor \\
\text{Tu} & \underline{\text{K}} & \underline{\text{Z}} \\
\text{W} & \underline{\text{O}} \,\rfloor \\
\text{Th} & \underline{\text{I}} \\
\text{F} & \underline{\text{U}}
\end{array}
$$

As this hypothetical is a viable solution, Tuesday is a day that Z can be scheduled, and answer choice (B) is correct.

Question #3: Global, Must Be True. The correct answer choice is (D)

This type of question would usually take a great deal of time because of the "ifs" present in each answer choice. Thus, generally it would be wise to do this type of question at the end of the game, after you have gathered as many hypotheticals as possible. In this case the hypothetical from question #2 eliminates answer choice (E). No other hypothetical from the game eliminates an answer choice, and you are forced to examine each answer choice on its own merits. Answer choice (D) is correct since U on Thursday fulfills the two-on-one-day rule, forcing the KO block into Monday, Tuesday, or Wednesday. This leaves the H > Z sequence, and since no more doubles are allowed, H must go on Monday or Wednesday, leaving only Z to go on Friday.

Question #4: Global, Justify. The correct answer choice is (D)

Similar to answer choice (D) in the previous question, Thursday plays the key role. If Z is placed on Thursday, the two-on-one-day rule is fulfilled. This forces K, O, and H to fill in Monday, Tuesday, and Wednesday in some order. Thus, U must go on Friday, and answer choice (D) is correct.

Question #5: Local, Could Be True. The correct answer choice is (A)

Answer choice (B) forces U and I on Thursday and H and Z on Friday, a violation of the two-on-one-day rule. Answer choice (C) forces a double on Tuesday and on Thursday, since either K or O would have to go on Thursday. Answer choice (D) forces three variables onto Thursday, a violation of the rules. Answer choice (E) forces three variables, U, H, and Z, onto Friday, again a violation of the rules. Answer choice (A), the correct answer, can be proven by the following hypothetical:

$$
\begin{array}{ll}
\text{M} & \underline{\text{U} \,|} \\
\text{Tu} & \underline{\text{H}} \\
\text{W} & \underline{\text{Z} \,|} \\
\text{Th} & \underline{\text{I}} \quad \underline{\text{O}} \\
\text{F} & \underline{\text{K}} \\
\end{array}
$$

PrepTest 8. June 1993 Game #2: *6. C 7. B 8. B 9. D 10. A 11. B 12. E*

This is a Circular Linearity, Identify the Possibilities game.

The first rule establishes that at least one of any three consecutively numbered lights is off, meaning three lights in a row cannot be on:

$$\boxed{\text{O } \cancel{\text{O}} \text{ O}}$$

The second rule establishes that light 8 is on:

O = on $\cancel{\text{O}}$ = off

$$\begin{array}{ccc} 1 & 2 & 3 \\ \text{O } 8 & & 4 \\ 7 & 6 & 5 \end{array}$$

The third rule states that lights 2 and 7 cannot be on when light 1 is on:

$$1 \longleftrightarrow\!\!\!| \;\; 2, 7$$

This rule will play a pivotal role in an inference to be discussed shortly.

The fourth rule indicates that at least one of the three lights on each *side* is on:

$$\boxed{\cancel{\text{O}} \; \cancel{\text{O}} \; \cancel{\text{O}}}$$

The fifth rule is another rule about sides and lights, and it indicates that if exactly one light on a side is on, then that light must be the center light:

$$\text{Side}_{1\,\text{light on}} \longrightarrow \text{Center}_{\text{on}}$$

The contrapositive of this rule is:

$$\cancel{\text{Center}}_{\text{on}} \longrightarrow \cancel{\text{Side}}_{1\,\text{light on}}$$

Since a side must have at least one light on and cannot have all three lights on, this contrapositive can be translated as:

$$\text{Center}_{\text{off}} \longrightarrow \text{Side}_{2\,\text{lights on}}$$

When a side has two lights on but the center is not on, then both corners must be on:

Center _off_ ⟶ Both corners on that side are on

The contrapositive of this inference is:

Both corners ~~on~~ that side are on ⟶ Center _on_

Thus, if one of the corners is off, then the center light is automatically on.

The final rule states that two lights on the north side are on. From the third rule we know that lights 1 and 2 cannot be on at the same time, so, by Hurdling the Uncertainty we can infer that light 3 must always be on (otherwise you could not fulfill the constraints of this rule):

O = on   ~~O~~ = off

```
                            O
        1     2     3
    O  8             4
        7     6     5
```

At this point, most students move on to the questions. But, there are six rules, and several of those rules establish general limitations on each side or section of three lights, and these rules, when combined with the fact that the status of two of the eight lights is already determined, indicate that the game cannot have a large number of solutions. The best decision, then, is to explore Identifying the Possibilities.

Start first with the third rule, which states that lights 2 and 7 are off when light 1 is on. By turning light 1 on, lights 2 and 7 automatically are off, leaving lights 4, 5, and 6 undetermined. But, from our discussion of the fifth rule, when a corner light is off (as light 7 is), then the center light on that side is on. Hence, light 6 must be on. Lights 4 and 5 cannot be precisely determined, but if one is on, the other is off (if both were on, the first rule would be violated), leading to a dual-option. Combining all of the information gives us only two possibilities when light 1 is on:

Template #1:

O = on   ~~O~~ = off

```
                O          ~~O~~         O
            1          2          3
        O  8                      4  O/~~O~~
            7          6          5
          ~~O~~        O        ~~O~~/O
```

Of course, light 1 could be off. In that case, light 2 must be on in order to meet the constraints of the final rule. With lights 2 and 3 on, light 4 must be off in order to conform to the first rule. With light 4 off, light 5 must be on in order to abide by the fifth rule. The only undetermined lights are 6 and 7, but both cannot be on (otherwise the first rule would be violated) and both cannot be off (otherwise the fifth rule would be violated). Thus, one of lights 6 and 7 is on, and the other is off, leading to two possibilities:

Template #2:

O = on   Ø = off   Ø   O   O
                                   1   2   3

                        O   8   4   Ø

                             7   6   5
                        O / Ø   Ø / O   O

Thus, because all possibilities have been explored when light 1 is on and when it is off, and light 1 has no more possible positions, we have explored all possibilities of the game, and there are only four possible solutions, as captured by the two templates above.

Question #6: Global, Could Be True, List. The correct answer choice is (C)

Template #2 proves that answer choice (C) is possible, and therefore correct.

Answer choice (A) is incorrect because when light 1 is on then light 7 must be off, and because light 8 is not on.

Answer choice (B) is incorrect because two lights on the north side must be on.

Answer choice (D) is incorrect because three consecutively numbered lights are on (6, 7, 8).

Answer choice (E) is incorrect because when light 1 is on then light 2 must be off, and also because three consecutively numbered lights are on (4, 5, 6).

Question #7: Global, Must Be True. The correct answer choice is (B)

As discussed during the setup, due to the combination of the third rule and the last rule, light 3 must always be on. Consequently, answer choice (B) is correct.

Question #8: Local, Must Be True. The correct answer choice is (B)

If light 1 is off, then only Template #2 is applicable. In Template #2, light 4 is always off, and so answer choice (B) is correct. Note that if light 1 is off, then lights 2 and 3 must be on. This forces light 4 to be off otherwise the first rule would be violated.

Question #9: Global, Must Be True. The correct answer choice is (D)

Normally, "5 if" questions such as this one should be avoided until the very end of a game. But, when a game is attacked with templates, "5 if" questions consume no more time on average than any other type of question. Template #1 shows that answer choice (D) must be true, and thus (D) is correct.

Answer choice (A) is incorrect because when light 6 is on then light 6 can be off or on. Note that the answer to question #6 can be used to disprove this answer as well.

Answer choice (B) is incorrect because light 1 could be on instead of light 2.

Answer choice (C) is incorrect because light 3 is always on.

Answer choice (E) is incorrect because when light 6 is off then light 1 is off.

Question #10: Local, Could Be True. The correct answer choice is (A)

This question is similar to the preceding question, with the addition that light 5 is on. When light 5 is on, then Template #1 or #2 can apply, with the specification that in Template #1 light 4 would be off.

Answer choice (A) is the correct answer. Under Template #2 it is possible for lights 1 and 6 to be off.

Answer choice (B) is incorrect because from the third rule, if light 1 is on then light 7 is off.

Answer choice (C) is incorrect because light 4 is always off when light 5 is on.

Answer choice (D) is incorrect because if light 2 is off, then light 6 is on.

Answer choice (E) is incorrect because this would cause four consecutively numbered lights to be on (5, 6, 7, 8), a multiple violation of the first rule.

Question #11: Local, Must Be True, Except. The correct answer choice is (B)

If light 4 is on, then only Template #1 applies, with the additional inference that light 5 is off. Under Template #1, light 2 is always off, and so answer choice (B) cannot be true and is thus correct.

Question #12: Local, Not Necessarily True, Suspension, FTT. The correct answer choice is (E)

The question stem suspends the final rule of the game, and instead specifies that exactly one light on the north side is on. From the fifth rule, then, the north-side light that is on must be light 2, and lights 1 and 3 are off:

O = on   Ø = off   Ø   O   Ø
                                         1   2   3

                                   O 8   4

                                       7   6   5

At this point, answer choices (A), (B), and (C) can be eliminated as each must be true.

From our discussion of the fifth rule, when any corner light is off, then the center light on that side must automatically be on. Thus, because light 3 is off, light 4 must be on:

O = on   Ø = off   Ø   O   Ø
                                         1   2   3

                                   O 8   4 O

                                       7   6   5

Because light 4 is on, answer choice (D) can be eliminated. Consequently, only answer choice (E) remains, and (E) is the correct answer.

PrepTest 8. June 1993 Game #3: *13. C 14. C 15. E 16. B 17. D*

This is an Advanced Linear: Balanced game.

B: F H I J ⁴

     *   *

G: R S T ³

	B	G	B	G	B	G	B	
w	F/	R/T	/F	T/R	I	S	H/J	e
	1	2	3	4	5	6	7	

B̶/B̶

F R
R F

The four boys must sit in chairs 1, 3, 5, and 7; the three girls must sit in chairs 2, 4, and 6. This occurs because of the Separation Principle™ in this game, a result of the second rule. With I sitting in chair 5 due to the third rule, and with the girls sitting in chairs 2, 4, and 6, from the fourth rule we can deduce that S must sit in chair 6. R and T must then sit in chairs 2 and 4, not necessarily in that order.

Because F and R must be adjacent to each other from the last rule, and because R is limited to chair 2 or chair 4, we can infer that F cannot sit in chair 7, and must instead sit in chair 1 or 3.

Because F cannot sit in chair 7, and because I is already seated in chair 5, only H or J can sit in chair 7.

Question #13: Global, Must Be True, Maximum. The correct answer choice is (C)

F and R can sit in three different pairs of chairs:

F	R		R	F		F	R
1	2		2	3		3	4

Consequently, the correct answer choice is (C).

Note that if you were concerned about time, this would be an excellent question to skip and return to later after you had seen the work in other questions. Questions #15, #16, and #17, for example, show two of the placements listed above.

Question #14: Global, Cannot Be True, FTT. The correct answer choice is (C)

Answer choices (A), (B), and (E) can all occur when F is in chair 1. Answer choices (B), (D), and (E) can occur when F is seat 3.

Only answer choice (C) cannot occur, and thus (C) is the correct answer. For both H and J to sit west of F, F would have to be in chair 7, and that placement would create a violation of the last rule.

Question #15: Local, Not Necessarily True, FTT. The correct answer choice is (E)

If T sits next to I, then T must sit in chair 4 (and, consequently, R must sit in chair 2). If F sits next to T, then F must sit in chair 3. The only remaining uncertainty involves J and H:

J/H	R	F	T	I	S	H/J
1	2	3	4	5	6	7

In a Not Necessarily True question (or a Could Be True question, for that matter), you should immediately search for an answer that addresses the variable or variables whose placement is uncertain. In this case, J and H are not completely determined, and a scan of the answer choices shows that only answer choice (E) contains J or H. Ultimately, a brief analysis shows that answer choice (E) is the correct answer.

Question #16: Local, Could Be True. The correct answer choice is (B)

If F does not sit next to any child seated next to I, then F cannot be chair 3, and F must sit in chair 1. From the last rule, R must then sit in chair 2, forcing T to sit in chair 4. Again, only the placement of J and H is uncertain:

F	R	J/H	T	I	S	H/J
1	2	3	4	5	6	7

As this is a Could Be True question, you should immediately look for an answer that references J or H, the two variables that have not been fully placed. Only answer choice (B) addresses one of those two variables, and ultimately answer choice (B) is correct.

Question #17: Local, Cannot Be True. The correct answer choice is (D)

If F seats east of R, then an RF block is created, and the only placement for this block is in chairs 2 and 3. With R seated in chair 2, T must sit in chair 4, leaving J and H as the only two unplaced variables:

J/H	R	F	T	I	S	H/J
1	2	3	4	5	6	7

As I is seated in chair 5 and R is seated in chair 2, they cannot sit next to each other and answer choice (D) is correct.

This is a Grouping: Partially Defined game.

Using WXYZ as the base is superior to using FGH since each of WXYZ must respond to at least one antibiotic, and the W ——→ X rule can easily be shown within the diagram. This leads to the following base diagram:

Organisms: W X Y Z [4]
Antibiotics: F G H [3]

$$\overline{}\quad\overline{}\quad\overline{}\quad\overline{}$$
$$\ \ \text{W}\quad\ \ \text{X}\quad\ \ \text{Y}\quad\ \ \text{Z}$$

From the first two rules, because each organism responds to at least one of the antibiotics, but not all three antibiotics, each of the organisms responds to either one or two of the antibiotics.

The third rule establishes that either two of the organisms or three of the organisms must respond to F.

The fourth rule is diagrammed as:

$$\text{W} \longrightarrow \text{X}$$

This should also be shown within the diagram.

The fifth rule is diagrammed as:

$$\text{F} \longrightarrow \text{G}$$

From an inference standpoint, no organism can respond to both H and F because F brings along G, and thus F and H together means that an organism responds to all three antibiotics, a violation of the second rule. This deduction is the key to the game.

Via the contrapositive, if an organism does not respond to G, then it cannot respond to F. Consequently, if an organism does not respond to G, it must respond to H. If an organism does not respond to H, then it must respond to G (either it responds to G alone, or if it responds to F, then it also responds to G under the fifth rule).

Combining all of the above leads to the final diagram for the game:

Organisms: W X Y Z ^{4}
Antibiotics: F G H ^{3}

W $\longrightarrow$ X

F $\longrightarrow$ G

F $\longleftarrow\!|\!\longrightarrow$ H

F $\longrightarrow$ 2/3

$$\overline{}\quad\overline{}\quad\begin{array}{c}G\\F\\\overline{Y}\\\cancel{H}\end{array}\quad\overline{Z}$$
$$\underset{W\longrightarrow X}{}$$

Question #18: Global, Could Be True, Except. The correct answer choice is (D)

Because Y responds to F, Y also must respond to G. Consequently, from the second rule, Y cannot respond to H, and answer choice (D) is correct.

Question #19: Global, Could Be True. The correct answer choice is (B)

Answer choice (A) is incorrect because under the proposed scenario all four organisms would respond to F, a violation of the third rule. Answer choice (D) is incorrect because if W responds to G, then X responds to G, but since Y already responds to G, the condition in the answer choice cannot occur. Answer choice (C) is incorrect because every antibiotic that W responds to is also responded to by X, as specified in the fourth rule. Answer choice (E) is incorrect because every organism that responds to F also responds to G, as specified in the fifth rule. As a result, (B) is the correct answer choice.

Question #20: Global, Could Be True. The correct answer choice is (E)

Answer choice (A) violates the third rule. Answer choice (B) is impossible because Y cannot respond to H. Answer choice (C) violates the inference made in the setup. Answer choice (D) cannot occur because then there would be no antibiotic for an organism to respond to, a violation of the first rule. Consequently, answer choice (E) is correct.

Question #21: Local, Must Be True. The correct answer choice is (D)

If X does not respond to F, then from the fourth rule W does not respond to F. To comply with the third rule, then, Z must respond to F:

$$\begin{array}{cccc} & & G & G \\ & & F & F \\ \overline{W} & \overline{X} & \overline{Y} & \overline{Z} \\ \cancel{F} & \cancel{F} & \cancel{H} & \cancel{H} \end{array}$$

Thus, answer choice (D) is correct.

Question #22: Local, Must Be True. The correct answer choice is (B)

Any organism responding to exactly two of the antibiotics must respond in accordance with one of the following two scenarios:

G	H
F	G

Since G is found in both of the scenarios, it follows that any organism responding to two of the antibiotics must respond to G. Therefore, (B) is the correct answer choice.

Question #23: Local, Must Be True. The correct answer choice is (E)

As discussed in the setup, if an organism does not respond to H, then it must respond to G. Accordingly, answer choice (E) is correct.

Question #24: Local, Must Be True, Except. The correct answer choice is (C)

The condition in the question stem forces the following scenario to occur:

$$\begin{array}{cccc} G & G & G & \\ \underline{F} & \underline{F} & \underline{F} & \underline{} \\ W & X & Y & Z \\ & & & \cancel{F} \end{array}$$

Only answer choice (C) does not have to occur, and thus (C) is correct.

POWERSCORE®

PREPTEST 9

OCTOBER 1993 LOGIC GAMES SETUPS

This is a Grouping: Defined-Fixed, Unbalanced: Underfunded, Numerical Distribution game.

The scenario and rules give us a very basic setup:

G O R V⁴

The game scenario contains a condition that partially controls the number of each type of flower. If each type must be represented, and the number of roses is *at least* twice the number of orchids, then the following possibilities exist for just the roses and orchids:

R	O
2	1
3	1
4	1
5	1
6	1
4	2
5	2

The presence of "at least" in the game scenario makes the number of distributions more difficult to determine. Had the condition specified "exactly" instead of "at least," the distributions could have been quickly and easily fixed (2-1 and 4-2). From the above, the minimum combined number of roses and orchids is three, and the maximum combined number of roses and orchids is seven (which leaves one gardenia and one violet in a 5-2-1-1 overall distribution). The table also reveals that the maximum number of orchids that can be used is two, and the minimum number of roses that must be used is two. The maximum number of roses that can be used is six, a fact that is tested in question #2.

Of course, when the gardenias and violets are added into the above distributions, the number of distributions grows rapidly. Because there are so many possibilities, the questions often specify further conditions so you can narrow the range of possible distributions in each question.

Note also that the second and third rules state "at least as many," and not "exactly."

Question #1: Global, Could Be True, List. The correct answer choice is (C)

Answer choice (A) is incorrect because corsage 3 cannot contain any orchids.

Answer choice (B) is incorrect because there must be at least twice as many roses as orchids.

Answer choice (C) is the correct answer choice.

Answer choice (D) is incorrect because corsage 1 must contain exactly two types of flowers.

Answer choice (E) is incorrect because corsage 2 contain have at least one rose.

Question #2: Global, Must Be True, Maximum. The correct answer choice is (D)

Because all four flower types must be used, to maximize roses simply minimize the other three types by using them once each. As discussed in the game setup, six roses is the maximum, and answer choice (D) is correct.

Question #3: Local, Could Be True, Maximum. The correct answer choice is (B)

If there are two orchids used, there must be at least four roses used. One is used in corsage 1, and the other three must be in the other two corsages. Those two corsages have room for six flowers: three roses, a gardenia, and at most two violets. Thus, answer choice (B) is correct.

Question #4: Local, Could Be True. The correct answer choice is (A)

Answer choice (A) is proven possible by the following hypothetical:

V	G	G
O	R	R
O	R	R
1	2	3

Question #5: Local, Must Be True. The correct answer choice is (C)

If two different corsages contain at least one orchid each, then there must be an orchid in corsage 1 and corsage 2 (no orchids can be included in corsage 3 per the last rule, and thus only corsages 1 and 2 can be used to meet the condition in the question stem). As there must be at least one rose in corsage 2 from the rules, we can infer that corsage 2 must include at least one orchid and one rose. Therefore, answer choice (C) is correct.

Question #6: Local, Must Be True, Maximum. The correct answer choice is (D)

To have the greatest number of violets, simply minimize the other flowers. Use one gardenia, one orchid, and two roses. That gives a maximum of five violets, and fixes the gardenia-orchid-rose-violet distribution at 1-1-2-5. Answer choice (D) must be true because exactly two roses would be used.

Question #7: Local, Could Be True. The correct answer choice is (A)

Because corsage 1 only has two types of flowers (gardenias and violets in this question), and no orchids can be used in corsage 3, an orchid must be used in corsage 2:

G/V	___	___
V	O	___
G	R	G
1	2	3
		Ø̸

This fact eliminates answer choices (C), (D), and (E), each of which do not contain an orchid.

Of course, if three different types of flowers are used in corsage 3, and orchids cannot be used, the three types of flowers must be G, R, and V:

G/V	___	V
V	O	R
G	R	G
1	2	3

Thus far, in total there are two roses and one orchid. Because of the specification that there are at least twice as many roses as orchids, the third flower in corsage 2 cannot be a orchid, because there are not enough remaining open spaces to add two more roses. This information eliminates answer choice (B), which indicates that there are two orchids in corsage 2. Thus, answer choice (A) is correct.

This is a Grouping: Defined-Fixed, Unbalanced: Overloaded game.

This game features a fixed group of four selections, with an overloaded group of seven variables available to fill those four spaces. Thus, four variables are always selected and three variables are not selected.

The game contains only four rules. The first two rules are quite powerful and "reserve" two of the four available spaces. These rules are represented directly on the game diagram with dual-options. The third and fourth rules are both simple conditional rules, and are represented with arrow diagrams in our setup:

J K L M N P Q ^{7}
    *

N ⟶ L

Q ⟶ K

$$\underline{\text{J/K}}\;\;\underline{\text{N/P}}\;\;\underline{\quad\quad}\;\;\underline{\quad\quad}$$
$$\text{4 people}$$

Of course, there are also inferences that can be made in the game:

> Because J, K, N, and P will collectively occupy exactly two of the spaces, the remaining two spaces are occupied by the group of L, M, and Q. Thus, we can infer that two people from the group of L, M, and Q must always be selected. This will be represented directly on the diagram using a parenthetical notation. Note that any time one of the members of the group of L, M, and Q is not selected, the other two *must* be selected.

> From the last rule, when Q is selected then K must be selected, and from the first rule when K is selected J cannot be selected. Thus, Q and J cannot be selected together. This rule is shown with a double-not arrow.

> Note that some students attempt to draw an inference between P and L by combining the second and third rules. There is no usable inference that can be drawn from these two rules (an inference is present, "Some Ls are not Ps" but that inference has no value in this game).

The final entire setup then appears as:

J K L M N P Q ^{7}
    *

N ⟶ L

Q ⟶ K

Q ⟷̸ J

$$\underline{\text{J/K}}\;\;\underline{\text{N/P}}\;\;\underline{\text{(L, M, Q)}}$$
$$\text{4 people}$$

With the information above, we are ready to attack the questions.

Question #8: Global, Could Be True, List. The correct answer choice is (D)

As always, apply each rule to all of the contending answer choices in order to solve a List question:

Answer choice (A) is incorrect because neither J nor K is selected, a violation of the first rule.

Answer choice (B) is incorrect because Q is selected but K is not selected, a violation of the last rule (the lack of K also leads to the pairing of J and Q, a violation of the inference made during the setup).

Answer choice (C) is incorrect because N is selected but L is not selected, a violation of the third rule. This answer also pairs J and Q, a violation of the inference made during the setup.

Answer choice (E) is incorrect because both J and K are selected, a violation of the first rule. Note how answer choices (A) and (E) play on both sides of the first rule. Many students will eliminate one of the two answers, but then forget to check the "other" side.

Thus, answer choice (D) is proven correct by process of elimination.

Question #9: Global, Must Be True. The correct answer choice is (B)

This is the most difficult question of the game. The difficulty arises from the wording of the question and the nature of the answer choices. Reworded, the question asks, "Of the people selected to attend the retirement dinner, there must be at least one from which one of the following pairs?" or, alternately, "Which one of the following pair of people cannot both be eliminated from attending the retirement dinner?"

The two easiest answers to this problem would be J or K, or N or P, because we know from the first two rules that at least one person from each of those pairs must be selected. Of course, because those answers are so obvious, they do not appear among any of the lettered answer choices. Instead, to find the solution to this question, we must return to the inference discussion in the setup. In the discussion of the selection pool, we noted that exactly two of L, M, and Q must be selected, and if one of those three variables is not selected, then the other two *must* be selected. Thus, no two of those variables can be eliminated from contention. Answer choice (B), which contains L and M, contains a pair of variables where one or both must be selected, and thus answer choice (B) is correct.

To consider this problem from another angle, if you remove both L and M from the retirement dinner, you will not be able to come up with a group of four people that also meets the requirements of the rules.

Question #10: Global, Cannot Be True. The correct answer choice is (B)

As discussed in the setup of the game, J and Q cannot be selected together. Hence, answer choice (B) is correct.

Question #11: Local, Must Be True. The correct answer choice is (B)

If M is not selected to attend the retirement dinner, from our analysis of the groups we can infer that L and Q must both be selected. Of course, when Q is selected then K must be selected, leading to the following setup:

$$\underline{\quad K \quad} \quad \underline{\quad N/P \quad} \quad \underline{\quad L \quad} \quad \underline{\quad Q \quad}$$

Accordingly, answer choice (B) is correct.

Question #12: Local, Must Be True. The correct answer choice is (C)

If P is not selected to attend the retirement dinner, then N must be selected, and when N is selected then L must be selected as well. The only remaining variable choices to consider are the pairings of J or K, and M or Q. Of these four variables, only one combination—J and Q—is impossible, and so there are three possible combinations when P is not selected:

#3:	J	N	L	M
#2:	K	N	L	M
#1:	K	N	L	Q

Answer choice (C) is thus correct.

Question #13: Global, Justify. The correct answer choice is (E)

The question stem asks you to identify a pair of variables that, when selected, allows for only one grouping of people to be selected. Answer choice (E) is correct because when M and Q are selected then L is not selected, and when L is not selected then N is not selected. From the second rule, then, P must be selected. And because Q has been selected, from the last rule K must be selected. Thus, when M and Q are selected, only the group of M, Q, P, and K can be selected.

Note that the work done in question #12 can be used to eliminate answer choice (C) because our hypothetical in #12 shows three different possible solutions when L and N are selected. In that same vein, the work from question #11 can be used to eliminate answer choice (D) because the selection of L and Q still allows for two possibilities (those possibilities are represented in the choice of N or P).

This is a Pattern game.

Some games are difficult because they contain a large number of rules or variables; other games are difficult because they are built around a complex concept that forces you to make several deep inferences. This game is one of the latter. And as is always the case with these type of games, creating an effective setup makes the game much easier. The first important decision in this game is how to display the dancing couples for each dance. Many students attempt to use a basic setup similar to the following:

Unfortunately, this setup does not offer you a concrete base to work with. In each of the three dances you are still making decisions about each of the six variables, eighteen total for all three dances. If at all possible, you would like a setup to fix some of the variables and thus allow you to reduce the number of variables you have to work with for each dance. The following basic setup achieves that goal:

R   ___   ___   ___
S   ___   ___   ___
T   ___   ___   ___
    1   2   3

By fixing R, S, and T, only the three boys remain to be placed for each of the three dances. This effectively reduces the total number of variables to be placed to nine, down from eighteen in the previous setup. Choosing to display R, S, and T is superior to choosing K, L, and M because it allows us to display the second rule within the diagram:

R   ___   ___   ___
S   ___   ___   ___
T   ___   ___   ___
    1   2   3

Note that this second rule involves a double arrow. If we know who partners Rita in dance 2, that person must partner Sarah in dance 3, and if we know who partners Sarah in dance 3, that same person must partner Rita in dance 2.

According to the last rule, "No two children can partner each other in more than one dance." By combining this rule with the second rule, we can make the essential inference that the boy who partners Rita in dance 2 and Sarah in dance 3 must partner Tura in dance 1. This pattern holds true for every possible game configuration. This inference can also be added to the setup:

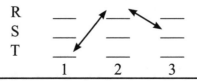

Since the game now has one established pattern, it is quite possible that other patterns exist. For example, let's examine the boy who dances with Rita in dance 1. In dance 2 this same boy can partner Sarah or Tura, and in dance 3 he can partner only Tura (remember, Sarah is already taken and he can't partner with Rita again). But wait—if he must partner Tura in dance 3, then he cannot partner her in dance 2, and thus he must partner Sarah in dance 2. It therefore follows that whomever partners Rita in dance 1 must partner Sarah in dance 2 and Tura in dance 3. Now that this second pattern exists, there can be only one possible pattern for the boy who partners Sarah in dance 1: Tura in dance 2 and Rita in dance 3 (remember each of the other two girls in dances 2 and 3 are involved in other patterns). Thus, by analyzing the interaction of the second and third rules we have established the three patterns that must exist in every game:

> One boy must partner T in dance 1, R in dance 2, and S in dance 3. (T - R - S)
> One boy must partner R in dance 1, S in dance 2, and T in dance 3. (R - S - T)
> One boy must partner S in dance 1, T in dance 2, and R in dance 3. (S - T - R)

Obviously, uncovering this pattern within the grouping rules will now allow us to easily conquer the game. But, as we begin the questions, we also need to keep in mind that Karl must partner with Sarah in dance 1 or 2 (essentially this means that he will be in either the STR pattern or the RST pattern).

Question #14: Local, Must Be True, List. The correct answer choice is (D)

If Luis partners Sarah in dance 3, he must partner Rita in dance 2 and Tura in dance 1. This leaves either Rita or Sarah for Miguel to partner in dance 1, and thus answer choice (D) is correct.

Question #15: Local, Could Be True. The correct answer choice is (B)

If Miguel partners Rita in dance 2, he must partner Sarah in dance 3 and Tura in dance 1. This information is sufficient to eliminate answer choices (A), (C), (D), and (E). It follows that answer choice (B) is correct.

Question #16: Local, Must Be True. The correct answer choice is (B)

If Miguel partners Sarah in dance 1, Karl must partner Sarah in dance 2. This being the case, Luis must partner Sarah in dance 3. Of course, if Luis partners Sarah in dance 3, he must partner Rita in dance 2 and Tura in dance 1. Adding this information to the patterns we have already established allows us to fill in the entire diagram:

$$
\begin{array}{cccc}
R & K & L & M \\
S & \underline{M} & \underline{K} & \underline{L} \\
T & \underline{L} & \underline{M} & \underline{K} \\
& 1 & 2 & 3
\end{array}
$$

It follows that answer choice (B) is correct.

Question #17: Local, Must Be True. The correct answer choice is (C)

Like the previous question, the information in the question stem fills in the entire diagram:

```
R     L      M      K
S     K      L      M
T     M      K      L
      1      2      3
```

Thus answer choice (C) is correct.

Question #18: Local, Must Be True. The correct answer choice is (D)

While the four previous questions can be answered without an understanding of the three patterns that control this game, this generally difficult question is made easy by applying the patterns:

```
R     M      L      K
S     K      M      L
T     L      K      M
      1      2      3
```

The setup indicates that answer choice (D) is correct.

This game was universally considered by students to be the hardest game on the October 1993 LSAT, if not one of the hardest games of the modern era. However, an application of the basic rules allows any student to answer at least the first four questions, and those students who discovered the three patterns found the game quite easy. Remember, just because a game contains a few simple rules doesn't necessarily mean that the setup is also simple or uninformative. Always examine the interaction of the rules, even if there are only two or three.

This is a Mapping—Supplied Diagram game.

The game provides a diagram that should be used for your main setup. In examining the diagram, note that the small squares in the middle of cities 1-2-3-4 and cities 3-4-5-6 are there so that cities that are diagonal from each other, such as 1 and 4 or 4 and 5, do not share a common border. This fact plays an important role when considering the fifth rule.

The first rule is a cleanup rule, one that limits the number of solutions in the game.

The second rule establishes that the maximum number of jails in a city is one, and the maximum number of hospitals in a city is also one.

The third rule is a negative grouping rule, and it establishes that jails and universities do not appear in the same city:

$$J \longleftarrow\!\!|\!\!\longrightarrow U$$

The fourth rule indicates that if a jail is in a city, then a hospital must also be in that city:

$$J \longrightarrow H$$

As a complete aside, these two rules are kind of funny if you think about them literally: prisoners and college kids can't be in the same city, but if you have a jail, you need a hospital (are they expecting a prison riot to break out?).

The fifth rule indicates that the universities are located in two cities that do not share a common border. More on this rule in a moment.

The sixth and final rule places two of the institutions: a university in city 3 and a jail in city 6. This can be diagrammed as:

Hospitals: H H H H [4]
Jails: ~~J~~ J [2]
Universities: ~~U~~ U [2]

1 ___	2 ___
3 _U_	4 ___
5 ___	6 _J_

With these two institutions placed, a number of inferences can be made. With a jail in city 6, from the fourth rule there must be a hospital in city 6, and from the third rule there cannot be a university in city 6. There can also not be another jail in city 6 according to the second rule:

Hospitals: H̶ H H H ⁴
Jails: J̶ J ²
Universities: U̶ U ²

1 ___   2 ___

3 _U_   4 ___

5 ___   6 J H U̶ J̶

With a university in city 3, from the fifth rule we can infer that there are no universities in cities 1, 4, and 5 (nor can there be another university in city 3 according to the second rule). Combining these inferences with the information above, we have one more university to place, but that university cannot be in cities 1, 3, 4, 5, or 6. Thus, the second university must be in city 2:

Hospitals: H̶ H H H ⁴
Jails: J̶ J ²
Universities: U̶ U̶ ²

1 ___ U̶   2 _U_

3 _U_ U̶   4 ___ U̶

5 ___ U̶   6 J H U̶ J̶

Finally, from the third rule, we can eliminate jails from cities 2 and 3, both of which contain universities:

Hospitals: H̶ H H H ⁴
Jails: J̶ J ²
Universities: U̶ U̶ ²

1 ___ U̶   2 _U_ J̶

3 _U_ U̶ J̶   4 ___ U̶

5 ___ U̶   6 J H U̶ J̶

The above diagram contains all of the institutions that can be placed, and all of the Not Laws that follow from the rules. At this point, there are only three hospitals and one jail that remain to be placed. Of course, the jail must be placed in a city with a hospital, and because the jail cannot be placed in cities 2, 3, and 6, we can infer that a jail and a hospital will be placed in city 1, 4, or 5:

$$\boxed{\text{J H}} \longrightarrow 1, 4, \text{ or } 5$$

The remaining two hospitals have no restrictions, and they can be located within any city.

Thus, the final diagram for the game is:

Hospitals: H̶ H H H ⁴
Jails: J̶J̶ ²
Universities: U̶U̶ ²

J ◄——┼——► U

J ——————► H

[J H] ——————► 1, 4, or 5

1 ____ U̶

2 _U_ J̶

3 _U_ J̶U̶

4 ____ U̶

5 ____ U̶

6 _J H_ U̶J̶

Question #19: Global, Could Be True. The correct answer choice is (E)

As examined during our discussion of the game and as shown by the Not Laws above, answer choices (A), (B), (C), and (D) each cannot be true. Answer choice (E) could be true, and is thus correct.

Question #20: Global, Could Be True. The correct answer choice is (A)

As examined during our discussion of the game and as shown by the Not Laws above, answer choices (B), (C), (D), and (E) each cannot be true. Answer choice (A) could be true, and is thus correct.

Question #21: Global, Must Be True, List. The correct answer choice is (D)

The inference involving the remaining jail was discussed at the end of the setup examination. The remaining jail cannot be placed in cities 2, 3, and 6, and only cities 1, 4, and 5 remain as candidates. Thus, answer choice (D) is correct.

Question #22: Local, Must Be True. The correct answer choice is (D)

From the setup, we know that cities 1, 4, and 5 do not currently contain any of the institutions. The only remaining unplaced institutions are three hospitals and one jail (H, H, H, and J). But, we know that the jail requires a hospital, which effectively creates a JH block, leaving just three entities to cover the three empty cities:

[J H]   H   H

Thus, although we cannot determine which city the jail is placed in, we can determine that there is a hospital placed in cities 1, 4, and 5. Thus, answer choice (D) must be true and is correct.

Question #23: Global, Must Be True. The correct answer choice is (B)

In the prior question, we discussed the fact that there are still three hospitals remaining to be placed. But, in that question, the hospitals had to be separated in order to "cover" cities 1, 4, and 5, each of which did not contain an institution. This is a Global question, and there is no restriction on the hospitals being together, so it is possible that the three hospitals could all be placed in any of those three cities, and thus we can eliminate cities 1, 4, and 5 from contention. This removes answer choices (A), (C), and (D) from consideration (another way of thinking about those three answers is that according to our diagram, cities 1, 4, and 5 are identical, so none of them is likely to be the correct answer).

Only cities 2 and 6 remain in consideration. City 6 already has a hospital, and there is no restriction on adding two more hospitals (which would leave the remaining hospital to pair with the jail in city 1, 4, or 5), and so city 6 can have three hospitals, and is eliminated from consideration.

City 2 cannot contain all three remaining unplaced hospitals because city 2 cannot contain a jail, and one of the three hospitals must be with the jail that goes in city 1, 4, or 5. Because the maximum number of hospitals in city 2 is thus two, answer choice (B) is the correct answer.

Question #24: Local, Could Be True, List. The correct answer choice is (A)

This question requires you to identify a list of three cities, none of which contain a hospital. Thus, for the three cities you choose, no hospitals can be assigned, and all of the hospitals in the game must be in the other three unlisted cities.

The question stem specifies that one of the cities contains an HHU block. This block must be placed in city 2 or city 3, because these are the only two cities with a university. Answer choice (C) can thus be eliminated because one of city 2 or 3 always contains two hospitals, and this answer lists both city 2 and 3 as part of a group of cities with no hospital.

Answer choice (B) can also be eliminated because we know from our initial discussion that a JH block must go in city 1, 4, or 5.

Answer choices (D) and (E) can also be eliminated because city 6 must contain a hospital, and both answer choice (D) and (E) list city 6 among the cities with no hospital.

Answer choice (A) is thus proven correct by process of elimination. In (A), the JH block would be placed in city 4, and the other two hospitals placed among some portion of cities 2, 4, or 6.

POWERSCORE

10 PREPTEST

FEBRUARY 1994 LOGIC GAMES SETUPS

This is a Pure Sequencing game.

This is an unusual game in that it presents a fairly standard sequence, but instead of placing the students in a 1-9 order, it instead assigns them to three groups—level 1, level 2, and level 3—each with three members.

The rules form the following sequence:

Variables: F G H I J K L M N [9]

$$I > G > \begin{array}{l} J > M > H > N \\ \text{- - - - - - - - - - -} \\ F \\ K > \text{- - -} \\ L \end{array}$$

This sequence allows for some immediate inferences. Because I must be first and G must be second, both I and G must be placed in the level 1 class:

I G		
Level 1	Level 2	Level 3

Because J or K must be third, the remaining slot in level 1 must be taken by either J or K:

I G J/K		
Level 1	Level 2	Level 3

Because J scores higher than at least three students (M, H, and N), J cannot be in level 3:

I G J/K		
Level 1	Level 2	Level 3
		J̸

F, H, K, L, M, and N are the only students who can be placed in the Level 3 class. Note that a variable such as N, which "appears" to have to be placed in the level 3 class due to the fact that it is at the end of a chain, does not have to be in the level 3 class because K, F, and L could have lower scores.

Question #1: Global, Could Be True. The correct answer choice is (B)

As discussed during the setup, I and G are in the level 1 class. The only uncertainty is whether J or K is the third member of the class. Thus, there two possible combinations for level 1—I, G, J and I, G, K—and answer choice (B) is correct.

Question #2: Global, Could Be True. The correct answer choice is (C)

G must be in the level 1 class, and thus answer choice (B) is eliminated. F, K, and N appear near the end of the chain, and all can be in the level 3 class, and thus answer choices (A), (D), and (E) are eliminated. As discussed during the setup, J cannot be in the level 3 class, and thus answer choice (C) is correct.

Question #3: Global, Could Be True. The correct answer choice is (C)

The correct answer is a student who can be placed in any of the three classes. As the level 1 class is very restricted, begin your analysis there. I and G are fixed in level 1, and so neither is a consideration. But, the one remaining spot must be occupied by J or K, and so either J or K must be the correct answer (because none of the other students can be in the level 1 class).

Based on the setup discussion and as confirmed in question #2, J cannot be in the level 3 class, and thus answer choice (B) is eliminated. At this point, we know that K must be the correct answer, and therefore (C) is correct.

If the above did not make perfect sense, consider the following: F and L both appear near the end of the chain, and each must score lower than at least G, I, and K. Since G, I, and K are always ahead of F and L, F and L can never appear in the level 1 class. It follows that answer choices (A) and (D) are eliminated. M can never appear in the level 1 class since G, I, and J must always appear ahead of him and therefore answer choice (E) is incorrect.

Question #4: Global, Justify. The correct answer choice is (C)

As in previous questions, J and K play a key role in this question. If we need to place two students in such a way that the composition of every class is determined, we will need to address which of J and K will be in the level 1 class. Thus, the correct answer is likely to include one of J and K. Answer choices (B) and (E), neither of which include J or K, are therefore less likely to be correct.

Of the three remaining answers, we can apply a different analysis, but one that is equally effective. J and K are somewhat similar, and the three students in answer choice (A), (C), and (D) besides J and K are F, H, and L. In examining F, H, and L, note that F and L are virtually identical in their basic characteristics: both are at the end of the same chain, behind K. Thus, pairing K with F or L (as do (A) and (D)) is likely to produce a similar result. The Uniqueness Theory of Answer Choices suggests that two answers with similar characteristics are unlikely to be correct. On the other hand, H sits in the middle of a different chain and automatically impacts N, who has a lower score. Thus, H appears to be more unique than F and L, and for our purposes this suggests that answer choice (C) is most likely to be correct.

Let's take a closer look at answer choice (C), then. If H and J are in the level 2 class, then M must be in the level 2 class with them. Consequently, K must be in the level 1 class, and N, F, and L must be in the level 3 class. Thus, answer choice (C) is correct.

Question #5: Global, Cannot Be True. The correct answer choice is (E)

This is the type of question where one might expect that J and K would be the correct answer (if J and K were in the same class as F, there would not be a third student for the level 1 class). However, that answer does not appear among the five lettered choices. Instead, we will need to find a different pair that creates a problem.

Answer choice (A) is incorrect because F, H, and N can be in the level 3 class, leaving L, M, and J or K for the level 2 class, and I, G and K or J for the level 1 class. Thus, as this student pair produces a workable solution, this answer choice is incorrect.

Answer choice (B) is incorrect because J, L, and F can be in the level 2 class, leaving M, H and N in the level 3 class, and I, G and K for the level 1 class. Thus, as this student pair produces a workable solution, this answer choice is incorrect.

Answer choice (C) is incorrect because K, L, and F can be in the level 3 class, leaving M, H and N for the level 2 class, and I, G and J for the level 1 class. Thus, as this student pair produces a workable solution, this answer choice is incorrect.

Answer choice (D) is incorrect because J, M, and F can be in the level 2 class, leaving L, H and N in the level 3 class, and I, G and K for the level 1 class. Thus, as this student pair produces a workable solution, this answer choice is incorrect.

In answer choice (E), placing F with L and M leaves only H and N for the level 3 class. Since each level must have three students, the scenario in answer choice (E) cannot occur, and therefore (E) is correct.

This is a Basic Linear: Unbalanced: Overloaded, Numerical Distribution, Identify the Possibilities game.

In this game, you must combine the numerical information and the two block rules to see the limitations inherent within the game.

The game scenario and the first rule establish a numerical situation where 6 reviewers review 4 movies, with each reviewer reviewing a movie, and each movie reviewed by at least one reviewer. This "6 into 4" scenario initially has two possible distributions:

$$\begin{array}{cccc} 3 & 1 & 1 & 1 \\ \text{and} & & & \\ 2 & 2 & 1 & 1 \end{array}$$

However, the second and third rules establish two blocks of two reviewers, and since neither distribution allows for four reviewers to review a movie, we can deduce that the two blocks must be separate. Hence, the 3-1-1-1 distribution is impossible, and the game must always have a 2-2-1-1 distribution.

Because of the blocks, the distribution of the variables is as follows:

Thus, G, J, and K can *never* review the same movie. Two of G, J, and K will review a movie alone, and the remainder will review a movie with L. The fourth movie will be reviewed by F and H.

While this information is inherently restrictive, there are still additional rules that further limit the game. The fourth rule states that G reviews Mystery, and the fifth rule states that J reviews either Mystery or else Wolves. As we can see from the distribution above, G and J can never review the same movie. Thus, with G already reviewing Mystery, we can conclude that J cannot review Mystery and must instead review Wolves:

F G H J K L ⁶

$$\frac{G}{M} \qquad \frac{}{R} \qquad \frac{}{S} \qquad \frac{J}{W}$$

With those two variables placed, the FH block is affected. Because F and H cannot review a movie with any other reviewers, they can no longer review Mystery or Wolves, and they must review either Retreat or Seasonings. K, the one variable in the G, J, K grouping that has not yet been addressed, also cannot review Mystery or Wolves (K either reviews a movie alone or with L), and must review either Retreat or Seasonings. However, because F and H cannot review the same movie as K, either F and H review Retreat and K reviews Seasonings, or F and H review Seasonings and K reviews Retreat. This leads to the following setup, with the only real uncertainty being which movie L reviews:

F G H J K L [6]

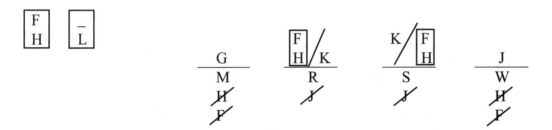

Note that L must review a movie with G, J, or K, and L cannot review the same movie as the FH block.

At this point, there are relatively few solutions, but there is no need to draw out the two templates that rely on the placement of FH and K because the diagram above does an excellent job of showing the various possibilities.

Question #6: Local, Must Be True. The correct answer choice is (A)

If L reviews S, then L must review S with K, and the following diagram results:

	F	K	
G	H	L	J
M	R	S	W

Hence, answer choice (A) is correct.

Question #7: Local, Must Be True. The correct answer choice is (E)

If K does not review S, then K must review R, and the following diagram results:

		F	
G	K	H	J
M	R	S	W

L's placement is uncertain, and L can review M, R, or W. Because F and H must review S, answer choice (E) is correct.

Question #8: Global, Could Be True, List. The correct answer choice is (E)

The third rule addresses L, and stipulates only that L must review the same movie as one other reviewer. This is a weak limitation, and ultimately L can review any of the four movies. Consequently, the correct answer choice is (E).

As with many Complete Variable List questions, if you do not immediately know the answer, one proven tactic is to skip the question and return to it after you have completed all of the other questions in the game. With that approach, you will typically see more of the options for L's placement, and the question will be less time-consuming to answer.

Question #9: Global, Could Be True. The correct answer choice is (E)

Answer choice (A): The 2-2-1-1 numerical distribution in this game forces F and H to review the same movie, and so no other reviewer aside from H can review a movie with F. This answer choice attempts to pair F and G, and is thus incorrect.

Answer choice (B): The 2-2-1-1 numerical distribution in this game forces F and H to review the same movie, and so no other reviewer aside from H can review a movie with F. This answer choice attempts to pair F and L, and is thus incorrect.

Answer choice (C): G must review M, and J must review W, and so the two can never review the same movie.

Answer choice (D): If K reviews W and L reviews M, then there is no solution to the game that would fit the 2-2-1-1 distribution. Because J must review M or W, either a 3-2-1 or a 2-2-2 distribution results, and in neither of those two distributions are all four movies reviewed. Thus, this answer choice cannot be true and is incorrect.

Answer choice (E): This is the correct answer choice. The hypothetical produced in question #7 helps show that this answer can be true.

Question #10: Global, Could Be True, Except. The correct answer choice is (B)

Because G must review M, if L and K also review M, that creates a violation of the 2-2-1-1 distribution. Thus, answer choice (B) cannot be true and is the correct answer.

Question #11: Local, Could Be True, List. The correct answer choice is (C)

The question stem stipulates that K reviews the same movie as exactly one other reviewer. From the initial setup, we can determine that the only other reviewer that can review a movie with K is L. The pairing of K and L cannot review M because G already reviews M, and K and L also cannot review W because J already reviews W. Thus, only R or S can be reviewed by K and L, and answer choice (C) is correct.

Question #12: Global, Could Be True, List. The correct answer choice is (B)

Answer choice (A): From the fifth rule J must review M or W, and so this answer choice is incorrect.

Answer choice (B): This is the correct answer choice.

Answer choice (C): From the fifth rule J must review M or W, and so this answer choice is incorrect.

Answer choice (D): The third rule stipulates that L reviews the same movie as exactly one other reviewer, and so this answer choice is incorrect.

Answer choice (E): From the fifth rule J must review M or W, and so this answer choice is incorrect. In addition, G must review M.

This is a Pattern game.

This game is unusual, to say the least. The "words" described in the scenario are just strings of letters, and there are no pre-existing words described in any of the rules. The rules themselves are odd, and do not describe any specific variables, just global applications of the rules. This lack of specificity about the variables is a classic signature of Pattern games, and one you must recognize when you see it.

The first rule establishes that each solution has five words, and the words are in alphabetical order:

$$\underline{\hspace{2cm}}\ \underline{\hspace{2cm}}\ \underline{\hspace{2cm}}\ \underline{\hspace{2cm}}\ \underline{\hspace{2cm}}$$
$$\quad 1 \qquad 2 \qquad 3 \qquad 4 \qquad 5$$

The second rule indicates that one of three operations is applied to a each word, either delete a letter, add a letter, or replace a letter. Thus, for example, if the first word was "armor," the second word could be:

> If a letter was deleted, a possible word would be: "rmor"

> If a letter was added, a possible word would be: "armors"

> If a letter was replaced, a possible word would be: "artor"

There are, of course, a huge number of other possible words that would fit each scenario above, but the above examples should give you an idea of what the test makers mean by the language in this rule. Note that in each instance above, the first and second words would be correctly alphabetically ordered.

The third rule affects the range of words, and limits the first letter in the words. At most three of the words can have the same first letter.

The final rule is crucial because it establishes that the same operation cannot be applied twice in a row. This means that, for example, if a letter is added to the first word to form the second word, when the third word is formed a letter cannot be added; a letter would have to be deleted or replaced.

Question #13: Global, Could Be True, List. The correct answer choice is (B)

This is a List question, so apply the rules to each answer choice and eliminate the incorrect answers.

Answer choice (A) is incorrect for two reasons: it is not in alphabetical order per the first rule ("bleak" follows "bzeak") and the last word, "pea," has only three letters, a violation of one of the conditions in the scenario.

Answer choice (B) is the correct answer.

Answer choice (C) is incorrect because the transition from the first word to the second word involves replacing two letters, not one ("dteam" to "gleam"), which is a violation of the second letter.

Answer choice (D) is incorrect because the last two operations performed are both replacements, a violation of the fourth rule.

Answer choice (E) is incorrect because the first four words start with "f," a violation of the third rule.

Question #14: Global, Could Be True. The correct answer choice is (D)

This is a tricky question, and you must remember that at most three of the five words can begin with the same letter as one another. If the first word of a sentence in the word game begins with the letter "z", then all five of the words in that sentence would have to begin with the letter "z" since all of the words in any sentence in the word game must appear in alphabetical order. Therefore, it follows that the first word of a sentence in the word game cannot begin with the letter "z", and consequently, answer choice (E) can be eliminated. The following hypothetical, however, proves that the first word of a sentence in the word game could begin with the letter "y":

year	yearn	zearn	zearns	zearnx
1	2	3	4	5

In this hypothetical all five of the words are in alphabetical order, and only three of the five words begin with the letter "z". Since "y" appears later in the alphabet than all other letters except "z", it follows that "y" is the last letter of the alphabet which the first word of a sentence in the word game can begin. Therefore, answer choice (D) is correct.

If you chose answer choice (C), do not feel bad. This is a tough question and the natural inclination is to step back two letters to "x," not just one letter to "y." This was, by far, the most commonly chosen incorrect answer.

Question #15: Local, Could Be True. The correct answer choice is (C)

Although the general pattern needed to answer this question can be evaluated and determined, it is far easier to solve this question by simply looking at each of the five candidates for the second word.

Answer choice (A) is incorrect because it is non-alphabetical.

Answer choice (B) is incorrect because "blender" requires two operations (remove a letter and replace a letter, not necessarily in that order) to be turned into "gender," a violation of the second rule.

Answer choice (C) is the correct answer.

Answer choice (D) is incorrect because "blender" requires two operations (remove a letter and replace a letter, not necessarily in that order) to be turned into "sender," a violation of the second rule.

Answer choice (E) is incorrect because "blender" requires two operations (remove a letter and replace a letter, not necessarily in that order) to be turned into "tender," a violation of the second rule.

Question #16: Local, Must Be True, Minimum. The correct answer choice is (D)

This questions tests your ability to manipulate the operations in order to minimize the number of letters in the fourth word.

If the first word has nine letters, then the optimal operation for the second word is to delete a letter, reducing the total number of letters in the word to eight. The next operation cannot be a deletion, so the most benign operation would be to replace a letter. Then to reach the fourth word, a letter could again be deleted, bringing the minimum number of letters possible in the fourth word to seven:

$$
\begin{array}{ccccc}
 & \text{delete} & \text{replace} & \text{delete} & \\
\dfrac{9}{1} & \dfrac{8}{2} & \dfrac{8}{3} & \dfrac{7}{4} & \dfrac{}{5}
\end{array}
$$

Accordingly, answer choice (D) is correct.

Question #17: Local, Could Be True, List. The correct answer choice is (E)

In this question, "learn" cannot be the second word in the sentence since it would take more than one operation to transform "clean" into "learn." Therefore, answer choices (A) and (D) can be eliminated. The following hypothetical, however, proves that "learn" could be the third word in the sentence:

$$
\begin{array}{ccc}
\dfrac{\text{clean}}{1} & \dfrac{\text{lean}}{2} & \dfrac{\text{learn}}{3}
\end{array}
$$

Answer choice (C) can be eliminated since it does not contain "third" in its list of potential positions for "learn."

The following hypothetical proves that "learn" could also be the fourth word in the sentence:

$$
\begin{array}{cccc}
\dfrac{\text{clean}}{1} & \dfrac{\text{lean}}{2} & \dfrac{\text{leapn}}{3} & \dfrac{\text{learn}}{4}
\end{array}
$$

Answer choice (B) can be eliminated since it does not contain "fourth" in its list of potential positions for "learn." Answer choice (E) is thus proven correct by process of elimination.

10

Question #18: Local, Must Be True, Maximum. The correct answer choice is (C)

This question is similar to question #16, except that in this question you are required to maximize the number of letters, instead of minimize the number of letters.

If the first word has four letters, then the optimal operation for the second word is to add a letter, increasing the total number of letters in the word to five. The next operation cannot be an addition, so the most benign operation would be to replace a letter. Then to reach the fourth word, a letter could again be added, bringing the number of letters possible in the fourth word to six. Finally, with another addition operation impossible, the best choice is to replace a letter:

$$
\begin{array}{ccccccccc}
 & \text{add} & & \text{replace} & & \text{add} & & \text{replace} & \\
\dfrac{4}{1} & & \dfrac{5}{2} & & \dfrac{5}{3} & & \dfrac{6}{4} & & \dfrac{6}{5}
\end{array}
$$

The maximum number of letters in the fifth word is thus six, and accordingly answer choice (D) is correct.

This is a Grouping/Linear Combination game.

Since the concertos from each composer produce the variables that are used in the linear setup, they are the logical starting point for our analysis. Each composer supplies two concertos, and the groups are as follows:

$$\text{Giuliani:} \quad \text{H, J, K}^3 \qquad \underline{\hspace{2em}} \ \underline{\hspace{2em}}$$
$$\text{Rodrigo:} \quad \text{M, N, O, P}^4 \qquad \underline{\hspace{2em}} \ \underline{\hspace{2em}}$$
$$\text{Vivaldi:} \quad \text{X, Y, Z}^3 \qquad \underline{\hspace{2em}} \ \underline{\hspace{2em}}$$

Of the three groups, Giuliani and Vivaldi are the most restricted, since they only have three concertos to fill the required two selections per composer. Thus, if any one concerto is unavailable from either the Giuliani or Vivaldi group, then the other two concertos must be selected. In a situation such as this, it is always best to immediately check the rules for any negative grouping rules among the members of the restricted groups. The third rule contains such a relationship:

$$X \longleftarrow\!\!\!\!\mid\!\!\!\!\longrightarrow Z$$

Since X and Z can never be selected together, we can Hurdle the Uncertainty and infer that Y must be selected from Vivaldi's group:

$$\underline{\text{Y}} \quad \underline{\text{X\textbackslash Z}}$$

The scenario above, three variables for two spaces, is perhaps the most common inference scenario that appears in Grouping games. Any negative grouping rule or any question stem that knocks out one of the three variables leads to the inference that some other variable must be selected. In the above scenario, the rule involving X and Z effectively knocks one of those two variables out of the selection pool, forcing Y to be selected. One of the best examples of this type of inference occurred in a game from the 1980s. In that game, seven basketball players were selected for five starting spots. Clearly, this leaves only two extra variables in the selection pool. However, as the rules unfold it turns out that two separate pairs of variables could not be selected together, in each case effectively reducing the candidate pool by one player. Since this occurred twice, it had to be that the three players not involved in the negative grouping rules were selected, a classic Hurdle the Uncertainties situation:

R S T U V W X ^{7}

$$U \longleftarrow\!\!\!\!\mid\!\!\!\!\longrightarrow S$$
$$W \longleftarrow\!\!\!\!\mid\!\!\!\!\longrightarrow V$$

$$\underline{\text{R}} \quad \underline{\text{T}} \quad \underline{\text{X}} \quad \underline{\text{U/S}} \quad \underline{\text{W/V}}$$
$$\text{5 Players}$$

Of course, a similar scenario can be produced with a wide variety of numerical combinations, four candidates for three spaces, eight candidates for six spaces, etc. It is also important to note that many questions introduce "if" statements that ultimately result in limited scenarios, such as three candidates for two spaces or four candidates for three spaces. The point is that any selection group that is limited in size relative to the number of members that must be selected will probably yield an important inference, and you must always watch for situations such as these in games. In the guitar concerto game under consideration, in Question #23 we benefit directly from our inference that Y must always be selected. Continuing with the setup of the game, we arrive at the following representation of the rules:

N $\longrightarrow$ J

M $\longleftarrow\!\!\!|\!\!\!\longrightarrow$ J

M $\longleftarrow\!\!\!|\!\!\!\longrightarrow$ O

X $\longleftarrow\!\!\!|\!\!\!\longrightarrow$ Z

X $\longleftarrow\!\!\!|\!\!\!\longrightarrow$ P

J, O $\longrightarrow$ J > O

$X_5 \longrightarrow$ M, N, or O_1

1	2	3	4	5	6
___	___	___	___	___	___

A combination of the first and second rules produces the following additional deduction:

N $\longleftarrow\!\!\!|\!\!\!\longrightarrow$ M

This deduction provides the answer to Question #24. There are also several other, less important inferences that can be made. For example, according to the second rule, when M is selected, J and O cannot be selected. Via the contrapositive, when J is not selected then N cannot be selected. From Rodrigo's group then, when M is selected, P is also selected:

M $\longrightarrow$ P

And since J is not selected, H and K must be selected from Giuliani's group:

M $\longrightarrow$ P, H, K

However, when P is selected, then X is not selected, and thus from Vivaldi's group Y and Z must be selected:

M $\longrightarrow$ P, H, K, Y, Z

So, if M is selected, the other five positions are automatically filled. A similar situation arises with X. When X is selected, Z and P are not selected. Since P is not selected, M cannot be selected (see the inference above). Since both M and P are not selected, N and O must be selected from Rodrigo's group. Of course, Y is always selected:

$$X \longrightarrow Y, N, O$$

According to the first rule, if N is selected, then J must be selected:

$$X \longrightarrow Y, N, O, J$$

These last two major inferences involving M and X are helpful, but they are not essential to answering the questions in the game. We discuss them here simply to indicate the type of inferences that can follow from restricted situations. The only other rule of note is the last rule, which states that if X is played on the fifth Sunday then one of Rodrigo's concertos must be played on the first Sunday. This rule is noteworthy because it is so specific. It should be easy to track while answering the questions, because it relies so heavily on two designated spaces.

Question #19: Global, Could Be True, List. The correct answer choice is (B)

This List question is easily answered by a systematic application of the rules. Answer choice (B) is correct. Answer choice (A) is incorrect because N is selected but J is not selected. Answer choice (C) is incorrect because both M and J are selected. Answer choice (D) is incorrect because both X and P are selected. Answer choice (E) is incorrect because J and O are both selected yet O is played before J.

Question #20: Local, Cannot Be True. The correct answer choice is (C)

This question provides a nice test of your linkage ability. Since the six variables are selected by the question stem, only the last two rules are applicable (both deal with the ordering of the variables). Since N (a concerto by Rodrigo) is to be played on the first Sunday, the conditions for the last rule (X on the fifth Sunday) are satisfied and this rule is not likely to play a role in answering the questions. However, since both J and O have been selected, the rule that states that J must be played before O is still in force. Since N will be played on the first Sunday, the sequencing relationship between J and O yields the Not Laws that J cannot be played on the sixth Sunday and O cannot be played on the second Sunday. Accordingly, answer choice (C) is correct.

Question #21: Local, Cannot Be True. The correct answer choice is (E)

The linkage chain in this question should be obvious. The question stem specifically refers to the fifth Sunday, a reference that also appears in the last rule. For X to play on the fifth Sunday, one of Rodrigo's concertos must be played on the first Sunday. According to the question stem, the only Rodrigo concerto that could be played on the first Sunday is O, but since J and O have both been selected, their sequencing relationship precludes O from being played on the first Sunday. It follows that X cannot be played on the fifth Sunday and thus answer choice (E) is correct.

Question #22: Local, Must Be True. The correct answer choice is (B)

If O is selected for the first Sunday, according to the sequencing rule involving J, J cannot be selected, and answer choice (A) is incorrect. Since J cannot be selected, the grouping restrictions come into play and H and K must be selected to represent Giuliani. Answer choice (B) is thus correct.

Question #23: Global, Must Be True. The correct answer choice is (D)

As previously discussed, answer choice (D) is correct.

Question #24: Global, Cannot Be True. The correct answer choice is (A)

As previously discussed, by combining the first two rules, we can infer that answer choice (A) is correct.

Perhaps the most important lesson of this game is to be mindful of the candidate restrictions in Grouping games. When some variables must be selected from a limited pool of candidates, invariably some powerful inferences will arise during the game, whether at the outset or during the questions.

POWERSCORE®

11
PrepTest

JUNE 1994 LOGIC GAMES SETUPS

11

This is a Defined-Moving, Balanced Grouping game.

The game establishes that eight counselors will supervise three activities, and the first rule creates a distribution of counselors to activities. Because each activity is supervised by at least two of the counselors but no more than three of the counselors, exactly two of the activities must be supervised by three counselors and exactly one of the activities must be supervised by two counselors, an unfixed numerical distribution of 3-3-2. Because the distribution is unfixed, the best diagram for the game is to show the minimum number of counselors for each activity (2), and then track the distribution throughout the questions:

F G H J K L N O⁸   3-3-2:
*   *

```
      ___  ___  ___
       S    T    V
```

The second and third rules place one of the counselors, and establish two Not Laws:

F G H J K L N O⁸   3-3-2:
*   *

```
      _H_  ___  ___
       S    T    V
           K̸
           Ø̸
```

The presence of the two Not Laws allows for two additional inferences (these will not be shown as dual-options because that would make it appear that swimming must have three counselors):

K ———→ S or V

O ———→ S or V

The fourth rule contains two negative grouping rules, which can be shown with blocks or arrows. We'll use arrows for the not-blocks as that has the greatest visual impact:

```
[J/K̸]      [J/N̸]
```

Combining this rule with the Not Laws specified in the third rule gives us two additional inferences:

J_s ———→ K_v

J_v ———→ K_s

The fifth rule establish a conditional relationship when G supervises swimming:

$$G_s \longrightarrow \begin{array}{c} N_v \\ + \\ O_v \end{array}$$

Combining all of the information above leads to the final setup for the game:

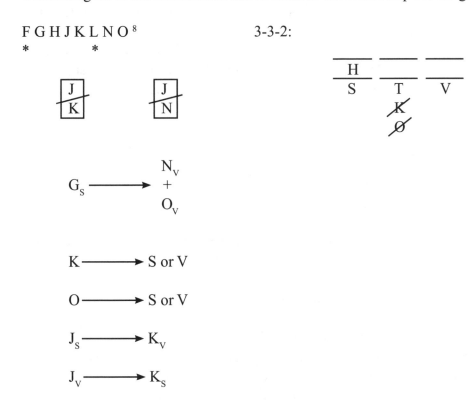

F G H J K L N O ^{8}
*   *

3-3-2:

Question #1: Global, Could Be True, List. The correct answer choice is (A)

Answer choice (B) is incorrect because it violates the last rule; when G supervises swimming, then N and O must supervise volleyball. Answer choice (C) is incorrect because swimming is assigned one counselor and tennis is assigned four counselors, a violation of the first rule. Answer choice (D) is incorrect because J and K cannot be assigned to supervise the same activity. Answer choice (E) is incorrect because K cannot be assigned to tennis. Thus, answer choice (A) is correct.

Question #2: Global, Could Be True. The correct answer choice is (E)

Answer choice (A) is incorrect since if G is assigned to swimming then N must be assigned to volleyball. Answer choice (B) is incorrect since G is assigned to swimming then O must be assigned to volleyball. Answer choice (C) is incorrect since K and J cannot supervise the same activity. Answer choice (D) is incorrect since J and N cannot supervise the same activity. Thus, answer choice (E) is proven correct by process of elimination.

Question #3: Global, Could Be True. The correct answer choice is (B)

According to the Not Laws, K and O cannot be assigned to supervise tennis. Accordingly, answer choices (A) and (E) can be eliminated. Since H is assigned to swimming, H cannot be assigned to tennis, and answer choice (C) can be eliminated. Answer choice (D) is incorrect since J and N cannot supervise the same activity. Thus, answer choice (B) is proven correct by process of elimination.

Question #4: Local, Could Be True. The correct answer choice is (D)

If G and K are assigned to swimming, then swimming has three counselors and no other counselors can be assigned to swimming. Because G is assigned to swimming, from the last rule we can determine that N and O must be assigned to volleyball. Because swimming is full and N is assigned to volleyball, J must be assigned to tennis. At least one of the remaining two counselors, F and L, must be assigned to tennis so that tennis is assigned at least two counselors. This information leads to the following setup:

$$
\begin{array}{ccc}
\underline{K} & & \\
\underline{G} & \underline{L/F} & \underline{O} \\
\underline{H} & \underline{J} & \underline{N} \\
S & T & V
\end{array}
$$

The remainder of L/F can be assigned to either tennis or volleyball. Accordingly, answer choice (D) is correct.

Question #5: Local, Must Be True. The correct answer choice is (C)

If F and L are assigned to supervise swimming, swimming is full, and thus O and K must be assigned to volleyball (remember, from the third rule they cannot be assigned to tennis). With K assigned to volleyball, from the fourth rule J must be assigned to tennis. The assignment of J to tennis forces N to be assigned to volleyball, and as volleyball now has the maximum of three counselors, G must be assigned to tennis:

$$
\begin{array}{ccc}
\underline{L} & & \underline{N} \\
\underline{F} & \underline{G} & \underline{K} \\
\underline{H} & \underline{J} & \underline{O} \\
S & T & V
\end{array}
$$

Consequently, answer choice (C) is correct.

Question #6: Local, Cannot Be True. The correct answer choice is (B)

This question can be solved by looking at the variables which are directly linked to both J and O. If J and O are assigned to supervise the same activity, then J and O would have to be assigned to either swimming or volleyball (O cannot be assigned to tennis). If J and O are assigned to swimming, then swimming is full and G cannot be assigned to swimming; on the other hand, if J and O are assigned to volleyball, then G still cannot be assigned to swimming. If G is assigned to swimming then N and O have to be assigned to volleyball, forcing N and J together, which is a violation of the rules. Thus, answer choice (B) is correct.

This is an Unbalanced: Underfunded Basic Linear game.

F G H I J ^{5}

A careful reading of the rules reveals that there are several numerical options available for the assignment of firefighters to days, and thus what appears to be a simple linear game is actually somewhat complex. Because numbers *always* play an important role in Logic Games, let us take a moment to review how you could have recognized that this game was not a simple 1-to-1 relationship:

1. The game scenario never specifies that each firefighter must work.

    Many students make the mistake of assuming that because five firefighters are listed, that all five must work. However, if that is the case, you will always see confirmation of that fact in either the game scenario or rules. This game contains no such confirmation, and so it is not the case that every firefighter must work. Do not make the mistake of assuming that the first rule states that every firefighter works. Instead, the first rule indicates that exactly one firefighter is assigned each day (and not that every firefighter is assigned).

    Remember, the statements that are omitted in the rules are just as important as the statements that are made.

2. The second rule reveals that some firefighters are able to work more than one day per week.

    The second rule directly addresses numbers, and so this is the most apparent tip-off that something is going on with the firefighter assignments in this game. While this rule limits firefighters to no more than two days worked, applying this rule in combination with the point made in item #1 above leads us to three unfixed numerical distributions for the game:

    2-2-1:   Two firefighters work two days each, one firefighter works one day. Two firefighters do not work.

    2-1-1-1:   One firefighter works two days, three firefighters each work one day. One firefighter does not work.

    1-1-1-1-1: Each firefighter works one day. When this distribution is in play, the game acts like a standard Basic Linear game.

With the understanding that not all of the firefighters must work, the rules are no longer simple blocks and sequences. Instead, for the rules to be in effect, you must know that all of the firefighters mentioned in each rule are working. Otherwise, the rule is not in force.

The third rule is shown as a CC not-block, which is more efficient than showing each of the five firefighters in individually lettered not-blocks.

The fourth rule is now conditional, as F and J must both work in order for the F > J sequence to apply. Because the rule only enacts if *both* F and J work, no Not Laws can be drawn.

The fifth rule is also conditional, and only occurs when H works. Of course, via the contrapositive, if G does not work, then H cannot work, and the other three firefighters would be in the 2-2-1 distribution. Note that the conditional nature of this rule means that G could be the first firefighter to work, a scenario that can occur if H does not work. Thus, no G Not Law appears under Monday.

Question #7: Global, Cannot Be True, List. The correct answer choice is (B)

Answer choice (B) is correct because when J works second and F works fifth, the fourth rule is violated. This is the case even though F also works first. Remember, the fourth rules states "F *never* works later in the week than J."

Question #8: Local, Could Be True, List. The correct answer choice is (D)

Answer choice (A) is incorrect because G does not have two consecutive days off during the week (remember, the wording in the question stem is explicit: "at least two consecutive days off *during* the *Monday-to-Friday workweek*"). Answer choice (B) is incorrect because, according to the last rule, when H works then G must work on the following day. In this answer choice, H works on Monday, but G does not work on Tuesday. This answer choice also violates the third rule. Answer choice (C) is incorrect because I works on consecutive days, a violation of the third rule. Answer choice (E) is incorrect because F works later in the week than J, a violation of the fourth rule. Hence, answer choice (D) is correct.

Question #9: Local, Cannot Be True. The correct answer choice is (B)

If both F and J work during the week, then the fourth rule comes into play, and from the Not Laws that follow from a sequence in a linear game, we know that J cannot work on Monday and F cannot work on Friday. Consequently, answer choice (B) cannot occur, and is correct.

Question #10: Local, Could Be True. The correct answer choice is (B)

If J works on Thursday, and F works twice during the week, then from the fourth rule F must work twice in the Monday-Tuesday-Wednesday span. From the third rule, we can then conclude that F works on Monday and Wednesday:

	F		F	J	
M	T	W	Th	F	

From this information, we can eliminate answer choices (A), (D), and (E). Answer choice (C) can also be eliminated because if H were to work on Tuesday, then G would have to work on Wednesday, which is not possible in this question. Hence, answer choice (B) is correct (Remember, G can work on any given day, irrespective of H—don't make a Mistaken Reversal!).

Question #11: Local, Must Be True. The correct answer choice is (D)

If G does not work during the week, then from the last rule we know that H cannot work during the week. Hence, only F, I, and J can work, and the only available numerical distribution is the 2-2-1. Despite this powerful information, and the application of the fourth rule, this is still a difficult question. If you make some good inferences, but still do not see an answer choice that is immediately and obviously correct, try to use hypotheticals to solve the problem. In this instance, answer choices (A) and (C) can both be eliminated with the following hypothetical:

F	I	F	I	J
M	T	W	Th	F

Note that a savvy student could use the hypothetical created in question #7 answer choice (A)—which is the same as the hypothetical above—to eliminate answer choices (A) and (C) in question #11 (remember, question #7 is a Cannot Be True question, so the four wrong answer choices are viable solutions).

Answer choices (B) and (E) can both be eliminated with the following hypothetical:

F	I	J	I	J
M	T	W	Th	F

Answer choice (D) is thus proven correct by process of elimination.

After reviewing the above information, some students still wonder why it must be that I works twice during the work week. If I only works once and F and J each work twice, then F and J are forced to "overlap" in a way that violates the fourth rule (to do otherwise causes a violation of the third rule). If you are uncertain of how this works, try to create a workable solution containing two F's, two J's, and one I. It cannot be done.

This is a Grouping: Defined-Moving, Unbalanced: Overloaded game.

This is a fairly standard Grouping game, except for the fact that there is a chairperson, and the chairperson affects the size of each group. Thus, the game actually has two different possible groupings:

T: F G J K M ^{5}
H: P Q R S ^{4}
    * *

$$\underline{\quad}\;\;\underline{\quad}\;\;\underline{\quad}\;\Big|\;\underline{\quad}\;\;\underline{\quad} \quad \text{or} \quad \underline{\quad}\;\;\underline{\quad}\;\Big|\;\underline{\quad}\;\;\underline{\quad}\;\;\underline{\quad}$$
$$\;\;\text{T}\quad\text{T}\quad\text{T}\;\;\;\text{H}_c\;\;\text{H} \qquad\qquad \text{T}_c\quad\text{T}\;\;\;\text{H}\quad\text{H}\quad\text{H}$$

The vertical bar has been placed between the tenant and homeowner groups to make the group separation in each scenario more clear.

The last four rules are each conditional, and each is relatively easy to diagram:

Third rule: F $\longrightarrow$ Q

Fourth rule: G $\longrightarrow$ K

Fifth rule: J $\longleftrightarrow$ M

Sixth rule: M $\longleftarrow\!\!\!\mid\!\!\!\longrightarrow$ P

The combination of the fourth and fifth rules leads to two interesting inferences. Because selecting G forces K to be selected, the JM block cannot be selected with G as that would mean that four tenants would be selected for the committee, a violation of the rules. Thus, G cannot be selected with either J or M:

G $\longleftarrow\!\!\!\mid\!\!\!\longrightarrow$ J

G $\longleftarrow\!\!\!\mid\!\!\!\longrightarrow$ M

The combination of the fifth and sixth rules allows for another inference:

J $\longleftarrow\!\!\!\mid\!\!\!\longrightarrow$ P

Thus, if J and M are selected, P cannot be selected (leaving only Q, R, and S left as homeowners possibly on the committee). Therefore, if either J or M is the chairperson, the five committee members must be J and M as the two tenants, and Q, R, and S as the three homeowners. This inference is tested on questions #14 and #17.

The combination of the information above leads to the final setup for the game:

T: F G J K M ^{5}
H: P Q R S ^{4}

$\quad\quad\quad$ * *

Rules:

$$\underline{\quad}\ \underline{\quad}\ \underline{\quad}\Big|\underline{\quad}\ \underline{\quad} \quad\quad \text{or} \quad\quad \underline{\quad}\ \underline{\quad}\Big|\underline{\quad}\ \underline{\quad}\ \underline{\quad}$$

$$\quad\text{T}\quad\text{T}\quad\text{T}\quad\text{H}_c\quad\text{H}\quad\quad\quad\quad\quad\text{T}_c\quad\text{T}\quad\text{H}\quad\text{H}\quad\text{H}$$

$\quad$ F $\longrightarrow$ Q

$\quad$ G $\longrightarrow$ K

$\quad$ J $\longleftrightarrow$ M

$\quad$ M $\longleftarrow\!\!|\!\!\longrightarrow$ P

Inferences:

$\quad$ G $\longleftarrow\!\!|\!\!\longrightarrow$ J

$\quad$ G $\longleftarrow\!\!|\!\!\longrightarrow$ M

$\quad$ J $\longleftarrow\!\!|\!\!\longrightarrow$ P

$\quad$ J$_c$
$\quad$ or $\longrightarrow$ J, M, Q, R, S
$\quad$ M$_c$

Finally, this game contains eight questions, a unique number in modern LSAT Games history. All other games contain either five, six, or seven questions. The presence of eight questions meant that this game represented one-third of all the questions in this section, and thus a test taker hoping for a reasonable score in the Games section *had* to do this game.

Question #12: Global, Could Be True, List. The correct answer choice is (D)

Answer choice (A) is incorrect because G is selected but K is not.

Answer choice (B) is incorrect because J is selected but M is not.

Answer choice (C) is incorrect because only one tenant is selected, a violation of the first rule.

Answer choice (E) is incorrect because both M and P are selected, a violation of the last rule.

Thus, answer choice (D) is the correct answer.

Question #13: Global, Could Be True, List. The correct answer choice is (C)

Each of the four incorrect answer choices attempts to pair G with either J or M. As discussed previously, this cannot occur, and thus answer choices (A), (B), (D), and (E) are incorrect.

Note that answer choices (A) and (D) are also incorrect because J is selected but M is not selected, a violation of the fifth rule.

Answer choice (C) is correct, and can be proven by the hypothetical F-J-M-Q-R.

Question #14: Local, Must Be True. The correct answer choice is (E)

If M is the chairperson, then M and J are the two tenants, and because M cannot be selected with P, the three homeowners must be Q, R, and S. Thus, answer choice (E) is correct.

Note that even if you did not see this inference during your setup, answer choices (A) and (B) can be eliminated because they are both tenants (and J and M are already the two tenants on the committee), and answer choice (D) can be eliminated because of the sixth rule. Thus, even without the "J or M as chairperson" super-inference, you can eliminate three of the answer choices, leaving you with the ability to use a hypothetical to choose between (C) and (E).

Question #15: Local, Must Be True. The correct answer choice is (B)

If F is selected to be the chairman, there can be only one additional tenant on the committee. Thus J, M, and G cannot be selected because each requires another tenant. It follows that K must be the additional tenant selected and thus answer choice (B) is correct.

Question #16: Local, Could Be True, Except. The correct answer choice is (A)

The information in the explanation for question #15 can be used to explain why answer choice (A) must be correct. Since F and G cannot be the only two tenants selected, it is impossible for G to be the chairperson if F is selected.

Question #17: Local, Could Be True. The correct answer choice is (C)

If K is not selected then from the contrapositive of the fourth rule G cannot be selected. Thus, if F, G, and K are not selected, then J and M must be the only two tenants selected, and either J or M must be the chairperson. If J or M is chairperson, as discussed earlier Q, R, and S must also be selected. Therefore, answer choice (C) is correct.

Question #18: Local, Must Be True. The correct answer choice is (A)

This is a "5 if" question, which is a type that can be quite time-consuming. Thus, you must use as many tricks as possible to narrow down the list of possible answer choices.

For example, the correct answer choice from question #12 can be used to eliminate answer choices (C) and (E). Since List questions such as #12 always produce full or partial hypotheticals, you can often use the correct answer in a List question to eliminate answer choices in other questions, as is the case here. List questions, which are among the easiest questions, are thus also among the most useful questions, and you must take special care to answer them correctly. By quickly and easily eliminating two answers on this difficult question you can save valuable time.

Answer choice (B) is unlikely to be correct because it posits that R, a random must be selected.

Answer choice (D) can be disproven by the hypothetical J-K-M-R-S.

Accordingly, answer choice (A) is correct.

Question #19: Global, Must Be True. The correct answer choice is (C)

This is a tricky question as well, and the question stem asks for you to identify the pair of variables where at least one of the two is always on the committee. Thus, if a scenario can be found where neither variable is on the committee, that answer choice is incorrect. In questions such as this, prior work is invaluable, so make sure to check the work you produced in solving the other questions in the game.

The hypothetical produced by the correct answer to question #12—J, K, M, Q, S—eliminates answer choice (A) because neither F nor P appears in the hypothetical. Other work in the game can be used to attack some of the other answers (#15 for answer choice (B), for example), but because many of those questions produced only partial hypotheticals, this can be challenging.

Let's take a different attack, and look at each answer choice from a more abstract standpoint, one that assesses the conditional value of each variable:

> Answer choice (A): contains two sufficient conditions
> Answer choice (B): contains two sufficient conditions (one is also a necessary condition)
> Answer choice (C): contains two necessary conditions
> Answer choice (D): contains two sufficient conditions (one is also a necessary condition)
> Answer choice (E): contains two randoms

In a game such as this one, where there is an Overloaded set of variables for the group being formed, variables that are necessary conditions are extremely powerful because when they are removed, another variable is typically also removed. Thus, answer choice (C) looks the most promising, followed by (B) and (D), then answer choice (A). answer choice (E) is the least likely to be correct as randoms are not likely to have to appear in every viable committee.

Given that (C) is the most promising answer, let's start our analysis there. Answer choice (C) contains two representatives who are necessary for other representatives to be selected. So, eliminating both K and Q would also eliminate F and G from the committee. That leaves only J, M, P, R, and S for the committee. However, from the sixth rule, M and P cannot be on the same committee, so removing K and Q does not leave enough representatives to form a viable committee. Thus, either K or Q must be on every viable committee, and answer choice (C) is correct.

This is a Pattern: Identify the Possibilities game.

This can be a very challenging game. The first line of the scenario establishes the key information that the apprentices are initially assigned to separate projects. T leads to a decision moment: there is a choice between using the variable set QRST as the base or using variable set LMNO as the base. QRST is the better choice as the base because two of the three rules focus on that variable set. Also, a quick glance at questions #22 and #23 indicates that Law Services uses QRST as the base in their answer choices. Answering the questions is always easier if you are looking at the test in the same way that the test makers are looking at the test.

The key is that exactly two reassignments will be made each year. Each of these reassignments uses one of three plans, and no plan can be used twice. Thus, with only three plans, only six possible arrangements of the three plans are possible:

> 1. Plan 1, then Plan 2
> 2. Plan 1, then Plan 3
>
> 3. Plan 2, then Plan 1
> 4. Plan 2, then Plan 3
>
> 5. Plan 3, then Plan 1
> 6. Plan 3, then Plan 2

The key to destroying this game is to take these six outcomes and use them to Identify the Possibilities:

Apprentices: L M N O⁴
Projects: Q R S T⁴

Initial Assignments / Plan 1 / Plan 2 / Plan 3 diagram

Question #20: Local, Must Be True. The correct answer choice is (E)

If N is assigned to T *after the second reassignment*, then the plans must have been either Plan 2 then Plan 3, or Plan 3 then Plan 2. In both cases O is assigned to project S, so answer choice (E) is the correct answer.

Question #21: Local, Could Be True. The correct answer choice is (E)

Answer choice (A) is incorrect because L must be assigned to Q, R, or S.

Answer choice (B) is incorrect because N must be assigned to Q, S, or T.

Answer choice (C) is incorrect because O must be assigned to R, S, or T.

Answer choice (D) is incorrect because when L stays on the same project, N is assigned to a different project (Plan 2), and when N stays on the same project, L is assigned to a different project (Plan 3).

Answer choice (E) is the correct answer choice. N and O are both assigned to the same projects in Plan 3.

Question #22: Local, Could Be True, List. The correct answer choice is (A)

This can be a confusing question because the answer must show the arrangement *prior* to L being reassigned to R.

If L is assigned to project R, then the plans could be Plan 3 then Plan 1 (previous arrangement was the original assignment), or Plan 3 then Plan 2 (previous arrangement after Plan 3), or Plan 2 then Plan 3 (previous arrangement was the rearrangement after Plan 2). Respectively, these previous assignments are:

> Original: Q: L   R: M   S: N   T: O
>
> After Plan 2: Q: L   R: M   S: O   T: N
>
> After Plan 3: Q: M   R: L   S: N   T: O

Answer choice (A) is correct because it gives the reassignment following Plan 2.

Note that this was fairly predictable answer once you identified the three possibilities. Because Plan 3 reassigns L to R, most students look at plan 3 immediately or its branch, Plan 3 then Plan 2. The one possibility that doesn't involve an initial use of Plan 3 is the Plan 2 then Plan 3 assignments, so this answer requires a bit more work to identify, making this answer more likely to be correct.

Question #23: Local, Could Be True, List. The correct answer choice is (B)

After only one reassignment you have the results of either Plan 1, Plan 2, or Plan 3. Answer choice (B) is correct because it gives the reassignment following Plan 3.

Question #24: Local, Must Be True. The correct answer choice is (A)

If the first reassignment is from Plan 1, then the second reassignment follows Plan 2 or Plan 3. Respectively, these give:

After Plan 1 then Plan 2: Q: N   R: O   S: M   T: L

After Plan 1 then Plan 3: Q: N   R: O   S: M   T: L

Answer choice (A) is correct because in both Plan 2 and Plan 3 (following Plan 1) L is assigned to T.

POWERSCORE®

12

PrepTest

12

OCTOBER 1994 LOGIC GAMES SETUPS

PrepTest 12. October 1994 Game #1: *1. E 2. B 3. C 4. B 5. C 6. D*

This is a Basic Linear: Balanced, Identify the Possibilities game.

At first glance, this game appears to be a standard Basic Linear game. However, the second and third rules combine to create a powerful block-sequence:

$$\boxed{G\ \_\_\ \_\_\ S} > U$$

By itself, the GS portion of this super-block-sequence can only be placed in days 1-4 or days 2-5 (days 3-6 are unavailable because S > U). By itself, then, this formation would suggest creating two base templates. However, the addition of the first rule (J > H) and the fourth rule (J ⟶ 1/3) further limits the possibilities, and the best approach is to Identify the Possibilities. Let's examine each:

<u>Template #1: GS block scheduled for days 1-4</u>

When the GS block is scheduled for days 1-4, then from the second rule U must be scheduled for day 5 or 6, and from the last rule J must be scheduled for day 3:

G		J	S	U/	/U
1	2	3	4	5	6

Because from the first rule J > H, H must be scheduled for day 5 or 6, and T, a random, must be scheduled for day 2:

G	T	J	S	U/H	H/U
1	2	3	4	5	6

This template captures two solutions to the game.

<u>Template #2: GS block scheduled for days 2-5, J scheduled for day 3</u>

When the GS block is scheduled for days 2-5, then from the second rule U must be scheduled for day 6. When J is scheduled for day 3, the following setup results:

	G	J		S	U
1	2	3	4	5	6

Because from the first rule J > H, H must be scheduled for day 4, and T, a random, must be scheduled for day 1:

T	G	J	H	S	U
1	2	3	4	5	6

This template captures one solution to the game.

When the GS block is scheduled for days 2-5, then from the second rule U must be scheduled for day 6. When J is scheduled for day 1, the following setup results:

J	G	__	__	S	U
1	2	3	4	5	6

The remaining two students—H and T—are then scheduled for days 3 and 4, not necessarily in that order:

J	G	H/T	T/H	S	U
1	2	3	4	5	6

This template captures two solutions to the game.

As all of the possibilities for the GS block have been explored, the five solutions above represent the only five solutions to the game.

Combining all of the information above leads to the final setup for the game:

G H J S T U^6

$\qquad$ *

J > H

$\boxed{G \_ \_ \_ S}$ > U

J $\longrightarrow$ 1/3

4 + 5:	J	G	H/T	T/H	S	U

3:	T	G	J	H	S	U

1 + 2:	G	T	J	S	H/U	U/H
	1	2	3	4	5	6

Although creating this setup takes some time, with all of the possibilities in hand the questions can be destroyed at a high rate of speed.

Question #1: Local, Must Be True. The correct answer choice is (E)

When J's lesson is scheduled for day 1, only the template containing possibilities 4 and 5 applies. In that template U is scheduled for day 6, and thus answer choice (E) is correct.

Question #2: Global, Must Be True. The correct answer choice is (B)

In the three templates only J, H, or T can be scheduled for the third day, and only H, S, or U can be scheduled for the fifth day. As H is the only student common to both those lists, H is the correct answer and answer choice (B) is correct.

Question #3: Global, Could Be True, List. The correct answer choice is (C)

A review of all five solutions shows only G or T scheduled for the second day, and thus answer choice (C) is correct.

Question #4: Local, Must Be True. The correct answer choice is (B)

H and T are consecutive only in the template containing possibilities 4 and 5. In that template G is second, and thus answer choice (B) is correct.

Question #5: Local, Could Be True. The correct answer choice is (C)

If J is scheduled for the third day, then only the first three possibilities apply. In a Could Be True question, look for the uncertainty, which occurs in possibilities 1 and 2 with H and U. Only answer choice (C) includes H and U, and, as it is possible for H's lesson to be scheduled for a later day than U's lesson, answer choice (C) is correct.

Question #6: Global, Could Be True, List. The correct answer choice is (D)

In possibilities 1 and 2, T is scheduled for the second day. In possibility 3, T is scheduled for the first day. In possibilities 4 and 5, T is scheduled for the third or fourth day. Hence, T can be scheduled for the first four days, and answer choice (D) is correct.

This is a Grouping: Defined-Fixed game.

This type of game has proven to be consistently difficult for the typical test taker. This particular game features nine people filling nine total spaces in three groups. From a theoretical standpoint, there is an advantage in the fact that all nine people (or variables) must be used, since unused variables will not be a concern. As a lengthy aside, if some variables were unused, it may or may not be an advantage to the test taker. For example, if there were nine people for seven group positions, this would be advantageous since knocking out any two candidates would force the remaining seven people to fill the seven positions. However, if there were nine people for five positions, this would probably be disadvantageous since there are more options to fill each position. Knocking out one or two of the people wouldn't necessarily produce any variables that would have to fill a position.

In this game, the nine variables themselves are split into two subgroups, children and adults, and you must make certain to keep this in mind throughout the game. The two groups can be represented as follows:

$$\frac{C}{F\,G\,H\,J\,K}^5 \qquad \frac{A}{Q\,R\,S\,T}^4$$

Any individual variable you work with can be symbolized with a C or A subscript (for example, Q_A) if necessary for clarity.

The first point of difficulty arises from the unbalanced separation of the adults. Since there are three groups and four adults, and each group must contain at least one adult, two groups contain a single adult and the remaining group contains two adults (a numerical distribution of 2-1-1, although not necessarily in that order). To partially combat this difficulty, you should reserve the bottom row of spaces for the adults that must be in each group, as follows:

Adults: ___ ___ ___
            1   2   3

It would not be wise to designate both of the top two rows as children-only since the remaining adult must be in one of those two rows. However, we can infer that each group contains either one or two children, so we can safely designate the top row for children.

The rule involving the FJ block is clearly beneficial since both are children and therefore they will fill the two available child spots in any given group. Because of this fact, F and J cannot be in a group with any of the other children, an inference we can symbolize as follows:

$$\boxed{\begin{matrix}F\\J\end{matrix}} \longleftrightarrow\!\!\!| \longrightarrow G, H, K$$

The next two rules are similar in nature and can be represented with either not-blocks or double-not arrows. Both work efficiently, but for our purposes we will use not-blocks since this game has a linear-type setup conducive to using the visually powerful blocks:

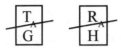

In this case we have chosen to designate the adults with a subscript since they are the smaller group and thus somewhat more restricted.

The last rule provides us with two Not Laws on the second group:

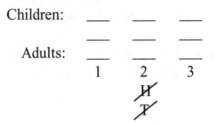

This final rule also allows us to make some critical inferences. First, H and T have been reduced to only two possibilities: group 1 or group 3. If for some reason one of those two groups should be completely filled by other variables, then both H and T must automatically go into the other group. As discussed previously, whenever variables are limited to only two options they are in a highly restricted state and will usually play a key role in the game. Also, if for some reason (as specified in a rule or "if" statement) another variable knocks either H or T out of group 1 or group 3, then H or T would have to go into the other group. In this game, the third and fourth rules act in such a way. According to the third rule G and T cannot be in the same group. Since T cannot be in group 2, we can make the following inferences:

$$G_1 \longrightarrow T_3$$
$$G_3 \longrightarrow T_1$$

Taking the contrapositive of the first inference, if T is not in group 3, then G is not in group 1. This is identical to saying that if T is in group 1, then G is in either group 2 or 3. The same reasoning applies to the second inference. These contrapositives, while helpful, simply reflect the not-block information in the rules and in fact in this case do not produce any truly helpful information. However, it is always of value to quickly examine the contrapositive of any conditional rule you see in a game. Some of the most important game insights have come from understanding the implications of the contrapositive.

The last rule also interacts with the fourth rule to produce the following inferences:

$$R_1 \longrightarrow H_3$$
$$R_3 \longrightarrow H_1$$

The same contrapositive reasoning as above applies to this set of inferences as well.

We have now exhausted the possible inferences from the initial set of rules and we should be ready to attack the questions. In approaching the questions, rely upon the restricted variables F, J, R, H, G, and T to help make deductions essential to answering the questions. A close examination of the restricted points in any game—whether variables or spaces—almost always yields some inferences of value.

Question #7: Local, Could Be True. The correct answer choice is (E)

The "if" statement specifies that F must be in group 1, which automatically indicates that J is in group 1 as well. Since the FJ block is in group 1, G, H, and K must be in either group 2 or 3. Looking at the restricted variable H, we can see that H must be in group 3 (note that H has been placed into the "third" space in group 3, signifying that the adult space is yet to be filled). Since H is in group 3, R cannot be in group 3, and we have the following setup:

$$
\begin{array}{ccc}
\text{F} & \underline{\quad} & \text{H} \\
\underline{\text{J}} & \underline{\quad} & \underline{\quad} \\
\underline{\quad} & \underline{\quad} & \underline{\quad} \\
1 & 2 & 3 \\
\cancel{H} & & \cancel{R}
\end{array}
$$

Answer choice (A) is incorrect since group 3 cannot contain three children. Answer choice (B) is incorrect since R cannot be placed into group 3 with H. Answer choice (C) is incorrect because J is in group 1. Answer choice (D) is incorrect because both K and R cannot fit into group 1 along with F and J. It follows that answer choice (E) is correct. Surprisingly, this question is correctly answered by only 47% of all test takers. In approaching games in general, there is often some value in bypassing "could be true" questions that appear early in the game. Perhaps a later question will emulate the "F in 1" criterion in question #7 and thus produce a hypothetical that could be used to eliminate wrong answer choices. Regrettably, in this game no such hypothetical appears. However, using this strategy does not cost the test taker any time and so the question could still be completed at the end of the game.

Question #8: Local, Must Be True. The correct answer choice is (A)

If F and S are in group 3, then J must be in group 3 as well. Since group 3 is now full, H and T must both be placed into group 1, and therefore R and G must be placed into group 2. K and Q are a dual option between groups 1 and 2:

$$
\begin{array}{ccc}
\text{K/Q} & \text{Q/K} & \text{J} \\
\underline{\text{H}} & \underline{\text{G}} & \underline{\text{F}} \\
\underline{\text{T}} & \underline{\text{R}} & \underline{\text{S}} \\
1 & 2 & 3
\end{array}
$$

Accordingly, answer choice (A) is correct.

Question #9: Local, Must Be True. The correct answer choice is (E)

After making our inference about G and T at the start of the game, this is the question we have been waiting for. If G is in group 3, then according to our inference T must be in group 1. Since this is a Must Be True question and one of our initial inferences applies, immediately scan the answer choices to see if "T is in group 1" appears among the answer choices. Answer choice (E) reflects the inference and is thus correct. This question acts as a separator among test takers. Those who have truly understood the grouping principle present in this game will likely answer the question in under 15 seconds, leaving them extra time to attack the more difficult questions in the section. Remember, if a question stem leads you to an immediate inference, scan the answer choices quickly to see whether or not that inference appears.

Question #10: Local, Cannot Be True. The correct answer choice is (D)

The "if" statement in the question stem specifies that two adults, Q and S, are in groups 1 and 3 respectively. Since the adults are already a restricted group and two of the four adults are now placed, immediately look at the second group and examine the two remaining adult candidates, R and T. According to the Not Laws, T cannot be placed into group 2 and thus R must be the adult in group 2. T must be in either group 1 or group 3:

$$\begin{array}{ccc} \overline{T/} & \overline{} & \overline{/T} \\ Q & R & S \\ 1 & 2 & 3 \end{array}$$

You might expect that making the inference that R is in group 2 would lead immediately to the correct answer, but this question is a bit more subtle. Interestingly, the answer choices come in two distinct types: answer choices (A) and (B) place specific variables into specific groups, and answer choices (C), (D), and (E) specify the number of children in a group. Since the number of children in a group is linked to the adults in a group, and we already have a large amount of information about the adults in this question, answer choices (C), (D), and (E) seem to offer greater prospects for the correct answer. In fact, since R is the only adult in group 2, there must be two children in group 2, and thus answer choice (D) is correct (remember, this is a Cannot Be True question).

Question #11: Local, Must Be True. The correct answer choice is (B)

As you might expect in a game with only five questions, the last question is relatively hard. The key word in the question stem is "only." Since G is the only child in group 1, there must be two adults in group 1. Also, since G is involved in one of our primary inferences, we know that when G is in group 1 then T must be in group 3:

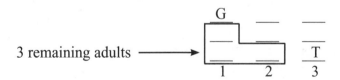

However, we can continue to make inferences because of the limited number of remaining spaces. The four remaining children, F, J, H, and K must be split between groups 2 and 3. Since F and J are a block, H and K must also form a block for this question. Since H cannot be placed into group 2, the H and K block must be placed into group 3, and F and J must then be placed into group 2:

These final inferences provide the justification for answer choice (B), the correct answer. Note that the positions of three remaining adults, Q, R, and S cannot be determined. Some students select answer choice (D), using the inference regarding H and R to incorrectly assume that since H is in group 3, then R must be in group 1. This is the Mistaken Reversal of the original inference and is thus incorrect.

As mentioned at the beginning of this discussion, the concepts in this game type are typically challenging for most test takers, and thus we strongly recommend that you work with this game and others like it until you have mastered these concepts.

This is a Grouping: Partially Defined game.

In an everyday scenario such as this one, where food is being matched with people, it makes sense to use the people as the base since most test takers think of giving the food to a person, not the other way around. Because this approach is more intuitive, it generally makes the game easier to understand. In general, if a base selection choice seems intuitive to you, go ahead and use that as the base.

The basic scenario and rules can be diagrammed as follows:

People: L M N ³
Foods: F H P S ⁴

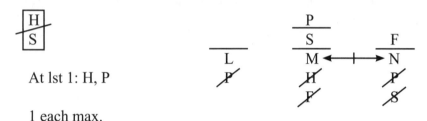

At lst 1: H, P

1 each max.

Let's briefly discuss each rule:

> The first rule simply means that multiples of each food are not available to each person. This serves to reduce the number of possibilities in the game.

> The second rule is represented by a vertical HS not-block, which is the most powerful visual representation of this rule.

> The third rule indicates that at least one hot dog and at least one pretzel are purchased.

> The fourth rule is represented with an S above Mendel in the diagram. When this rule is combined with the second rule, we can infer that Mendel does not buy a hot dog, which is shown with an H Not Law under Mendel.

> The fifth rule is represented with an F above Nastassia in the diagram.

> The sixth rule is shown with P Not Laws under Lara and Nastassia. This rule, when combined with the third rule, allows us to infer that Mendel must buy a pretzel, and so a P appears above Mendel.

> The seventh rule is shown by internal diagramming, which means that a double-not arrow is placed within the diagram between M and N. This makes the rule easier to remember and work with. Also, because Mendel buys a shish kebab and a pretzel, from this rule we know Nastassia cannot buy a shish kebab and a pretzel, and those inferences are represented with S and P Not Laws under Nastassia.

In addition, although part of the third rule is now satisfied (at least one person buys a pretzel), the portion stipulating that at least one person buys a hot dog is not yet fulfilled. Because Mendel cannot buy a hot dog, either Lara or Nastassia must buy a hot dog. And, because from the second rule a person who buys a shish kebab cannot also buy a hot dog, we can infer that if Lara has a shish kebab, Nastassia must have a hot dog:

$$L_S \longrightarrow N_H$$

Normally we could infer the other side of this dual-option inference (if Nastassia buys a shish kebab, then Lara buys a hot dog), but Nastassia can never buy a shish kebab so that side of the inference is non-applicable.

Finally, the last rule, which states that Mendel and Nastassia do not buy any similar foods, is the key to questions #14 and #17. As there are only four available foods, and since neither can select a food that overlaps with the other's selection, the maximum number of foods the two can jointly select is four. This inference is especially crucial for question #17, where some restrictions are lifted.

Question #12: Global, Must Be True. The correct answer choice is (D)

As discussed during the game setup, according to the third rule, at least one P must be purchased, and the sixth rule tells us that neither Lara nor Nastassia will be ordering a P—this means that Mendel must purchase a P. Accordingly, answer choice (D) is the correct answer choice;

Question #13: Global, Must Be True, Minimum. The correct answer choice is (B)

From the setup, we know that Mendel must purchase, at the very least, one S and one P (2 items = $2). We know from the fifth rule that Nastassia purchases an F (1 item = $1). The game scenario indicates that everyone buys at least on kind of food, and third rule dictates that someone must order an H; if we give the H to Lara (1 item = $1), all rules are satisfied. Thus, a minimum of four items must be purchased, and so the correct answer choice is (B).

Question #14: Global, Must Be True, Maximum. The correct answer choice is (B)

Since there can be no overlap between the purchases of Mendel and Nastassia, the most food types that we can distribute between those two is four (4 items = $4), provided that Nastassia orders an H. As for Lara, she is prohibited from purchasing a P but she can buy an F. However, she cannot purchase both an S and an H (only one or the other) due to the second rule. This leads to the following arrangement:

S/H	P	H
F	S	F
L	M	N

Thus, the greatest number of items that can be purchased in total would be six, so the correct answer choice is (B).

Question #15: Local, Must Be True. The correct answer choice is (A)

As established in the diagram for question #14 above, if Lara wishes to purchase exactly two types of food, she must buy an F and either an S or an H (remember, from the sixth rule she cannot buy a P, and from the second rule H and S cannot be purchased together). Therefore, the correct answer choice is (A).

Question #16: Local, Must Be True. The correct answer choice is (C)

According to the second rule, if Lara buys an S, she cannot buy an H. But the third rule dictates that someone must buy an H. Since Mendel cannot buy an H, Nastassia must be the one to buy an H in this case, so the correct answer choice is (C).

Question #17: Local, Must Be True, Maximum, Suspension. The correct answer choice is (C)

Because we still have the last rule, which prohibits Mendel and Nastassia from buying any of the same products, the best that we can do in maximizing their two orders is to have Nastassia order an H, as we did with question #14 above. As for Lara, since the second rule is suspended, she can order every food but P:

$$\frac{\text{S}}{\frac{\text{H}}{\frac{\text{F}}{\text{L}}}} \qquad \frac{\text{P}}{\frac{\text{S}}{\text{M}}} \qquad \frac{\text{H}}{\frac{\text{F}}{\text{N}}}$$

The greatest number of foods that the three could order would be seven, so the correct answer choice is (C).

This is a Pattern: Identify the Possibilities game.

The initial scenario and rules provide the following information:

$$1 + 2 = R$$
$$2 + 3 = O$$
$$1 + 3 = B$$
$$3 + 4 = B$$
$$1 + 4 = G$$
$$2 + 4 = G$$

R	B	G	O
1	2	3	4

The game hinges on the colors produced by combining the flasks. The key is to examine the results that occur when one or two experiments are conducted. Because each experiment combines two of the flasks, and no result of an experiment can be used, there is a limited number of possible outcomes in this game.

If only one experiment occurs there are six possibilities, and each possibility encompasses the results of the experiment and the colors of the other two, non-used flasks. These possibilities are based on the order of the rules, so possibility #1 reflects what occurs when the second rule (which is the first rule that addresses specific flasks) is implemented:

#1.	$1 + 2 = R$,	$3 = G$,	$4 = O$	(R, G, O)
#2.	$2 + 3 = O$,	$1 = R$,	$4 = O$	(O, R, O)
#3.	$1 + 3 = B$,	$2 = B$,	$4 = O$	(B, B, O)
#4.	$3 + 4 = B$,	$1 = R$,	$2 = B$	(B, R, B)
#5.	$1 + 4 = G$,	$2 = B$,	$3 = G$	(G, B, G)
#6.	$2 + 4 = G$,	$1 = R$,	$3 = G$	(G, R, G)

If only two experiments occur there are only three possibilities, and each encompasses the results of the two experiments:

#7.	$1 + 2 = R$,	$3 + 4 = B$	(R, B)
#8.	$1 + 3 = B$,	$2 + 4 = G$	(B, G)
#9.	$1 + 4 = G$,	$2 + 3 = O$	(G, O)

Thus, there are only nine outcomes (or solutions) to this game, and once you have identified all nine, the questions are considerably easier.

Question #18: Local, Could Be True, List. The correct answer choice is (D)

If only one experiment is performed you will get one mixed color result, as well as the colors of the two unmixed flasks. Answer choice (D) is correct because G, G, R are the colors that result from mixing flasks 2 + 4 (green), leaving flask 1 as is (red), and leaving flask 3 as is (green). This is possibility #6 in the master list.

Question #19: Local, Could Be True, List. The correct answer choice is (C)

If two experiments are performed there are only three possibilities: R + B, B + G, or G + O. Answer choice (C) is correct because blue and red are produced by mixing flasks 1 + 2 (red), and flasks 3 + 4 (blue). This is possibility #7 in the master list of possibilities.

Question #20: Local, Could Be True, List. The correct answer choice is (B)

If only one experiment is performed and no red flasks remain, then the original red flask (flask 1) must have been used in the experiment. Flask 1 cannot be mixed with flask 2 because that would produce a red chemical, so the experiment must be either 1 + 3 (leaving 2 and 4 unused, producing a B, B, O result), or 1 + 4 (leaving 2 and 3 unused, a G, B, G result). Answer choice (B) is correct because it presents B, G, G (2, 1 + 4, 3). This is possibility #5 in the master list.

Question #21: Local, Must Be True. The correct answer choice is (A)

If only one experiment is performed and at the end exactly one blue flask is present, the experiment must have been 1 + 4 (leaving 2 and 3 unused, a G, B, G result). This is possibility #5 in the master list. Answer choice (A) is correct because the two non-blue flasks are both green.

Question #22: Local, Could Be True. The correct answer choice is (E)

If the first experiment performed results in a single orange flask being present, then the experiment was either 1 + 2 (leaving 3 and 4 unused), or 1 + 3 (leaving 2 and 4 unused). These are possibilities #1 and #3 in the master list.

Thus, the second experiment could either mix flasks 3 and 4, or flasks 2 and 4. Answer choice (E) is correct because mixing 3 and 4 is possible.

Question #23: Local, Must Be True. The correct answer choice is (E)

If only one experiment is performed and no orange flasks remain, then the original orange flask (flask 4) must have been mixed with one of the other flasks (this occurs under possibilities #4, #5, and #6). Thus, because flask 4 must have been used in an experiment, answer choice (E) is correct.

Question #24: Local, Must Be True. The correct answer choice is (D)

If two experiments are performed and a single orange flask is produced (which occurs in possibility #9), the experiments must have been 1 + 4 (green) and 2 + 3 (orange). Because the other flask is green, the correct answer choice is (D).

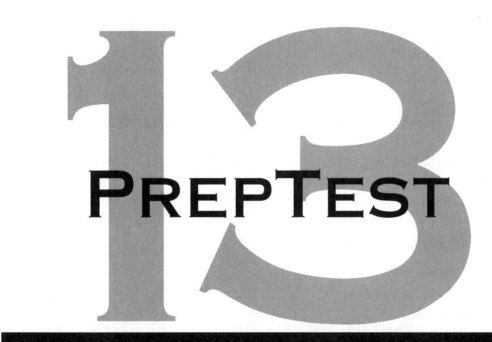

PowerScore®

13 PrepTest

December 1994 Logic Games Setups

13

This is a Grouping: Defined-Fixed, Balanced game.

The first key to this game comes from the second rule, and involves physically placing a G/M dual-option into both groups. This placement serves as a visual reminder that one space is already occupied in each group by either G or M. Thereafter, the basic setup and rule representation is fairly straightforward:

Next, let us examine some of the important inferences that can be drawn from the rules:

This Defined Grouping game involves placing 8 variables into 8 positions. Because all 8 variables must be in one of the two groups, the game uses a two-value system, which means that if a variable is not in one group, then it must automatically be in the other. Because of this feature, the second key to the game comes from taking the contrapositives of the third and fourth conditional rules and then translating them to account for the two-value system:

Third Rule:	$H_1 \longrightarrow L_1$
Direct Contrapositive:	$\cancel{L}_1 \longrightarrow \cancel{H}_1$
Translated Contrapositive:	$L_2 \longrightarrow H_2$

Thus, when H is in group 1, then L is in group 1. Via the translated contrapositive, when L is in group 2 then H is in group 2. Does this mean that H and L are always a block? No, because L could be in group 1 and H could be in group 2.

Fourth Rule:	$N_2 \longrightarrow G_1$
Direct Contrapositive:	$\cancel{G}_1 \longrightarrow \cancel{N}_2$
Translated Contrapositive:	$G_2 \longrightarrow N_1$

Thus, when N is in group 2, then G is in group 1 (and, incidentally, from the second rule, M is in group 2). Via the translated contrapositive, when G is in group 2 then N is in group 1 (and, incidentally, from the second rule, M is in group 1). Does this mean that N and G are always in separate groups? No, because G could be in group 1 and N could be in group 1.

The third rule allows for another inference. Because of the limited number of spaces per group, we can further deduce that if H is in group 1 (that is, the third rule is activated and thus L is also in group 1), then the FJ block created by the first rule must be in group 2 (remember, G or M is also in group 1, so there is only one remaining space when H and L are in group 1). Also, if L is in group 2, then H is in group 2, and the FJ block must be in group 1. These two inferences can be diagrammed as:

$$H_1 \longrightarrow \boxed{\begin{matrix} F \\ J \end{matrix}}_2$$

$$L_2 \longrightarrow \boxed{\begin{matrix} F \\ J \end{matrix}}_1$$

With the above information, we are ready to attack the questions.

Question #1: Global, Could Be True, List. The correct answer choice is (D)

Answer choice (A) is incorrect because H is in group 1 but L is not, a violation of the third rule.

Answer choice (B) is incorrect because F and J are not in the same group.

Answer choice (C) is incorrect because G and M are in group 2 together, a violation of the second rule.

Answer choice (D) is the correct answer.

Answer choice (E) is incorrect because G and M are in group 1 together, a violation of the second rule.

Question #2: Local, Must Be True. The correct answer choice is (B)

If K and N are in a group together, they create a block. F and J are also a block, and the two blocks cannot be in the same group due to lack of space. Thus, the two blocks are in separate groups, and we can reserve two more spaces in each group, even though we cannot determine exactly which variables are in each group:

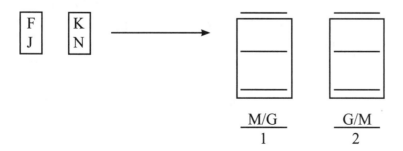

With three spaces in each group reserved, we can Hurdle the Uncertainty and determine the placement of the remaining two variables, H and L. Because from the third rule if H is in group 1 then L must be in group 1, and there is insufficient room in group 1 for two more variables, we can infer that H cannot be in group 1 and therefore must be in group 2. Accordingly, answer choice (B) is correct.

To complete the diagram, as there is no more space in group 2, L must be in group 1.

Question #3: Local, Must Be True. The correct answer choice is (C)

The question stem forms a FJH super-block. This block is obviously quite space-consuming, and the space restriction should be your starting point. If the FJH block is in group 1, then L must also be in group 1 from the third rule, which is impossible due to space restrictions (again, note how important it is to show the G/M dual option on the diagram). Thus, the FJH block must be in group 2, and the other three variables—K, L, and N—must be in group 1. Consequently, answer choice (C) is correct.

Question #4: Local, Could Be True. The correct answer choice is (E)

If L and M are in group 2, then G must be in group 1 (because of M), and H must be in group 2 (because of the contrapositive of the third rule). With H, L, and M in group 2, there is not enough room for the FJ block, and thus we can infer that the FJ block is in group 1. Only N and K remain, and each variable could be in group 1 or 2.

K/N	N/K
J	H
F	L
G	M
1	2

N is not among the choices, but K is, and hence answer choice (E) is correct:

Question #5: Global, Could Be True, Except. The correct answer choice is (B)

Answer choice (B) is correct because F and H in group 1 automatically bring along J (from the first rule) and L (from the third rule). However, that means FJHL completely occupy group 1, forcing G and M into group 2 together, a violation of the second rule.

Note that the hypothetical produced in question #1 eliminates answer choices (D) and (E), and the hypothetical produced in question #4 eliminates answer choice (A). The hypothetical produced in question #2 also helps in eliminating answer choice (C).

Question #6: Local, Could Be True, Except. The correct answer choice is (D)

If L is in group 2, then from the contrapositive of the third rule H must be in group 2. Due to space restrictions, F and J must be in group 1, leaving K and N to form another dual-option:

K/N	N/K
J	H
F	L
M/G	G/M
1	2

The problem is still tricky because the dual-options are not completely free to rotate. The fourth rule affects both G and N, and assigning K and M—the remainder in each dual-option—to group 1 forces G and M into group 2 together, a violation of the fourth rule. Hence, answer choice (D) is correct.

Note that answer choice (B) is possible because G and N can be in group 1 together; the fourth rule just prohibits them from being in group 2 together, as discussed in the setup.

This is a Basic Linear: Balanced game.

The game features five people scheduled as contestants on a television show, one contestant per day. Because the days of the week have an inherent order, they should be chosen as the base for the game:

H I K N V ^{5}

$$\overline{}\quad\overline{}\quad\overline{}\quad\overline{}\quad\overline{}$$
$$\text{M}\quad\text{Tu}\quad\text{W}\quad\text{Th}\quad\text{F}$$

The first rule provides us with an N Not Law under Monday:

H I K N V ^{5}

$$\overline{}\quad\overline{}\quad\overline{}\quad\overline{}\quad\overline{}$$
$$\text{M}\quad\text{Tu}\quad\text{W}\quad\text{Th}\quad\text{F}$$
$$\cancel{\text{N}}$$

The second and third rules are both conditional in nature, and specify what occurs when a particular person is scheduled for a specific day:

Second rule: $H_M \longrightarrow N_F$

Third rule: $N_T \longrightarrow I_M$

Note that these two rules both involve N and both involve Monday, which in this case means the rules work together to some extent. For example, if H is scheduled for Monday, then I cannot be scheduled for Monday (none of the other contestants could be scheduled for Monday either, of course). If I cannot be scheduled for Monday, then via the contrapositive N cannot be scheduled for Tuesday. Thus, if H is scheduled for Monday, then N is not scheduled for Tuesday (which in part should be obvious because the second rule states that if H is scheduled for Monday then N is scheduled for Friday, but its still good to explicitly recognize what occurs).

The fourth rule creates a VK block:

$$\boxed{\text{V K}}$$

This block creates Not Laws for K under Monday, and for V under Friday:

HIKNV ^{5}

M	Tu	W	Th	F
N̶				V̶
K̶				

The two Not Laws under Monday allow for the deduction that only H, I, or V can be scheduled for Monday. This can be shown on the diagram with a triple-option, and this inference plays an important role in the game.

Combining all of the information leads to the following final setup:

HIKNV ^{5}

$H_M \longrightarrow N_F$

$N_T \longrightarrow I_M$

$\boxed{VK}$

H/I/V				
M	Tu	W	Th	F
N̶				V̶
K̶				

This final setup is not overly complicated, and so as you move to the questions you should feel good about the prospects for finishing this game quickly, especially since there are only five questions.

Question #7: Global, Could Be True, Except. The correct answer choice is (E)

As discussed during the examination of the fourth rule, the block prohibits V from being scheduled on Friday. Consequently, answer choice (E) is correct.

Question #8: Local, Could Be True, List. The correct answer choice is (E)

The question stem creates an HI block and then requests a list of all of the days that H could be scheduled. The block creates two Not Laws: H cannot be scheduled for Friday, and I cannot be scheduled for Monday. Of course, from the third rule, I is not scheduled for Monday. Thus, either H or V must be scheduled for Monday. H can go on Monday—Monday appears in every answer choice—but V is part of the VK block, and so if H is not on Monday, V must be on Monday and K must be on Tuesday. This effectively prohibits H from ever being scheduled for Tuesday (if H is scheduled for Tuesday, V must be scheduled for Monday, but then there is no room for K). With Tuesday out of contention, answer choices (A) and (D), each of which list Tuesday, can be eliminated.

The question is now whether H can be scheduled for Wednesday, Thursday, or both. The following hypothetical proves that H can be scheduled for Wednesday:

V	K	H	I	N
M	Tu	W	Th	F

The following hypothetical proves that H can be scheduled for Thursday:

$$\frac{V}{M} \quad \frac{K}{Tu} \quad \frac{N}{W} \quad \frac{H}{Th} \quad \frac{I}{F}$$

Consequently, H can be scheduled for Monday, Wednesday, and Thursday, and answer choice (E) is correct.

Question #9: Local, Could Be True. The correct answer choice is (C)

If K is scheduled for Wednesday, then from the fourth rule V must be scheduled for Tuesday. Consequently, only H and I are available to be scheduled for Monday.

If H is scheduled for Monday, then N must be scheduled for Friday, forcing I to be scheduled on Thursday:

$$\frac{H}{M} \quad \frac{V}{Tu} \quad \frac{K}{W} \quad \frac{I}{Th} \quad \frac{N}{F}$$

If I is scheduled for Monday, then H and N rotate between Thursday and Friday

$$\frac{I}{M} \quad \frac{V}{Tu} \quad \frac{K}{W} \quad \frac{H/N}{Th} \quad \frac{N/H}{F}$$

The above two diagrams encompass all of the possibilities for this question, and in combination prove that answer choice (C) is correct.

Question #10: Local, Must Be True. The correct answer choice is (C)

If K is scheduled for Friday, then from the fourth rule V must be scheduled for Thursday. Consequently, only H and I are available to be scheduled for Monday. However, H cannot be scheduled for Monday because from the second rule N would have to be scheduled for Friday, and that is impossible in this question. Thus, only I can be scheduled for Monday:

$$\frac{I}{M} \quad \frac{H/N}{Tu} \quad \frac{N/H}{W} \quad \frac{V}{Th} \quad \frac{K}{F}$$

Accordingly, answer choice (C) is correct.

Question #11: Local, Must Be True. The correct answer choice is (C)

If I is scheduled for Wednesday, the VK block must be scheduled for either Monday-Tuesday or Thursday-Friday. Let's examine each possibility.

If VK is scheduled for Monday-Tuesday, then H and N are unrestricted, and they rotate between Thursday and Friday, creating the following diagram:

$$\frac{V}{M} \quad \frac{K}{Tu} \quad \frac{I}{W} \quad \frac{H/N}{Th} \quad \frac{N/H}{F}$$

If VK is scheduled for Thursday-Friday, then H must be scheduled for Monday (I and V are scheduled elsewhere), but from the second rule, when H is scheduled on Monday then N is scheduled for Friday, which is impossible here as K is already scheduled for Friday. Thus, V and K cannot be scheduled for Thursday-Friday.

As the only two possibilities in this question are the ones where the VK block is scheduled for Monday-Tuesday, K must always be scheduled for an earlier day than H, and answer choice (C) is correct.

Answer choice (A) could be true but does not have to be true, and answer choices (B), (D), and (E) each cannot be true.

This is a Grouping/Linear Combination game.

This Grouping/Linear combination game features eight lectures filling six spaces, and thus whenever two lectures are eliminated from the scheduling, the remaining six lectures must be scheduled. Questions #16 and #17 are excellent examples of this principle in action. The morning and afternoon variable sets also add an advanced linear element to the game, and consequently the game is difficult. The setup to the game is as follows:

F H L N O P S W[8]

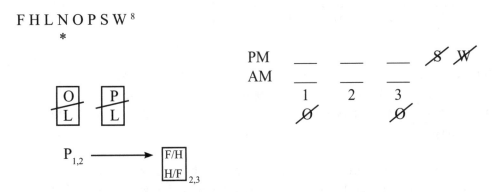

Since the three days contain an inherent sense of order, they are chosen as the base and the morning and afternoon variable sets are stacked on top. "Morning" and "afternoon" have been abbreviated as AM and PM because they are too time-consuming to write out. It makes no difference whether your diagram has the AM set as the top row or as the bottom row.

Because of the vertical component, the OL and PL rules are written in block form. For convenience L has been placed on the bottom in both rules, but it is essential to understand that O and L (and P and L) can never be scheduled for the same day, regardless of which one is in the AM or PM. If this confuses you, each rule can be written out both ways for clarity:

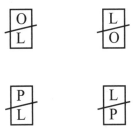

Note also that the first rule has not been written out. Instead of showing that O could go on day 2 (O should not be placed on day 2 on the diagram because we cannot be sure O is one of the six scheduled lectures), it is preferable to show that O cannot go on day 1 and day 3. Superior representations always reflect the absolutes—what must occur and what cannot occur. In examining the diagram it is also important to note that the O Not Laws on day 1 and day 3 apply to both the AM and PM. They can be placed on each row for each day if you feel that is necessary.

The last rule is difficult to diagram concisely. There are two scenarios under the rule: when P is scheduled for day 1, then F and H are scheduled for day 2, and when P is scheduled for day 2 then F and H are scheduled for day 3. In the form we have chosen, we have combined the two possibilities and represented them through the "1, 2" and "2, 3" subscripts. If you find this confusing, write out each scenario separately. This rule is especially important because it needs a lot of space. Also, do not forget to take the contrapositive of the rule: if any variable other than F or H is scheduled for day 2, then P cannot be scheduled for day 1, and if any variable other than F or H is scheduled for day 3, then P cannot be scheduled for day 2. This important inference is tested.

Because each appears in two rules, O and P are the key variables in the game and you must always be aware of them. In contrast to O and P, N is a random and relatively weak variable. Remember that in games with a large number of variables—say 9 or 10—randoms are relatively weak, and that in games with few variables—5 or 6—randoms are stronger and need to be given more consideration.

Finally, it is notable that this game does not contain any extremely deep inferences. There are some obvious inferences—for example, if L is scheduled for day 2, then O cannot be scheduled at all—but nothing truly challenging. This may in part explain why five of the six questions are local: to create challenging situations the test makers had to supply local conditions to create limitation. Some games with deep inferences or limited possibilities have a large number of global questions to test your knowledge of the inferences. The first game from the June 1999 LSAT is a good example (only several possibilities exist and consequently all five questions are global).

Question #12: Global, Could Be True, List. The correct answer choice is (B)

Remember to apply the simplest and most visually powerful rules first. In this case that happens to be the order in which the rules are presented. The first rule eliminates answer choice (C). The second rule eliminates answer choice (D). The third rule eliminates answer choice (A). And the fourth rule eliminates answer choice (E). Answer choice (B) is thus correct.

Question #13: Local, Could Be True. The correct answer choice is (A)

Irrespective of the Local conditions, answer choices (B), (D), and (E) can be eliminated by the PM and day 1 Not Laws. With the answers narrowed to (A) and (C), we can consider the Local condition in the question stem. The stem produces the following mini-diagram next to the question:

$$
\begin{array}{cccc}
\text{PM} & \underline{} & \underline{\text{L}} & \underline{\text{F}} \\
\text{AM} & \underline{} & \underline{} & \underline{} \\
 & 1 & 2 & 3
\end{array}
$$

Note that in doing the question on the test, we would not take the time to write out AM, PM, 1, 2, and 3.

This setup automatically rules out P's being scheduled on day 1, since if P is scheduled for day 1, then both F and H have to be scheduled for day 2. Since F is already scheduled for day 3, answer choice (C) can be eliminated. Answer choice (A) is therefore correct.

Question #14: Local, Could Be True. The correct answer choice is (E)

Irrespective of the Local conditions, answer choice (C) can be eliminated by applying the Not Laws. The conditions produce the following diagram:

$$\overline{\underset{\cancel{O}}{}} \quad \overline{\underset{\cancel{O}}{L}} \quad \overline{\underset{\cancel{O}}{H}}$$

Once L is scheduled for day 2, O cannot be scheduled for day 2, and, consequently O cannot be scheduled for any of the days. The other lecture affected by the local conditions is P. As in question #2, P cannot be scheduled on day 1, since if P is scheduled for day 1 then both F and H have to be scheduled for day 2. Since H is already scheduled for day 3, answer choice (D) can be eliminated.

There are now three answer choices remaining: F, N, and S. Forced to guess with just the information at hand, you might suspect that S could be scheduled for the morning of day 1 because S is a variable already confined to the morning spaces. Although answer choice (E) is correct, it is important to understand why both answer choices (A) and (B) are incorrect. Consider that for the three afternoon spaces there are initially eight lectures: F, H, L, N, O, P, S, and W. From the second rule both S and W cannot lecture in the afternoon, so the pool is now down to six: F, H, L, N, O, and P. The conditions in the question place L and H in the morning and eliminate O from scheduling, and so the candidate pool is now three: F, N, and P. Thus, F, N, and P must be the three afternoon lectures in this question. If any of the three is placed in a morning space then there would not be enough lectures for the afternoon. **This illustrates a critical grouping concept: it is as important to evaluate the variables left for consideration as it is to evaluate the variables already placed.**

Question #15: Local, Cannot Be True. The correct answer choice is (D)

Since L is scheduled for day 3, P cannot be scheduled for day 2 (because of the contrapositive of the last rule) or day 3 (because of the third rule). Since O is scheduled for day 2, again because of the second rule, P cannot be scheduled for day 1. It follows that answer choice (D) is correct.

Question #16: Local, Must Be True. The correct answer choice is (B)

Irrespective of the Local conditions, answer choice (C) can be eliminated by applying the Not Laws.

Since neither F nor N is scheduled, it follows that H, L, O, P, S, and W must be scheduled. And since F is not scheduled, P cannot be scheduled for day 1 or day 2 (the contrapositive of the final rule). Consequently P must be scheduled for day 3 and thus answer choice (D) is incorrect. Since O is scheduled for day 2 and P is scheduled for day 3, the third rule can be applied, and it follows that since L cannot be scheduled with O or P, then L must be scheduled for day 1. Thus, answer choice (B) is correct.

Question #17: Local, Could Be True. The correct answer choice is (E)

Since F, H, and L are scheduled for the three morning slots, the pool of afternoon lectures is S, W, N, O, and P. However, because S and W cannot be scheduled in the afternoon, only N, O, and P can be scheduled for the afternoon slots. Accordingly, O must be scheduled for day 2, P must be scheduled for day 3 (apply the last rule!), and thus N is scheduled for day 1. Since O and P are scheduled for days 2 and 3 respectively, L must be scheduled for day 1. F and H represent a dual-option on the mornings of days 2 and 3:

$$
\begin{array}{cccc}
\text{PM} & \underline{\text{N}} & \underline{\text{O}} & \underline{\text{P}} \\
\text{AM} & \underline{\text{L}} & \underline{\text{H/F}} & \underline{\text{F/H}} \\
 & 1 & 2 & 3
\end{array}
$$

Answer choice (E) is therefore correct.

This is a Pattern game.

This game from December 1994 was repeated as the third game of the February 1997 LSAT. The repeat version featured a train making five trips around a circle containing stops P, Q, R, S, and T. On each trip the train stopped at exactly three of the five stops. No stop could be repeated three trips in a row, and each stop had to be visited at least once in any two-trip period.

Let's first examine the participation of the clans and the overall cycle. Each cycle ends when each of the five clans has participated exactly three times each, so there are a total of fifteen participations during the life of the cycle. Because there are only three participations each year, a cycle must last for exactly five years (this is the correct answer to question #20). This can be diagrammed as:

N O P S T [5]

$$
\begin{array}{ccccc}
\underline{\quad} & \underline{\quad} & \underline{\quad} & \underline{\quad} & \underline{\quad} \\
\underline{\quad} & \underline{\quad} & \underline{\quad} & \underline{\quad} & \underline{\quad} \\
\underline{\quad} & \underline{\quad} & \underline{\quad} & \underline{\quad} & \underline{\quad} \\
1 & 2 & 3 & 4 & 5
\end{array}
$$

Determining the length of the cycle effectively makes the third rule "dead" (meaning it has been appropriately captured and no longer needs to be considered actively in each question). The fourth rule is captured by understanding that each clan must be used three times within each cycle:

N N N [3]   O O O [3]   P P P [3]   S S S [3]   T T T [3]

Those fifteen clan participations make up each cycle, and once identified are easy to understand and represent.

Now that the basic setup is established, we move to the most difficult part of the game. With the third and fourth rules under control, only the first and second rules require constant monitoring in this game. But, as in most Pattern games, these two rules do not address any specific variables, but instead address the global behavior of all variables. As is often the case in Pattern games, there is a broad-based pattern that controls the variables in a predictable way. Let's look at the two rules more closely and see if we can deduce the pattern.

The first rule establishes that each clan participates *at least once* in *any* two consecutive years (italics added for emphasis). The "any two consecutive years" is the most critical part. That means each clan has to participate at least once in years 1-2, at least once in years 2-3, at least once in years 3-4, and at least once in years 4-5. That is an extremely restrictive rule and it dramatically affects how the clans are used. For example, let's assume that clans N, O, and P participate in the first year:

NOPST[5]

	P				
	O				
	N				
	1	2	3	4	5

With the first year filled, for Q and R to comply with the first rule they *must* participate in the second year:

NOPST[5]

	P				
	O	R			
	N	Q			
	1	2	3	4	5

The third clan in the second year would then be one of N, O, or P. Let's say that N was the clan participating in the second year. If that's the case, then from the action of the second rule, N could not participate in the third year:

NOPST[5]

	P	N			
	O	R			
	N	Q			
	1	2	3	4	5
			N̶		

Let's take a moment to review how N stands in respect to the first rule :

N participates twice in years 1-2.

N participates once in years 2-3.

Currently, N does not participate in years 3-4. Thus, because N cannot participate in the third year, N *must* participate in the fourth year:

NOPST[5]

	P	N			
	O	R			
	N	Q		N	
	1	2	3	4	5
			N̶		

With N participating in the fourth year, N participates once in years 3-4 and years 4-5.

Thus, N participates a total of three times, and conforms to both the first and second rules.

Note that N now participates in years 1-2-4. O and P, the other two clans that participated in the first year, would have to participate in the third year (establishing both with a 1-3 start to the cycle). This reveals an interesting fact: for the three clans who participate in the first year, one of the three participates in the second year (1-2) and the other two participate in the third year (1-3). This is the start of the pattern, and as you might expect, if the cycle starts with a pattern, it ends with one too.

We could continue to show how the variables work to construct the entire pattern, but we recommend that you play with some of the options and watch how the patterns form. What you will ultimately find is that the rules produce a pattern where each cycle contains five distinct participation sequences. Each clan must fit one of the five sequences, and each cycle must contain all five of the sequences. The five sequences are:

$$1 - 3 - 5$$
$$1 - 2 - 4$$
$$1 - 3 - 4$$
$$2 - 4 - 5$$
$$2 - 3 - 5$$

In our example, N fit the 1-2-4 sequence, and one of O and P would fit the 1-3-4 sequence and the other would fit the 1-3-5 sequence.

But, what if you can't determine the pattern during the setup? Admittedly, the patterns above are difficult to deduce during the game. Pattern game setups typically contain minimal information, and if you do not see the patterns for this game (or any Pattern game) during the setup, move to the following two types of questions first:

1. List questions

    List questions allow you to work with pre-made solutions and to simply use the rules to eliminate answer choices. Deriving the correct answer gives you a hypothetical that adds to your overall game knowledge. In this game questions #18 and #24 are List questions.

2. Questions with the greatest amount of local information

    These questions give you the best chance to work directly with the variables while still solving questions, and hopefully working with the questions will give you a better sense of what is occurring in the game on a global level. In this game, then, to apply that approach you would begin with questions #22, #23, or #24 and use the hypotheticals produced by those questions to gain an understanding of how the rules interact.

Question #18: Local, Could Be True, List. The correct answer choice is (E)

If N, O, and P participate in the first year, then from the first rule we know that S and T *must* participate in the second year. Only answer choice (E) contains both S and T, and answer choice (E) is correct.

Question #19: Global, Could Be True. The correct answer choice is (C)

Answer choices (A) and (B) can quickly be eliminated because they violate the second rule. Answer choices (C), (D), and (E) are similar in nature, but note that (D) and (E) place two variables in three years, whereas (C) places two variables in only two years. Theoretically then, answer choice (C) is less restrictive and one would expect that (C) is far more likely to be correct than (D) or (E). This is especially so if you realize that on an abstract level each clan is more or less the same, as is each year.

Answer choice (C) is ultimately correct, and our patterns reveal that two of the clans that participate in the first year will also participate in the third year. Oddly, if you examine the question stem to question #24, you will note that this question stem provides sufficient information to correctly choose (C) in question #19.

Question #20: Global, Must Be True. The correct answer choice is (A)

In the setup to the game we determined that the length of the cycle was 5 years, and so answer choice (A) is correct.

Question #21: Global, Must Be True. The correct answer choice is (A)

This is a question where understanding the pattern provides a significant benefit. As noted in our example in the setup explanation, exactly two of the clans participating in the first year will participate in the third year, and so answer choice (A) is correct. If you examine the patterns for the game, you can easily dismiss the remaining answer choices.

Question #22: Local, Must Be True. The correct answer choice is (D)

Answer choice (A) can immediately be eliminated because it would violate the second rule. After this point, however, without the patterns the question is very difficult. If you do not have the patterns, the best approach is to use hypotheticals to solve the problem.

If N, O, and S participate in the first year, then P and T must participate in the second year:

N O P S T[5]

$$\begin{array}{ccccc} S & & & & \\ \hline O & T & & & \\ \hline N & P & & & \\ \hline 1 & 2 & 3 & 4 & 5 \end{array}$$

As shown in the patterns, the two clans who participate in the second year but do not participate in the first year follow these two patterns:

$$2 - 4 - 5$$

$$2 - 3 - 5$$

Thus, P and T, who both participate in the second year but not the first, must both participate in the fifth year, and answer choice (D) is correct.

Question #23: Local, Could Be True, Except. The correct answer choice is (C)

The question stem establishes the following information:

N O P S T[5]

T				
O			P	
N			O	
1	2	3	4	5

If N, O, and T participate in the first year, then S and P must participate in the second year. Because P participates in the second year and the fourth year, from the second rule we can infer that P does not participate in the third year:

T				
O	S		P	
N	P		O	
1	2	3	4	5
		P̶		

Thus, answer choice (C) is correct.

Question #24: Local, Could Be True, List. The correct answer choice is (A)

The question stem establishes the following information:

N O P S T⁵

```
 S  ___  S  ___ ___
 O  ___  O  ___ ___
 N  ___  T  ___ ___
 1   2   3   4   5
```

Because O and S participate in both the first and third years, from the second rule they cannot participate in the second year. With O and S removed from consideration, N, P, and T must be the three clans that participate in the second year:

```
 S   T   S  ___ ___
 O   P   O  ___ ___
 N   N   T  ___ ___
 1   2   3   4   5
     S̸
     Ø
```

With T participating in both the second and third years, according to the second rule T cannot participate in the fourth year, and thus to meet the conditions of the first rule T must participate in the fifth year:

```
 S   T   S  ___ ___
 O   P   O  ___  T
 N   N   T  ___  T
 1   2   3   4   5
             T̸
```

Only answer choice (E) contains T among its list of clans participating in the fifth year, and thus answer choice (E) must be correct.

Note that we can also infer that P participates in the fourth and fifth years, but that alone does not prove any individual answer choice correct, although it does eliminate answer choice (B).

PREPTEST

14

FEBRUARY 1995 LOGIC GAMES SETUPS

This is a Grouping: Defined-Moving, Balanced, Numerical Distribution game.

In this game, five employees each hold one of three positions. The twist comes in that two of the employee levels—manager and technician—are supervised. Let's examine the numerical spread of the positions first.

The first rule establishes that there is exactly one president. The next two rules establishes that there is at least one manager and at least one technician. Thus, all three positions must be filled by the five employees, which establishes a minimum of a 1-1-1 spread for the distribution:

	P	M	T		
Minimum:	1	1	1	=	3

Thus, two employees remain to be distributed. Because there is only one president, those two employees must be distributed between the managers and technicians. This leaves three possibilities:

	P	M	T		
Remaining 2 are M:	1	3	1	=	5
1 is M and 1 is T:	1	2	2	=	5
Remaining 2 are T:	1	1	3	=	5

However, take a closer look at the statement in the scenario that "employees are supervised by exactly one employee." For this to be true, the 1-3-1 distribution cannot occur because the three managers would all have to supervise the same technician. Thus, there can be only two distributions in this game:

P	M	T		
1	2	2	=	5
1	1	3	=	5

From a supervisory standpoint, these are the rules for each employee:

President: Is not supervised. Must supervise one or two managers; can supervise technicians as well in the 1-1-3 distribution.

Manager(s):   Is/are supervised by the president. Must supervise one or more technicians.

Technicians: Are supervised by president or manager. Do not supervise anyone.

Let's now combine the distributions with the supervision possibilities, with the last two rules as well:

Employees: F G H K L [5]   Possible Fixed Numerical Distributions:
            * * *

Positions: P M T [3]

P	M	T
1	2	2
1	1	3

1-2-2 Distribution: 1-1-3 Distribution:

P ___|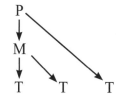

M

∅ T   F

In the distributions above, the arrows indicate supervision assignments.

H, K, and L are all randoms, so your focus must be on F and G as you assess the game. Because F does not supervise any employee, F must always be a technician. Consequently, G is the only employee who has any restrictions, and these restrictions can be applied to the two distributions:

In the 1-2-2 fixed distribution, G cannot be a manager because each manager supervises only one employee, and the last rule indicates that G must supervise exactly two employees. Hence, in the 1-2-2 fixed distribution G must be the president.

In the 1-1-3 fixed distribution, G could be either the president or a manager. Because of the last rule, however, the supervision assignments are fixed: if G is the president, the G must supervise the manager and one technician, and if G is the manager, then G must supervise two technicians. Therefore, regardless of G's assignment, in the 1-1-3 fixed distribution the president always supervises exactly two employees and the manager always supervises two employees.

With the information above, we are ready to attack the questions.

14

Question #1: Global, Could Be True, List. The correct answer choice is (B)

Answer choice (A) is incorrect because the three managers would all supervise the same employee
   (F), a violation of the game scenario stipulations.

Answer choice (C) is incorrect because F must be a technician.

Answer choice (D) is incorrect because there is only one president per the first rule.

Answer choice (E) is incorrect because the four managers would have no employees to supervise.

Note that answer choices (A), (D), and (E) also violate the numerical distributions of the game.

Accordingly, answer choice (B) is correct.

Question #2: Global, Must Be True. The correct answer choice is (A)

As established during our discussion of the numbers in this game, there are at most three technicians.
Thus, answer choice (A) is correct.

Question #3: Global, Could Be True. The correct answer choice is (E)

F can never be a manager because F does not supervise any employees. Thus, answer choices (A)
and (B) can be eliminated.

When there are two managers, G must always be the president, and thus answer choices (C) and (D)
can be eliminated.

Thus, answer choice (E) is correct.

Question #4: Global, Could Be True. The correct answer choice is (B)

As determined in the discussion of the numerical distributions, there can be exactly two managers.
Thus, answer choice (B) is correct.

Question #5: Local, Must Be True. The correct answer choice is (D)

Because F is a technician, only the 1-1-3 distribution allows F to be supervised by the president.
Hence, answer choice (D) is correct.

Question #6: Local, Must Be True. The correct answer choice is (C)

If K supervises two employees, and G supervises two employees, the employees must be in the 1-1-
3 distribution, with G and K as the president and manager, not necessarily in that order. The other
three employees are each technicians. Note also that answer choices (D) and (E) both reflect the 1-2-2
distribution.

This is an Advanced Linear: Balanced, Identify the Templates game.

In the modern era, this ranks as one of the easiest LSAT games. In the scenario, the game threatens to be challenging because seven objects subdivided into three groups could be difficult to track, but the last sentence of the game scenario—which establishes that each sub-group was washed together—makes the game considerably easier. Effectively, that sentence creates three blocks, and that limits the number of possibilities in the game.

The first and fourth rule are cleanup rules that limit the number of possible solutions to the game.

The second rule creates two mutually exclusive sequences, which further limit the game:

$$\boxed{C\ C} \quad > \quad \boxed{G\ G} \quad > \quad \boxed{U\ U\ U}$$

or

$$\boxed{U\ U\ U} \quad > \quad \boxed{G\ G} \quad > \quad \boxed{C\ C}$$

The third rule is really two rules in one, and can be diagrammed as:

$$K > S$$

$$\boxed{MP}$$

MP is a block above because there are only two pieces of china, and if M is washed before P, they form an MP block. K and S are not a block because there are three utensils.

The sequences are so powerful that you should immediately realize that the best approach to this game is to Identify the Templates. There are two templates, which appear as follows when the third rule is added in:

C: M P ^{2}

G: W J ^{2}

U: F K S ^{3}

$\boxed{MP}$

K > S

Template 1:	C	C	G	G	U	U	U
	M	P	W/J	J/W	(K >	S,	F)
	1	2	3	4	5	6	7
					~~S~~		~~K~~

Template 2:	U	U	U	G	G	C	C
	(K >	S,	F)	W/J	J/W	M	P
	1	2	3	4	5	6	7
	~~S~~		~~K~~				

The two scenarios above provide sufficient information to easily answer most of the questions.

Question #7: Global, Cannot Be True. The correct answer choice is (E)

The two templates show that Ron either washes a glassware item or a utensil third, and so answer choice (E) cannot be true, and is correct.

Question #8: Global, Could Be True. The correct answer choice is (A)

Under Template 2, the utensils are washed first, second, and third. Thus, K could be washed second under the following hypothetical: F-K-S-J-W-M-P. Accordingly, answer choice (A) is correct.

Question #9: Global, Could Be True, List. The correct answer choice is (B)

According to the third rule, K > S, and so answer choice (B) cannot be true and is correct. In that answer, S would be first, K second, and F third, causing the violation.

Question #10: Global, Cannot Be True. The correct answer choice is (C)

Under the first template, because K is a utensil and K > S, when the utensils are washed 5-6-7 then K cannot be washed seventh. However, this is not one of the answer choices. Under the second template, when the utensils are washed 1-2-3, then K cannot be washed third. Hence, answer choice (C) is correct.

Question #11: Local, Could Be True. The correct answer choice is (E)

The condition in the question stem creates the following sequence:

$$K > \boxed{SF}$$

However, because K, S, and F are all utensils, they must be washed consecutively, and therefore they must form a block:

$$\boxed{K\ S\ F}$$

Accordingly, in Template 2 neither answer choice (A) nor answer choice (B) can be true. Answer choices (C) and (D) can be eliminated because they conform to neither template. Thus, answer choice (E) is proven correct by process of elimination, and it could occur under Template 2.

Question #12: Local, Cannot Be True, FTT. The correct answer choice is (A)

The condition in the question stem forces the objects into Template 1, with K washed fifth:

M	P	W/J	J/W	K	F/S	S/F
1	2	3	4	5	6	7

Accordingly, answer choice (A) cannot be true and is correct. By the way, Template 2 would not be applicable because K would have to be third, which is impossible due to the third rule.

This is a Grouping: Partially Defined, Numerical Distribution game.

The game scenario indicates that there are two cages and one exhibition for ten birds. At least two birds and at most four birds are on exhibition, and there are at most four birds in each of two cages:

Cage	Cage	Exhibition
Maximum 4	Maximum 4	1 or 2 pairs (2 or 4 birds)

This leads to some easy distributions, such as a 4-4-2 (cage-cage-exhibit) or 4-2-4 and 2-4-4, etc. However, the distributions do not play a major role in this game. Instead, it is the grouping rules and the restrictions between all of the birds that answers the questions.

These are the ten birds:

3 Goldfinches	2 Lovebirds	5 Parakeets
m: H	m: M	m: Q, R, S
f: J, K	f: N	f: T, W

The second rule states that birds that are both of the same sex and of the same kind cannot be caged together. Therefore, only one male parakeet can be assigned to each cage. Since there are three male parakeets and only two cages, it follows that at least one male parakeet must always be exhibited, along with a corresponding female parakeet. Thus, one of Q, R, or S and one of T or W is *always* on exhibit.

So, at least one pair of parakeets must always be exhibited. However, one of the initial rules states that at most two pairs of birds can be exhibited at a time. Therefore, a pair of goldfinches and a pair of lovebirds can *never* be exhibited together. This inference is tested directly in question #17.

The second rule states that two birds of the same sex and kind cannot be caged together. Thus, J and K (two female goldfinches) cannot be caged together. Same for Q and R (two male parakeets), Q and S (two male parakeets), R and S (two male parakeets), and T and W (two female parakeets). These inferences can be diagrammed as:

Cage Inferences

1.	J ←——┼——→ K
2.	Q ←——┼——→ R
3.	Q ←——┼——→ S
4.	R ←——┼——→ S
5.	T ←——┼——→ W

While the cage inferences are all based on the second rule, there is more variation in the exhibit inferences.

First, from the third rule, S cannot be exhibited with J or W:

$$S \longleftrightarrow\!\!\!| \quad J, W$$

Of course, if S cannot be exhibited with W, then we can infer that S must be exhibited with T, the only other female parakeet:

$$S \longrightarrow T$$

The next few inferences derive from the stipulation that pairs of one male and one female of the same type must be exhibited. Because S can only be exhibited with T, and not with W, neither Q nor R can be exhibited with S:

$$S \longleftrightarrow\!\!\!| \quad Q, R$$

Again, this occurs because Q or R would require W, and S cannot be exhibited with W.

Another inference in that same vein involves J and K, the two female goldfinches. J and K can never be exhibited together, because there is only one male goldfinch, and for both J and K to be exhibited, there would have to be two male goldfinches:

$$J \longleftrightarrow\!\!\!| \quad K$$

The final inference on the exhibition list reflects the inference discussed above that goldfinches and lovebirds cannot be exhibited together.

$$H, J, K \longleftrightarrow\!\!\!| \quad M, N$$

Combining all of the above rules and inferences leads to the following:

	Cage Inferences		Exhibit Rules/Inferences
1.	J ⟷⫴ K	1.	S ⟷⫴ J, W
2.	Q ⟷⫴ R	2.	S ⟶ T
3.	Q ⟷⫴ S	3.	S ⟷⫴ Q, R
4.	R ⟷⫴ S	4.	J ⟷⫴ K
5.	T ⟷⫴ W	5.	H, J, K ⟷⫴ M, N

With this information in hand, we are ready to attack the questions.

Question #13: Global, Could Be True, List. The correct answer choice is (D)

Answer choice (A) is incorrect because J and K—two birds of the same sex—are caged together.

Answer choice (B) is incorrect because J and S are exhibited together.

Answer choice (C) is incorrect because Q and S—two birds of the same sex—are caged together.

Answer choice (D) is the correct answer choice.

Answer choice (E) is incorrect because the first cage contains 5 birds, a violation of the first rule.

Question #14: Global, Could Be True, List. The correct answer choice is (D)

Since a pair of parakeets must be exhibited, and answer choices (A) and (C) do not contain a pair of parakeets, both answer choices can be eliminated. Answer choice (B) can be eliminated since J and S cannot be exhibited together. Answer choice (E) can be eliminated since W and S cannot be exhibited together. It follows that answer choice (D) is correct.

Question #15: Local, Must Be True. The correct answer choice is (D)

If Q and R are assigned to the cages, then S must be exhibited. If S is exhibited, then from the third rule J and W must be assigned to the cages. Accordingly, answer choice (D) is correct.

Question #16: Local, Must Be True. The correct answer choice is (D)

If T is assigned to a cage, then W must be exhibited since there must always be one male and one female parakeet on exhibit. If W is exhibited, then S cannot be exhibited. Since T and S are not exhibited, R must be exhibited. It follows that answer choice (D) is correct.

Question #17: Global, Cannot Be True. The correct answer choice is (B)

The correct answer choice, (B), reflects the major inference of the game as discussed in the setup.

Question #18: Local, Must Be True. The correct answer choice is (E)

If S is exhibited, T must be exhibited and W must be caged. As there are no more female parakeets available for exhibition, both Q and R must be assigned to the cages. Accordingly, answer choice (E) is correct.

PrepTest 14. February 1995 Game #4: *19. B 20. A 21. C 22. B 23. B 24. C*

This is an Advanced Linear: Unbalanced: Overloaded game

This game uses a repeating variable set—the sports—to fill in the seasonal slots for each of the two children. Within the game there are three important restrictions:

1. From the first rule, each child participates in four different sports, and thus once a child participates in a sport, he or she does not participate in that sport in another season.

2. From the second-to-last rule, the two children cannot participate in the same sport during the same season. Thus, once one of the children participates in a particular sport, the other child cannot participate in that same sport during that same season.

3. The winter season is particularly restricted because the children have only two sport options: H and V. And, H is offered only during the winter.

Let's use the above information to make some inferences. As stipulated in the last rule of the game, Otto's summer sport is V. Using the restrictions above, we can infer that Otto must participate in H during winter. And, because Nikki and Otto do not participate in the same sport in the same season, we can infer that Nikki must participate in V during winter. This inference is directly tested in question #19.

In addition, because H is offered only during the winter, Nikki will not participate in H during the year. This inference is tested in question #20.

Because Otto participates in V during summer, Otto will not participate in V in any other season, meaning that Otto's only options for fall are M and R, and Otto's only options for spring are K, M, and R.

Because Nikki participates in V during winter, Nikki will not participate in V in any other season, meaning that Nikki's only options for fall are M and R, Nikki's only options for spring are K, M, and R, and Nikki's only options for summer are K and M. These options combine to form the final diagram for the game:

Sports: H K M R V [5]

F: M, R, V

W: H, V

Sp: K, M, R, V

Su: K, M, V

	F	W	Sp	Su
Otto:	R/M	H	K/M/R	V
Nikki:	M/R	V	K/M/R	K/M

Otto and Nikki are linked by a vertical double arrow between them.

Question #19: Global, Must Be True. The correct answer choice is (B)

As discussed during the setup, Nikki's winter sport must be V, and thus answer choice (B) is correct.

Question #20: Global, Cannot Be True. The correct answer choice is (A)

As discussed during the setup, Nikki cannot participate in H, and thus answer choice (A) is correct.

Question #21: Local, Must Be True. The correct answer choice is (C)

If Nikki's fall sport is R, then Otto's fall sport cannot be R, and Otto's fall sport must be M:

Otto:	M	H	K/M/R	V

Nikki:	R	V	K/M/R	K/M
	F	W	Sp	Su

Consequently, answer choice (C) is correct:

Question #22: Global, Could Be True. The correct answer choice is (B)

The four incorrect answers can be eliminated by applying the dual-options and triple-options in the game:

Answer choice (A): According to the setup diagram, Nikki's fall sport is either M or R. Answer choice (A) attempts to assert that Nikki need not participate in either M or R in the fall, and therefore (A) can be eliminated.

Answer choice (C): According to the setup diagram, Nikki's summer sport is either K or M. Answer choice (C) attempts to assert that Nikki need not participate in either K or M in the summer, and therefore (C) can be eliminated.

Answer choice (D): According to the setup diagram, Otto's fall sport is either M or R. Answer choice (D) attempts to assert that Otto need not participate in either M or R in the fall, and therefore (D) can be eliminated.

Answer choice (E) can be eliminated because Otto has only three options for spring—K, M, or R—and answer choice (E) removes all three options.

Answer choice (B), which eliminates only two of Nikki's three spring options, is therefore correct.

Question #23: Local, Cannot Be True, FTT. The correct answer choice is (B)

If Otto does not participate in R during the year, then Otto must participate in M during the fall (and Nikki must participate in R during the fall). Because Otto does not participate in R and he participates in M during the fall, the only available sport for Otto in the spring is K. With Otto's sports fully determined, Nikki's sports can also be determined. We have already inferred that she must participate in R during the fall, and we determined during the setup that she must participate in V during the winter. For spring, she can no longer participate in R (because she participates in R during the fall), and because Otto participates in K during the spring she can no longer participate in K. Thus, in the spring Nikki must participate in M. Accordingly, in the summer her only option is K, and all of the season sports have been determined:

Otto:　　　__M__　__H__　__K__　__V__

Nikki:　　　__R__　__V__　__M__　__K__
　　　　　　　 F　　 W　　 Sp　　Su

In this Cannot Be True question, answer choice (B) is thus correct.

Question #24: Global, Could Be True. The correct answer choice is (C)

The hypothetical produced in question #23 proves that answer choice (C) is possible, and thus answer choice (C) is correct.

Answer choice (A) is incorrect because if Nikki's spring sport is M, then Otto's fall sport must be R, meaning his spring sport could not also be R.

Answer choice (B) is incorrect because if Nikki's spring sport is R, then her *fall* sport must be M, which is in conflict with the remainder of this answer choice which specifies that her summer sport is also M.

Answer choice (D) is incorrect because if Otto's fall sport is M, then Nikki's fall sport must be R, which conflicts with the remainder of this answer choice which specifies that her spring sport is also R.

Answer choice (E) is incorrect because in this answer choice both Nikki and Otto participate in M in seasons other than fall. Yet, from our setup we know that either Nikki or Otto must participate in M during the fall.

POWERSCORE®

15
PREPTEST

JUNE 1995 LOGIC GAMES SETUPS

15

This is a Basic Linear: Balanced game.

This is a fairly standard linear game, although the first two rules are unusual in that they jointly address all six variables. The first two rules create two not-blocks, and in each rule any two of the members can be consecutive, but all three members cannot be consecutive, regardless of their order. No Not Laws can be drawn directly from the two rules, but they clearly will play a significant role in the game.

The third rule can be diagrammed as H > S, and two Not Laws are created, one for S under the first speech, and one for H under the sixth speech.

The fourth and fifth rules both include J. The fourth rule creates J Not Laws under the first and sixth speeches, and the fifth rule creates TJ and JT not-blocks. Because J's speech must be second, third, fourth, or fifth from the fourth rule, when the fifth rule is considered, J's options are limited by where T speaks, leading to two inferences:

$$T_3 \longrightarrow J_5$$

and

$$T_4 \longrightarrow J_2$$

The information above combines to form the final diagram:

H J K R S T [6]

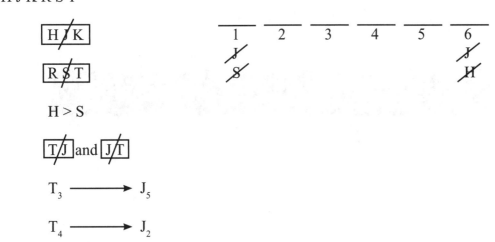

$$T_3 \longrightarrow J_5$$

$$T_4 \longrightarrow J_2$$

Question #1: Global, Could Be True, List. The correct answer choice is (D)

Answer choice (A) is incorrect because R, S, and T are consecutive.

Answer choice (B) is incorrect because J cannot deliver the last speech.

Answer choice (C) is incorrect because J and T cannot deliver consecutive speeches.

Answer choice (E) is incorrect because H's speech must be earlier than S's speech.

Thus, answer choice (D) is correct.

Question #2: Local, Must Be True. The correct answer choice is (B)

If T delivers the third speech, then from the last rule J cannot deliver the second or fourth speech. When this information is combined with the fourth rule prohibiting J from giving the first and last speech, we can infer that J must give the fifth speech. Consequently, answer choice (B) is correct.

Note that this question reflects one of the inferences drawn during the game setup.

Question #3: Local, Must Be True. The correct answer choice is (C)

When S is third and T is fourth, J must be second (J cannot be fifth due to the last rule, and J cannot be first or last due to the fourth rule). Because H > S, we can then deduce that H must speak first. We can then deduce that R must speak last (if R speaks fifth there would be a violation of the second rule). Finally, K must speak fifth as that is the only remaining slot:

$$\frac{\text{H}}{1} \quad \frac{\text{J}}{2} \quad \frac{\text{S}}{3} \quad \frac{\text{T}}{4} \quad \frac{\text{K}}{5} \quad \frac{\text{R}}{6}$$

Accordingly, answer choice (C) is correct.

Question #4: Local, Must Be True. The correct answer choice is (A)

When H delivers the fifth speech, then from the third rule we know that S must deliver the last speech. This leaves J, R, and T to occupy the second, third, and fourth slots. Because J and T cannot give consecutive speeches, they must be separated by R, who must give the third speech:

$$\frac{\text{K}}{1} \quad \frac{\text{J/T}}{2} \quad \frac{\text{R}}{3} \quad \frac{\text{T/J}}{4} \quad \frac{\text{H}}{5} \quad \frac{\text{S}}{6}$$

Accordingly, answer choice (A) is correct.

Question #5: Local, Could Be True. The correct answer choice is (D)

The question stem creates a super-rule:

$$H > \boxed{S\ R\ K}$$

This powerful configuration naturally has a limited number of placement options, but those options are further limited by the fact that the two variables not involved in the super-rule—J and T—cannot be consecutive. Remember, look not just at the variables in a rule configuration, but also at the variables left out.

Consider how the interaction of J and T affects the super-rule:

If H, S, R, and K attempt to fill the first four slots, a violation occurs because J and T are consecutive in the last two slots (in whatever order).

If H speaks first, and then S, R, and K attempt to fill the last three slots, a violation occurs because J and T are consecutive in the second and third slots (in whatever order).

If H, S, R, and K attempt to fill the last four slots, a violation occurs because J and T are consecutive in the first two slots.

Consequently, only two placements of H, S, R, and K exist:

1. H speaks first, and S, R, and K speak third, fourth, and fifth respectively:

H	J	S	R	K	T
1	2	3	4	5	6

2. H speaks second, and S, R, and K speak fourth, fifth, and sixth respectively:

T	H	J	S	R	K
1	2	3	4	5	6

Accordingly, answer choice (D) could be true and is correct.

Question #6: Local, Could Be True, Except. The correct answer choice is (A)

If K delivers the third speech, there is no immediate inference that follows. The question stem asks for which variable cannot give the fourth speech, and the rule that seems most likely to come into play is the first rule about H, J, and K. Answer choice (A) is correct because if K is third and H is fourth, then J must be second or fifth (because J cannot give the first or last speech). Thus, no matter where J is placed, there is a violation of the first rule.

15

This is a Mapping game.

On the surface this game appears to be a drawing exercise, and most students diagram the game as follows:

Planes: J K L M [4]
Areas: R S T U [4]

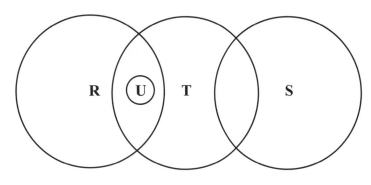

However, much like the Islands game on the October 1992 LSAT, this is actually a Grouping game masquerading as a Mapping game. Especially indicative are the third and fourth rules, both of which are negative grouping rules. Grouping is so prevalent on the test that it is essential to examine and understand a game such as this one that has mapping elements but is controlled by grouping principles.

Although every student inevitably draws out the detection areas, it is probably easier to set this game up in a more linear fashion:

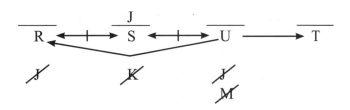

In this setup, we convert the air zones into a grouping relationship. For example, since U is inside of R and T, in our setup we show U with arrows heading towards R and T, meaning that any variable that is in U must also be in R and T. The game scenario indicates R and S do not overlap; our diagram puts a double not-arrow between R and S to indicate that any variable in one of R or S cannot be in the other. The same relationship holds for S and U.

Note that the grouping rules involving areas R, S, T, and U are easily displayed internally within this diagram. Also, since the detection areas are now represented linearly, it is easier to show the Not Laws that apply to each plane. The game is now diagrammed in a much more familiar format and should therefore be easier to attack.

Before moving on to the questions, let's take a moment to examine some of the Not Laws above. In considering these Not Laws, remember that the game is about where each plane is at exactly noon, and thus this is a snapshot at a given time.

Following the relationships above, we can begin to make inferences about the variables. For example, we are told that J is in S. From the relationships, we can deduce that J cannot be in R and U, and we make J Not Laws under R and U. We know that J and K cannot be in the same air zone. Hence, K cannot be in S and we can make a Not Law there. We also know that M can only be in one air zone, and thus M cannot be in U. Consequently, a corresponding M Not Law appears.

Remember, many games that would generally be classified as Mapping Games are actually Grouping games, and so often the best approach is to diagram the Grouping relationship as your primary diagram.

Question #7: Global, Could Be True, List. The correct answer choice is (D)

Answer choices (A) and (B) are eliminated since J cannot be in area R. Answer choice (C) is eliminated since M cannot be in area U. Answer choice (E) is eliminated since K cannot be in area S. It follows that answer choice (D) is correct.

Question #8: Local, Cannot Be True. The correct answer choice is (A)

If K is within exactly two areas, K cannot be in area U, since area U is also within areas R and T. Since K also cannot be in area S, K must be in areas R and T:

$$
\begin{array}{cccc}
\underline{K} & \underline{J} & \underline{\quad} & \underline{K} \\
R & S & U & T \\
\cancel{J} & \cancel{K} & \cancel{K} & \cancel{J}
\end{array}
$$

Since K is in area T, J cannot be in area T, and answer choice (A) is correct.

Question #9: Global, Could Be True, List. The correct answer choice is (E)

A perfect situation to refer to earlier work. According to question #7, J can be in area T. Thus, answer choices (A) and (D)—which fail to include J—must be incorrect. According to question #8, K can be in area T, and thus answer choices (B) and (C)—which fail to include K—must be incorrect. Answer choice (E) is proven correct by process of elimination.

Question #10: Global, Cannot Be True. The correct answer choice is (E)

According to the Not Laws in our initial setup, M cannot be in area U, and thus answer choice (E) is correct.

Question #11: Global, Cannot Be True. The correct answer choice is (D)

Again, according to the relationships diagrammed in the initial setup, no individual plane can be within areas S and U at the same time, and thus answer choice (D) is correct.

Question #12: Local, Cannot Be True. The correct answer choice is (E)

The information in the "if" statement can be diagrammed as follows:

$$
\begin{array}{cccc}
 & J & & M \\
\hline
R & S & U & T \\
\cancel{M} & \cancel{M} & \cancel{M} & \cancel{L} \\
 & & \cancel{L} & \\
\end{array}
$$

Note that the Not Law concerning plane L and area U occurs because L cannot be in area T (M and L cannot be in the same detection area). Any plane that cannot be in area T, area R, or both also cannot be in area U, and so L cannot be in area U. Furthermore, since no plane can be in both areas R and S, it follows that answer choice (E) is correct since L can be in only one detection area (R or S).

Remember, this is a Cannot Be True question, and thus the four incorrect answer choices could occur. For example, answer choice (D) could be true because K could be in both areas R and T.

Question #13: Local, Could Be True. The correct answer choice is (A)

If L is within exactly three areas, L cannot be in area S (if L were in S, then it could only be in S and T) and therefore L must be in areas R, U, and T:

$$
\begin{array}{cccc}
 & M & & \\
L & J & L & L \\
\hline
R & S & U & T \\
\cancel{M} & \cancel{L} & \cancel{M} & \cancel{M} \\
\end{array}
$$

Since L and M cannot be in the same detection areas, M cannot be in areas R, U, and T, and therefore answer choices (D) and (E) are incorrect. Since M must be in at least one detection area, it follows that M must be in area S. According to the Not Laws in our initial setup, K can never be in area S, and therefore answer choice (C) is incorrect. In answer choice (B), it is impossible for J to be in three areas since any plane in area S cannot be in area R and U. Thus, J can only be in at most two areas. Since answer choice (B) is incorrect, answer choice (A) is proven correct by process of elimination.

When you begin a logic game, you should read through all of the rules *before* you begin diagramming. As you read, consider the true nature of the game. Law Services is often able to confuse test takers who fail to completely examine the nature of the rules and their interrelationships. This game provides a fine example of how a thorough and knowledgeable test taker can gain a significant advantage by recognizing the true nature of the rules.

PrepTest 15. June 1995 Game #3: *14. D   15. E   16. C   17. A   18. B   19. E*

This is a Basic Linear: Unbalanced: Underfunded, Numerical Distribution game.

This game features four people driving a total of six days. The first rule specifies that each person drives at least once, and this creates two unfixed numerical distributions for the 6 days to the 4 drivers: 2-2-1-1 and 3-1-1-1. In the 2-2-1-1, two people drive twice, and two people drive once. In the 3-1-1-1, one person drives three times and three people drive once. The distribution directly answers question #17 and helps to answer question #19.

The second rule indicates that no person drives on two consecutive days. Instead of representing each of the four not-blocks (one of each driver), we will represent this rule as a DD not-block, where "D" stands for "driver":

$$\boxed{\cancel{D/D}}$$

The third rule is represented by an F Not Law under Monday.

The fourth rule is a conditional and can be represented as:

$$J \longrightarrow W/S \text{ or both}$$

The fifth rule is also conditional, and can be represented as:

$$G_M \longrightarrow \cancel{S}_S$$

This rule can be added to the fourth rule, to create a chain:

$$G_M \longrightarrow \cancel{S}_S \longrightarrow J_W$$

H is the only random in the game, which leads to the final setup:

$$F \ G \ H \ J^4 \longrightarrow 2\text{-}2\text{-}1\text{-}1 \text{ or } 3\text{-}1\text{-}1\text{-}1$$
$$*$$

$$\boxed{\cancel{D/D}} \qquad \overline{M} \quad \overline{Tu} \quad \overline{W} \quad \overline{Th} \quad \overline{F} \quad \overline{Sa}$$
$$\cancel{F}$$

$$J \longrightarrow W/S \text{ or both}$$

$$G_M \longrightarrow \cancel{S}_S \longrightarrow J_W$$

Question #14: Global, Could Be True, List. The correct answer choice is (D)

Answer choice (A) is incorrect because G drives on two consecutive days.

Answer choice (B) is incorrect because G drives on Monday, and J drives on Saturday, a violation of the last rule.

Answer choice (C) is incorrect because J must drive on Wednesday or Saturday according to the fourth rule.

Answer choice (D) is the correct answer.

Answer choice (E) is incorrect because D does not drive, a violation of the first rule.

Question #15: Global, Could Be True. The correct answer choice is (E)

Answer choice (A) is incorrect because it would cause a violation of the fourth rule.

Answer choice (B) is incorrect because if G drives on Monday, then according to the last rule J does not drive on Saturday, and consequently, according to the fourth rule, J must drive on Wednesday.

Answer choice (C) is incorrect because if J drove on both Tuesday and Friday, then in complying with the fourth rule J would drive either Wednesday or Saturday, which would create a violation of the second rule.

Answer choice (D) is incorrect because, like answer choice (C), it would lead to a violation of the second rule. If G drives on Monday, then J cannot drive on Saturday and J must drive on Wednesday. Because the answer choice also specifies that J drives on Thursday, the second rule would be violated.

Answer choice (E) is the correct answer.

Question #16: Local, Must Be True. The correct answer choice is (C)

If J drives on both Wednesday and Saturday and on no other day, then according to the contrapositive of the last rule G cannot drive on Monday. Since F cannot drive on Monday from the third rule, the only driver available to drive on Monday is H. Hence, answer choice (C) is correct.

Question #17: Local, Must Be True. The correct answer choice is (A)

If G drives exactly twice, then the four drivers must be in the 2-2-1-1 distribution, and consequently answer choice (A) is correct.

Question #18: Global, Cannot Be True. The correct answer choice is (B)

If G drives on Monday, then J must drive on Wednesday. According to answer choice (B), G drives on Monday and J drives on Tuesday. But, this creates a situation where J drives on both Tuesday and Wednesday, a violation of the second rule. Consequently, answer choice (B) cannot be true and is correct.

Question #19: Local, Could Be True. The correct answer choice is (E)

If F drives exactly twice, but does not drive on either Tuesday or Wednesday, F must drive on Thursday and Saturday, and this forces J to drive on Wednesday:

$$
\begin{array}{cccccc}
 & & J & F & & F \\
\hline
M & Tu & W & Th & F & Sa \\
\not{F} & \not{F} & \not{F} & & &
\end{array}
$$

The diagram is sufficient to eliminate answer choices (C) and (D). In addition, because F drives exactly twice, we can determine that the drivers are in a 2-2-1-1 distribution. This information can be used to eliminate answer choices (A) and (B). By process of elimination, answer choice (E) is proven correct.

Another way to eliminate answer choices (A) and (B) is to realize that they are functionally identical, and any two identical answer choices must both be wrong because each correct answer choice is unique (the Uniqueness Theory of Answer Choices).

This is a Defined-Fixed, Unbalanced: Overloaded Grouping game.

This game is Unbalanced because there are nine plumbers, but there are only eight slots (4 teams of 2), so one plumber is always "out" in this game. In this sense, the game has a 2-2-2-2-1 distribution:

Exp plumbers: F G J K M [5]
Inex plumbers: R S T V [4]

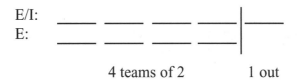

In this case, we have decided to show the "1 out" space as it is unusual to have 8 variables in and just 1 out, and the nature of the 8—two teams of four—could make it easy to forget that one plumber is always out.

The first two rules are fairly easy to understand. The first rule limits the numerical options for each plumber, and the second rule establishes that at least one plumber on each team must be experienced. The other plumber can be inexperienced or experienced. Thus, we can infer that none of the inexperienced plumbers can be assigned to the same team. This results in a slew of inferences, which we will show shortly.

The third rule is a negative grouping rule (we'll use arrows instead of vertical not-blocks because so many variables are involved):

$$F \longleftrightarrow M, R, V$$

Under this rule, F has limited options for which plumber he can be paired with.

The fourth rule limits the plumbers that T can be assigned with to G or K:

$$T \longrightarrow G \text{ or } K \text{ or Out}$$

If T cannot be assigned to G or K, then T must be the one plumber that is not assigned to a team. This rule plays a critical role in the game.

The fifth rule is another negative grouping rule, and prevents J and R from being assigned to the same team:

$$J \longleftrightarrow R$$

From these rules, a number of inferences can be drawn. The first set of inferences involves the fourth rule. Because T, an inexperienced plumber, must be with G or K or out, we also know that none of the other experienced plumbers can team with T:

$$F \longleftrightarrow T$$

$$J \longleftrightarrow T$$

$$M \longleftrightarrow T$$

Of course, for all three experienced plumbers above, these plumbers already had other negative grouping relationships, which we can add in here:

$$F \longleftrightarrow M, R, V, T$$

$$J \longleftrightarrow R, T$$

$$M \longleftrightarrow F, T$$

Thus, of the experienced plumbers, only G and K remain, and even they are restricted in that one of them must pair with T if T is on a team.

On the inexperienced side, the inexperienced plumbers each cannot be assigned with each other,

$$R \longleftrightarrow S, T, V$$

$$S \longleftrightarrow R, T, V$$

$$T \longleftrightarrow R, S, V$$

$$V \longleftrightarrow R, S, T$$

Of course, some of these inexperienced plumbers were already limited by other rules, and there are additional negative relationships that can be shown for each:

$$R \longleftrightarrow F, J, S, T, V$$

$$S \longleftrightarrow R, T, V$$

$$T \longleftrightarrow F, J, M, R, S, V$$

$$V \longleftrightarrow F, R, S, T$$

Note that in R's case, R must be with G or K or M or out.

This results in the final setup for the game:

Exp plumbers: F G J K M ^{5}
Inex plumbers: R S T V ^{4}

The rules:

$$F \longleftarrow\!\!\!|\!\!\!\longrightarrow M, R, V$$
$$T \longrightarrow G \text{ or } K \text{ or Out}$$
$$J \longleftarrow\!\!\!|\!\!\!\longrightarrow R$$

E/I: ___ ___ ___ ___ |
E: ___ ___ ___ ___ |

4 teams of 2   1 out

The rules with inferences:

$$F \longleftarrow\!\!\!|\!\!\!\longrightarrow M, R, V, T$$
$$J \longleftarrow\!\!\!|\!\!\!\longrightarrow R, T$$
$$M \longleftarrow\!\!\!|\!\!\!\longrightarrow F, T$$

$$R \longleftarrow\!\!\!|\!\!\!\longrightarrow F, J, S, T, V$$
$$S \longleftarrow\!\!\!|\!\!\!\longrightarrow R, T, V$$
$$T \longleftarrow\!\!\!|\!\!\!\longrightarrow F, J, M, R, S, V$$
$$V \longleftarrow\!\!\!|\!\!\!\longrightarrow F, R, S, T$$

$$T \longrightarrow G \text{ or } K \text{ or Out}$$
$$R \longrightarrow G \text{ or } K \text{ or } M \text{ or Out}$$

Note that if you have difficulty tracking the plumbers by experience level, simply use I and E subscripts to designate each plumber in the appropriate group.

Question #20: Global, Could Be True. The correct answer choice is (C)

Answer choice (A) is eliminated because K is an experienced plumber, and the question stem specifies that an inexperienced plumber is sought.

Answer choices (B) and (E) are eliminated by the application of the third rule.

Answer choice (D) is eliminated by the fourth rule.

Thus, answer choice (C) is correct.

Question #21: Global, Could Be True. The correct answer choice is (C)

Answer choices (A) and (B) are eliminated by the application of the third rule.

Answer choices (D) and (E) are eliminated because they both contain a pair of inexperienced plumbers.

Answer choice (D) is also eliminated because T must be assigned to a team with G or K.

Answer choice (C) is thus correct.

Question #22: Local, Could Be True. The correct answer choice is (B)

The condition in the question stem assigns G and K to T and S:

E/I:	T	S			
E:	G/K	K/G	F		

This information eliminates answer choice (A).

The application of the third rule eliminates answer choices (C), (D), and (E).

Thus, answer choice (B) is correct.

Question #23: Local, Must Be True. The correct answer choice is (A)

If G is not assigned to a team, then each team features one experienced plumber and one inexperienced plumber. From the fourth rule, T must be assigned to K. F is the next logical plumber to examine due to the number of restrictions on F, and of the remaining inexperienced plumbers F must be assigned to a team with S. Because J cannot be assigned to a team with R, J must be assigned to a team with V, leaving M to team with R:

E/I:	R	S	T	V	G
E:	M	F	K	J	

Answer choice (A) is thus correct.

Question #24: Local, Must Be True. The correct answer choice is (A)

The condition in the rule forces K to be assigned to T, M to be assigned to R, and J to be assigned to V. The only choice remaining is whether F or G teams with S:

E/I:	R	S	T	V	G/F
E:	M	F/G	K	J	

Answer choice (A) is therefore correct.

PrepTest 16

September 1995 Logic Games Setups

This is a Grouping: Defined-Fixed, Balanced game.

R S T V W X Y Z [8]

The combination of the second, third, and fifth rules leads to the following inferences involving W and Y:

$$W_1 \longrightarrow Y_2$$

$$W_2 \longrightarrow Y_1$$

The application of the final rule leads to a single solution:

$$T_1 \longrightarrow Z_1$$

Because this rule is so limiting, you should expect it to be tested at most once or twice during the game.

Question #1: Global, Could Be True, List. The correct answer choice is (D)

Answer choice (A): From the last rule we know that when T is added to class 1 then Z must also be added to class 1. This answer violates that rule, and thus cannot be true.

Answer choice (B): The second rule stipulates that S must be added to class 3. Because S is in class 2 in this answer, this answer is incorrect.

Answer choice (C): The fourth rule indicates that V and Z cannot be added to the same class. This answer is thus therefore incorrect because V and Z both appear in class 2.

Answer choice (D): This is the correct answer choice.

Answer choice (E): The third rule states that W and Y cannot be added to the same class. This answer is thus therefore incorrect because W and Y both appear in class 2.

The information from the hypothetical discovered in this question (namely that V can be added to class 2) can then be used to eliminate answer choices (A), (B), and (C) in question #2. The same hypothetical can be used to eliminate answer choices (C) and (E) in question #3.

Question #2: Global, Could Be True, List. The correct answer choice is (E)

As noted in question #1, by re-using the information in the question, we can quickly eliminate answer choices (A), (B), and (C) in this question. The difference between the two remaining answers choices (D and E) is class 1. While you can stop and create a hypothetical that shows that V can be added to class 1, the better choice would be to skip this question and return to it later, after you have completed all of the remaining questions and produced more hypotheticals. As we will see, the hypotheticals from questions #4, #5, and #6 each clearly show that V can be added to class 1.

Because V can be added to class 1, answer choice (E) is correct.

Question #3: Local, Must Be True. The correct answer choice is (A)

The key to this question, and questions #4 and 5, is to Hurdle the Uncertainty™. When X is added to class 1, the following diagram results:

$$\begin{array}{ccc} \underline{\quad} & \underline{\quad} & \underline{\quad} \\ \underline{X} & \underline{\quad} & \underline{\quad} \\ \underline{R} & \underline{\quad} & \underline{S} \\ 1 & 2 & 3 \end{array}$$

The remaining variables are V, Z, W, Y, and T. Because the VZ pair and the WY pair cannot be added to the same class, they must occupy spaces in difference classes. But, space is limited in class 1 and class 3. Because no pair can be added to class 2, and in the reverse, no pair can be added to class 1 and class 3 (otherwise the remaining pair would have to both be added to class 2), we can deduce that one pair must be added to classes 1 and 2, and the other pair must be added to classes 2 and 3, as indicated by the straight lines in the diagram below:

$$\begin{array}{ccc} \underline{X} & \underline{\quad} & \underline{\quad} \\ \underline{R} & \underline{\quad} & \underline{S} \\ 1 & 2 & 3 \end{array}$$

This arrangement leaves only one remaining space, and that space must be filled by T:

$$\begin{array}{ccc} & \underline{T} & \\ \underline{X} & \underline{\quad} & \underline{\quad} \\ \underline{R} & \underline{\quad} & \underline{S} \\ 1 & 2 & 3 \end{array}$$

Accordingly, answer choice (A) is correct.

Questions #3, #4, and #5 each trade on the same principle, but question #3 is considerably harder than questions #4 and #5. After you review the explanations to #4 and #5, return to this question and note how assigning the variable (X, in this case) to class 1 instead of class 3 changed the appearance of the problem. The underlying Hurdle the Uncertainty remains, but this problem is harder to solve because of that difference in variable assignment.

Question #4: Local, Could Be True, Except. The correct answer choice is (E)

When X is assigned to class 3, the diagram appears as follows:

$$
\begin{array}{ccc}
\underline{\quad} & \underline{\quad} & X \\
R & \underline{\quad} & S \\
1 & 2 & 3
\end{array}
$$

The remaining variables are V, Z, W, Y, and T. Because the VZ pair and the WY pair cannot be added to the same class, they must occupy spaces in difference classes. Thus, they must each occupy a space in class 1 and class 2:

$$
\begin{array}{ccc}
W/Y & & \\
V/Z & Y/W & X \\
R & Z/V & S \\
1 & 2 & 3
\end{array}
$$

T is the only remaining variable, and thus T must be added to class 2:

$$
\begin{array}{ccc}
W/Y & T & \\
V/Z & Y/W & X \\
R & Z/V & S \\
1 & 2 & 3
\end{array}
$$

Accordingly, answer choice (E) cannot be true and is correct.

Question #5: Local, Must Be True. The correct answer choice is (C)

This question is interesting because it is functionally identical to question #4 in how it is diagrammed, with the only difference being that T is substituted for X.

When T is assigned to class 3, the diagram appears as follows:

$$
\begin{array}{ccc}
\underline{\quad} & \underline{\quad} & T \\
R & \underline{\quad} & S \\
1 & 2 & 3
\end{array}
$$

The remaining variables are V, Z, W, Y, and X. Because the VZ pair and the WY pair cannot be added to the same class, they must occupy spaces in difference classes. Thus, they must each occupy a space in class 1 and class 2:

$$
\begin{array}{ccc}
W/Y & & \\
V/Z & Y/W & T \\
R & Z/V & S \\
1 & 2 & 3
\end{array}
$$

16

X is the only remaining variable, and thus X must be added to class 2:

$$
\begin{array}{ccc}
\text{W/Y} & \text{X} & \\
\text{V/Z} & \text{Y/W} & \text{T} \\
\hline
\text{R} & \text{Z/V} & \text{S} \\
\hline
1 & 2 & 3
\end{array}
$$

Accordingly, answer choice (C) is correct.

Question #6: Global, Must Be True. The correct answer choice is (D)

This is a "5 if" question, and because each answer choice presents a new scenario, this question can be quite time-consuming. Because this question is clearly intended to take longer to complete, and because this is the last question in the game, the best approach is to change course and consider the answers in reverse order, from (E) to (A). Given that this question is supposed to take more time than average to complete, and that each answer requires the test taker to consider a new scenario that will require a separate diagram, it is unlikely that the test makers will place the correct answer first or second. Thus, the chances are that the correct answer will be (C), (D), or (E), so start with answer choice (E) to maximize your efficiency.

Answer choice (E): When Y and Z are added to class 2, X can be added to class 1 or class 3, and so this answer choice is incorrect.

Answer choice (D): This is the correct answer choice.

Answer choice (C): If V and W are added to class 1, then Z can be added to class 2 or 3, and so this answer choice is incorrect.

Answer choice (B): If V and W are added to class 1, then T can be added to class 2 or 3, and so this answer choice is incorrect.

Answer choice (A): If T and X are added to class 2, then V can be added to class 1, 2, or 3, and so this answer choice is incorrect.

This is an Advanced Linear: Balanced, Identify the Templates game.

This game features six animals being assigned to six stalls, one animal per stall. The game is made slightly more challenging because the six animals are divided into two types: lions and tigers. The initial game scenario appears as:

Lions: F G H J [4]
Tigers: K M [2]

1	2	3

4	5	6

The first rule establishes that the two tigers cannot face each other:

K		M
M		K

The second rule assigns a lion to stall 1, which eliminates K and M from being assigned to the stall:

1	2	3
K̸		
M̸		

4	5	6

The third rule assigns H to stall 6:

1	2	3
K̸		
M̸		

4	5	H
		6

This additionally has the effect of removing H from consideration for stall 1, leaving only F, G, or J as candidates for the first stall.

The fourth rule is an important rule in the game, and, for some, a problematic rule. The rule is properly diagrammed as:

$$\boxed{\text{K J}}$$

One of the mistakes made by many students is to misinterpret this rule as being diagrammed as JK. The rule states that J is assigned to a stall *numbered one higher* than K's stall. Numerically, 2 is numbered one higher than 1, 3 is numbered one higher than 2, etc. Thus, if K is assigned to stall 2, then J must be assigned to stall 3. This produces a KJ representation, not JK.

With the addition of this rule, J cannot be assigned to stall 1, and K cannot be assigned to stall 5 (stall 6 is already occupied, and thus it is not the last "open" space). With J removed from consideration for stall 1, we can deduce that F or G must be assigned to stall 1. Of course, with F or G occupying stall 1, the earliest the KJ block could appear is 2-3, meaning J cannot be assigned to stall 2:

The last rule brings an important restriction: K cannot face H, and so K cannot be assigned to stall 3:

This final rule limits K's options to stall 2 or stall 4. With this limitation, and the other rules in the game, you must make the decision to show the two templates based on the position of the KJ block:

<u>Template #1</u>: KJ in stalls 2-3. When K is assigned to stall 2, M cannot be assigned to stall 5 due to the first rule, and must be assigned to stall 4. F and G rotate between stall 1 and stall 5.

$$\frac{F/G}{1} \qquad \frac{K}{2} \qquad \frac{J}{3}$$

$$\frac{M}{4} \qquad \frac{G/F}{5} \qquad \frac{H}{6}$$

<u>Template #2</u>: KJ in stalls 4-5. When K is assigned to stall 4, stalls 2 and 3 are occupied by M and the remainder of F/G.

$$\frac{F/G}{1} \qquad \frac{(\ G/F\ ,\ M\ )}{2 \qquad\qquad 3}$$

$$\frac{K}{4} \qquad \frac{J}{5} \qquad \frac{H}{6}$$

The two templates above capture all six of the possibilities in the game. This game can be somewhat difficult without the templates; with the templates, the game is easy.

This game is also the start of some interesting test construction elements used the test makers. Consider the following features of the second, third, and fourth games:

Game #2:   Features two rows, slots are numbered sequentially in horizontal fashion. Numerically, "2" is higher than "1," etc.

Game #3:   Features two rows, slots are numbered in non-sequential fashion (one odd row, one even row)

Game #4:   Numerically, "1" is higher than "2," etc.

In the second and third games, the slots are numbered in different ways, and in the second and fourth games, the numerical ranking relationships are opposite. These differences have the subtle effect of keeping test takers off-balance. For example, in the second game the slots line up 1-2-3, and in the third game they line up 1-3-5-7. Psychologically, it is difficult to develop a rhythm when the slots appear similar but are numbered differently. This type of construction is just another example of the psychological ploys used by the test makers.

Returning to this game, using the templates allows you to answer the questions extraordinarily quickly.

Question #7: Global, Must Be True. The correct answer choice is (E)

As discussed during the setup, K can be assigned to only stall 2 or stall 4, and so answer choice (E) is correct.

Question #8: Global, Could Be True. The correct answer choice is (B)

Under Template #2, H's stall can face M's stall, and so answer choice (B) is correct.

Question #9: Global, Must Be True. The correct answer choice is (C)

As shown in the two templates, K's stall is always in a different row than M's stall, and thus answer choice (C) is correct.

Question #10: Local, Must Be True. The correct answer choice is (E)

The condition in the question stem can only occur under Template #2. In that template M's stall and G's stall are always in the same row (the first row), and thus answer choice (E) is correct.

Question #11: Local, Could Be True. The correct answer choice is (C)

J's can only be assigned stall 3 under Template #1. In that template, F or G can be assigned to stall 1, and so answer choice (C) is correct.

Question #12: Global, Must Be True. The correct answer choice is (B)

In Template #1, M is assigned to stall 4, and in Template #2, K is assigned to stall 4. Thus, a tiger is always assigned to stall 4, and answer choice (B) is correct.

This is an Advanced Linear: Unbalanced: Underfunded game.

The first rule establishes that houses of the same style cannot be adjacent:

The HH designation indicates that two Houses of the same style cannot stand next to each other. This representation is faster and easier than drawing out not-blocks for each style.

The second rule establishes a vertical block that removes the possibility that split-level houses face each other:

The third rule is conditional, and stipulates that every time a ranch house appears, there is a Tudor next to it:

$$R \longrightarrow \boxed{\begin{array}{c} R\ T \\ \text{or} \\ T\ R \end{array}}$$

The fourth and fifth rules assign house styles to houses 3 and 6:

R S T ^{3}

	R		
1	3	5	7

		S	
2	4	6	8

Of course, with these two houses determined, a slew of Not Laws immediately follows from the first two rules. From the first rule, houses 1 and 5 cannot be R, and houses 4 and 8 cannot be S:

```
           R
 ___      ___      ___      ___
  1        3        5        7
  R̶                 R̶

                    S
 ___      ___      ___      ___
  2        4        6        8
           S̶                 S̶
```

From the second rule, house 5 cannot be S, which means that house 5 must be T. Consequently, house 7 cannot be T:

```
           R        T
 ___      ___      ___      ___
  1        3        5        7
  R̶                 R̶        T̶
                    S̶

                    S
 ___      ___      ___      ___
  2        4        6        8
           S̶                 S̶
```

Applying the third rule, house 3 now satisfies the rule because house 5 is T. But, we can also infer that house 8 *cannot* be R, because if house 8 was R, there would be no way for a T to be adjacent, a violation of the third rule. Thus, because house 8 cannot be S or R, it must be T:

```
           R        T
 ___      ___      ___      ___
  1        3        5        7
  R̶                 R̶        T̶
                    S̶

                    S        T
 ___      ___      ___      ___
  2        4        6        8
           S̶                 S̶
                             R̶
```

Of course, there are only three house styles, so each time one is removed, a dual-option results (for example, house 1 cannot be R, so it must be S or T). Adding all of the dual-options leads us to the final diagram for the game:

RST^3

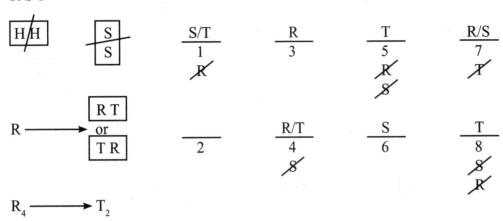

R$_4$ ⟶ T$_2$

Note that from the action of the third rule, if house 4 is R, then house 2 must be T, which is represented above as:

$$R_4 \longrightarrow T_2$$

This is the easiest game of the test; the first two rules produce numerous Not Laws, and each results in a dual-option or style assignment. This greatly limits the possibilities of the game. One approach would be to draw out each possibility, but the setup above is so powerful that it appears that showing each solution would not be worth the extra time.

Question #13: Global, Could Be True, Except. The correct answer choice is (D)

From the Not Laws above, house 7 can never be a Tudor house, and thus answer choice (D) is correct.

Question #14: Local, Could Be True. The correct answer choice is (B)

The condition in the question stem stipulates that two ranch houses face each other. That can only happen with houses 3 and 4. And, of course, if house 4 is a ranch then from the third rule house 2 must be a Tudor:

S/T	R	T	R/S
1	3	5	7

T	R	S	T
2	4	6	8

Houses 1 and 7 are the only uncertainties, and you should look for them in the answers of a Could Be True question. Answer choice (E) addresses house 1, but house 1 can never be a ranch house, so it can be eliminated. Answer choice (B) indicates that house 7 is a split-level house, which is possible, and so answer choice (B) is correct.

Question #15: Local, Could Be True. The correct answer choice is (A)

If house 4 is a Tudor house, then house 2 cannot be a Tudor house, and must instead be a ranch or split-level house:

S/T	R	T	R/S
1	3	5	7

R/S	T	S	T
2	4	6	8

Because this is a Could be True question, and only houses 1, 2, and 7 are uncertain, you should look for those houses in the answer choices. They appear in answer choices (A), (B), and (D), and only answer choice (A) includes an outcome that is possible, and thus (A) is correct.

Question #16: Global, Could Be True. The correct answer choice is (A)

Answer choice (B) can be eliminated since there are already 2 Tudor houses.

Answer choice (C) can be eliminated because having exactly two Tudor houses would leave just houses 5 and 8 as T. While house 1 could be S instead of T, if house 4 is R instead of T, then house 2 could only be S, which be a violation of the second rule since house 1 is already S. Literally, having exactly two Tudor houses does not leave enough options for the remaining open spaces.

Answer choices (D) and (E) can be eliminated since there can only be 3 Ranch houses maximum. House 3 is already an R, and house 7 can easily be an R as well. Between houses 2 and 4, a maximum of one can be R (remembered the first rule!), and so the maximum number of ranch houses is 3.

Thus, answer choice (A) is correct.

Question #17: Local, Must Be True. The correct answer choice is (E)

If no house faces a house of a similar style, then house 4 cannot be a ranch house, and it must be a Tudor:

S/T	R	T	R/S
1	3	5	7

R/S	T	S	T
2	4	6	8

Accordingly, answer choice (E) is correct.

Question #18: Local, Could Be True, List, Except, Suspension. The correct answer choice is (A)

This is a Suspension question, but, it is also a List question and so it is less time-consuming than other Suspension questions. In general, if you have time problems, avoiding a Suspension question is a reasonable strategy. But, do not avoid Suspension List questions as they can be solved as quickly as normal List questions!

This time Law Services is very clever, for although one of the rules is suspended, of course the third rule ("Ranch has a Tudor next to it") is still in force and this proves answer choice (A) correct in this Except question. Remember, this is still a List question and proper List question technique applies.

This is a Pattern game.

R J S M L [5]

	Initial Ranking:	
<u>Odd</u>	1	R
3 vs 2	2	J
5 vs 4	3	S
	4	M
<u>Even</u>	5	L
2 vs 1		
4 vs 3		

As with most Pattern games, this game has a minimal setup.

The first rule indicates that there odd and even rounds. The second and third rules indicate what each round consists of from a matchup standpoint. The fourth rule indicates what happens when a lower-positioned team wins (they move up a spot), and the losing team then drops down. If the lower-positioned team loses, the two teams stay in the same positions.

One of the critical inferences of the game is that one team does not participate in each round. For example, during an odd-position round, the team in position 1 does not play; during an even-position round, the team in position 5 does not play. Also, it is critical to understand that players can only move up or down a maximum of one position from one round to the next. This information is particularly helpful on questions #19 and #24.

Because this is a Pattern game, no further inferences can be made, and you should move on from the setup quickly and get to the questions. Use the questions to get a better understanding of how the game works.

As is the case in many Pattern games, all of the questions are Local. This occurs because the very nature of Pattern games requires that more information be added before any specific inferences can be made.

Question #19: Local, Could Be True, List. The correct answer choice is (D)

Question #19 provides an excellent example of the usefulness of the insight that one team does not play in each round. If exactly one even-position round has been played, then L, the team in position 5, has not played and cannot have moved. Only answer choice (D) lists L in position 5, and thus answer choice (D) is correct.

Question #20: Local, Must Be True, Except. The correct answer choice is (E)

This is an easy question to solve; simply apply the rules in the question stem. The question stem indicates that two rounds have been played, starting with an odd position round. If the lower-positioned team won every match, then after the first round the positions would have appeared as follows:

Original	#1: Odd
R	R
J	S
S	J
M	L
L	M

The next round would be even, and if every lower-positions team won, the results would appear as follows:

Original	#1: Odd	#2: Even
R	R	S
J	S	R
S	J	L
M	L	J
L	M	M

Accordingly, answer choice (E) is correct.

Question #21: Local, Could Be True. The correct answer choice is (A)

Answer choices (A) is possible when the rounds are odd-even: when 3 plays 2, J first defeats S and holds position, and then when 2 plays 1, J defeats R and rises to position 1. Thus, answer choice (A) is possible and correct.

Answer choices (B) and (C) are the same type of answer: a player at one of the "ends" trying to win or lose two matches. This is not possible due to the way the matches leave a player out each time. As the position 5 player, if L plays in the first round, it must be an odd round. If L loses the first match, then L would not play in the second round, which would be even. Similarly, as the position 1 player, if R plays in the first round, it must be an even round. If R wins the first match, then R would not play in the second round, which would be odd.

Answer choice (D) is incorrect because J and L are too far apart for L's only match to be against J.

Answer choice (E) is incorrect since there cannot be consecutive identical matches as part of the pattern of the game.

Question #22: Local, Could Be True. The correct answer choice is (C)

Because J wins all of his matches, he must end up as player 1. This eliminates answer choices (A), (B), and (D).

Here is the hypothetical that proves answer choice (C) correct:

Original	#1: Odd	#2: Even	#3: Odd
R	R	J	J
J	J	R	L
S	S	L	R
M	L	S	M
L	M	M	S

Question #23: Local, Must Be True. The correct answer choice is (A)

The question stem reveals that after three rounds where M has won three matches, and the other teams are in the same relative order, one of the teams *must* be in position 3. So, any hypothetical will work for this question because apparently all possible solutions result in the same team being positioned third.

Only one hypothetical is required to solve this question. Either of these hypotheticals will work:

Results after three rounds:

Even-Odd-Even			Odd-Even-Odd	
1	M		1	R
2	R		2	M
3	J		3	J
4	S		4	S
5	L		5	L

In each instance, J is third, and thus answer choice (A) is correct.

Question #24: Local, Could Be True. The correct answer choice is (C)

If you are given the order of teams in any round, then in the *previous round* for the first and fifth positions there can be only two possible teams that occupied that position: for position 1, the teams in position 1 and 2; for position 5, the teams in position 4 and 5. Question #24 uses this information to great effect. In question #24, the order of teams after *three* rounds is:

1	R
2	J
3	L
4	S
5	M

In attempting to determine the order of teams after the *second* round, it is important to realize that teams can only move up or down one position at a time at most. Thus, at the end of the second round either J or R *must* have been in position 1. Unfortunately, every answer choice lists J or R in position 1. Let us try position 5. At the end of the second round either M or S *must* have been in position 5. Because only answer choice (C) lists M or S in position 5, answer choice (C) must be the correct answer.

POWERSCORE®

17

PREPTEST

DECEMBER 1995 LOGIC GAMES SETUPS

This is a Basic Linear: Balanced game.

This is a standard Balanced Linear game featuring a lot of sequencing. Overall, this is an excellent beginning to the games section. The basic structure of the game is:

P Q R S T U W [7]

__	__	__	__	__	__	__
1	2	3	4	5	6	7

The first rule is sequential, and can be diagrammed as Q > W. Two Not Laws are created:

P Q R S T U W [7]

Q > W

__	__	__	__	__	__	__
1	2	3	4	5	6	7
W̸						Q̸

The second rule is also sequential, and can be diagrammed as U > P. Two more Not Laws are created:

P Q R S T U W [7]

Q > W

U > P

__	__	__	__	__	__	__
1	2	3	4	5	6	7
W̸						Q̸
P̸						U̸

The third rule creates a dual-option for appointment 3:

P Q R S T U W [7]

Q > W

U > P

__	__	R/T	__	__	__	__
1	2	3	4	5	6	7
W̸						Q̸
P̸						U̸

The fourth rule creates an unfixed block, which can be diagrammed as:

$$\boxed{\begin{array}{|c|c|}\hline R & S \\\hline S & R \\\hline\end{array}}$$

Although no direct inferences follow from this rule, a series of fairly obvious linkage inferences can be drawn from this rule. For example, is S is 7th, then R is 6th, and T must be 3rd, etc. There are so many of these inferences that it is not worth writing down; instead, note the connection and move on.

The final setup to the game is:

P Q R S T U W⁷

Q > W

U > P

$$\boxed{\begin{array}{|c|c|}\hline R & S \\\hline S & R \\\hline\end{array}}$$

```
                     R/T
___  ___  ___  ___  ___  ___  ___
 1    2    3    4    5    6    7
 W̸                              Ø̸
 P̸                              U̸
```

Question #1: Global, Could Be True, List. The correct answer choice is (E)

This question can be easily solved using proper List question technique.

Answer choice (A) is incorrect because it violates the second rule.

Answer choice (B) is incorrect because it violates the third rule.

Answer choice (C) is incorrect because it violates the fourth rule.

Answer choice (D) is incorrect because it violates the first rule.

Answer choice (E) is the correct answer.

Question #2: Local, Must Be True. The correct answer choice is (E)

The Local condition in the question stem places two of the variables. When W is 2nd, then from the first rule Q must be first, and when P is 5th, then U must be 4th. There is no room for the RS block to be 3rd, so T must be 3rd, and the RS block rotates between 6th and 7th:

$$\frac{Q}{1} \quad \frac{W}{2} \quad \frac{T}{3} \quad \frac{U}{4} \quad \frac{P}{5} \quad \frac{R/S}{6} \quad \frac{S/R}{7}$$

Accordingly, answer choice (E) is correct.

Question #3: Local, Must Be True. The correct answer choice is (B)

The condition in the question stem creates the following sequence:

$$\boxed{T\ U\ R\ S} > P$$

Because this block includes R and T (the two variables from the third rule), the block in this sequence can only go in two positions: 1-4 or 3-6.

If the block is in 1-4, then Q, W, and P are in the final three spaces, with the rule that Q > W. If the block is in 3-6, then P must be last from the second rule, and Q is 1st and W is 2nd from the first rule. These are the two options:

Block in 1-4:
Block in 3-6:

$$\frac{T}{} \quad \frac{U}{} \quad \frac{R}{} \quad \frac{S}{} \quad \frac{(\ Q > W,}{} \quad \frac{}{} \quad \frac{P\ )}{}$$

$$\frac{Q}{1} \quad \frac{W}{2} \quad \frac{T}{3} \quad \frac{U}{4} \quad \frac{R}{5} \quad \frac{S}{6} \quad \frac{P}{7}$$

Accordingly, answer choice (B) is correct.

Question #4: Local, Could Be True, Except. The correct answer choice is (B)

This is the most difficult question of the game. The condition in the question stem creates the following block-sequence:

$$U > \boxed{P\ S\ R}$$

Because the earliest R could be is 4th, from the third rule we can deduce that T must be 3rd. Thus, the PSR block has only two options: 4-6 or 5-7.

When the block is in 4-6, U must be 1st or 2nd. Because Q > W, Q must also be 1st or 2nd, and W must be last. When the block is in 5-7, the remaining three unplaced variables—U, Q, and W—have several options, although from the first rule Q can never be 4th and W can never be 1st.

These are the resulting two diagrams:

Block in 4-6:	U/Q	Q/U	T	P	S	R	W
Block in 5-7:			T		P	S	R

positions: 1 (W̶) 2 3 4 (Q̶) 5 6 7

Accordingly, T can never be immediately in front of Q, and answer choice (B) is correct.

Question #5: Local, Must Be True. The correct answer choice is (D)

The condition in the question stem produces the following sequence:

$$\begin{matrix} U \\ \text{-----} > \boxed{P\ T\ W} \\ Q \end{matrix}$$

Because the earliest that T could appear is 4th, from the third rule R must be 3rd. At this point it appears that the PTW block could be 4-6 or 5-7. But, if the block is 4-6, then there is no way to fit the RS block in and still conform to the remaining rules. Thus, the PTW block must be in 5-7:

		R		P	T	W
1	2	3	4	5	6	7

With that block placed, the remaining variables are Q, S, and U. Because S must be next to R from the fourth rule, we can make two templates based on the position of S:

S is 2:	Q/U	S	R	U/Q	P	T	W
S is 4:	Q/U	U/Q	R	S	P	T	W

positions: 1 2 3 4 5 6 7

R must always have an earlier appointment than P, and accordingly answer choice answer choice (D) must be true and is correct.

17

This is a Grouping: Defined-Fixed, Unbalanced: Underfunded, Numerical Distribution game.

This game is more challenging than the first game. Although the setup is straightforward, there are some interesting inferences. Let's take a look at the game by examining each rule.

The first rule reserves one space in each group for an officer:

Off: F G H ³
Super: K L M ³

Officer:

P   Q   S

Of course, if an officer must be assigned to each committee, then all three supervisors can never be assigned to the same committee:

The second rule establishes the minimum assignments—one per employee—in a numerical distribution. With six employees, that minimum translates to 1-1-1-1-1-1. Thus, there are three additional assignments remaining. All three cannot be assigned to the same person as that would result in four total assignment when there are only three possible committee assignments, so the three assignments must either be split 2-1 or 1-1-1. Adding those to the minimums produces two separate unfixed numerical distributions:

　　　　　　　#1:　　3-2-1-1-1-1
　　or
　　　　　　　#2:　　2-2-2-1-1-1

The third rule very nicely fills the Policy Committee with all three officers:

Off: F G H ³
Super: K L M ³

Officer:

H
G
F
P   Q   S

The fourth rule is a negative grouping rule between G and L. Because this game contains fixed groups in a vertical array, we will show this rule as a vertical not-block:

Because G and L cannot be assigned together, and from the second rule each must be assigned to at least one committee, we can infer that neither G nor L can be assigned to all three committees:

$$\boxed{G \not{} G}$$

As G is already assigned to the Policy Committee from the third rule, this means that G cannot be assigned to both the Quality and Sales Committees. L, who cannot be assigned to the Policy committee because it is full, must then be assigned to either the Quality or Sales Committees, or both:

$$L \longrightarrow Q/S \text{ or both}$$

The fifth and final rule assigns K to the Sales Committee. Because K is a supervisor, K will be placed in the second available slot, in order to reserve the first slot for an officer per the first rule:

Off: F G H [3]
Super: K L M [3]

Officer:	H		
	G		K
	F		
	P	Q	S

Combining all of the rules and inferences leads to the final setup for the game:

Off: F G H [3]
Super: K L M [3]

Officer:	H		
	G		K
	F		
	P	Q	S

#1:   3-2-1-1-1-1
#2:   2-2-2-1-1-1

L ⟶ Q/S or both

Question #6: Global, Could Be True, List. The correct answer choice is (D)

This is an easy List question—apply correct List question technique and you can solve the question quite quickly.

Answer choice (A) is incorrect because it violates the fifth rule.

Answer choice (B) is incorrect because it violates the fifth rule.

Answer choice (C) is incorrect because it violates the fourth rule.

Answer choice (D) is the correct answer.

Answer choice (E) is incorrect because it violates the first rule as there is no officer assigned to the committee.

Question #7: Local, Must Be True. The correct answer choice is (C)

This can be a difficult question. From a theoretical standpoint, it would have been preferable if the question #9 preceded this question since ultimately the two question are quite similar, and the theory behind question #7 is a more complex version of the theory behind question #9. There are really two ways to solve this question: abstractly or by using hypotheticals. We will examine both methods.

Abstract Solution

> Rule: H is assigned only once per the question stem.
>
> Rule: F cannot serve on both the Quality and Sales committees (due to the local FM rule) and G cannot serve on both the Quality and Sales committees (due to the global GL rule).
>
> Inference: G serves once on either the Quality or Sales committee, and F serves once on either the Quality or Sales committee.
>
> Inference: Since G must be assigned to either the Quality or Sales committee, L is assigned to the committee G is not on, and since F must be assigned to either the Quality or Sales committee, M is assigned to the committee G is not on.
>
> Inference: H, G, L, F, and M have now been assigned to their maximum number of spaces, and one space still remains on the Quality Committee and the Sales Committee.
>
> Inference: K must fill those final two spaces, and thus K is assigned to exactly two committees.

Essentially, K Hurdles the Uncertainty and must be assigned to both committees.

Hypotheticals

Only two hypotheticals exist for this question:

Off: F G H [3]
Super: K L M [3]

Officer:

H	K	K
G	L	M
F	F	G
P	Q	S

or

Officer:

H	K	K
G	M	L
F	G	F
P	Q	S

Accordingly, answer choice (C) is correct.

Question #8: Global, Cannot Be True. The correct answer choice is (B)

As discussed during the setup, if G is assigned to all three committees, then according to the fourth rule L will be unable to be assigned to a committee, a violation of the second rule. Accordingly, answer choice (B) is correct.

Question #9: Local, Must Be True. The correct answer choice is (E)

This question also hinges on Hurdling the Uncertainty. With G assigned to two committees, G must be assigned to either the Quality or Sales committee, we can infer that L must be assigned to the committee that G is not on from the action of the fourth rule. Thus, although we cannot be certain which committee G or L is assigned to, we can jump over this uncertainty and prove that because M must be assigned to one of the committees, and there is only space available on the Quality Committee, M must be assigned to the Quality committee.

Officer:

H	M	L/G
G	G/L	K
F	F	F
P	Q	S

Accordingly, answer choice (E) is correct.

Question #10: Global, Could Be True, List. The correct answer choice is (E)

Answer choice (A) is incorrect because according to the distribution in this answer, F, G, and H each work twice, meaning that none of them would be available to work on the Sales Committee. As that violates the first rule, this answer choice is incorrect.

Answer choice (B) is incorrect because either L or M would be left off of the Sales Committee, a violation of the second rule.

Answer choice (C) is incorrect because either L or M would be left off of the Sales Committee, a violation of the second rule.

Answer choice (D) is incorrect because it violates the fourth rule.

Answer choice (E) is the correct answer. Oddly, if you wait until completing all of the other questions to do question #10, you will find that the hypothetical in question #11 proves this answer correct.

Question #11: Local, Must Be True. The correct answer choice is (E)

This is another Hurdle the Uncertainty question. If L is assigned to two committees, the following results:

Officer:	H	L	L
	G		K
	F		
	P	Q	S

However, from the second rule, M must be assigned to a committee, and so M must be assigned to the Quality Committee. G cannot be on either the Quality or Sales Committee due to the fourth rule, and so the officer spaces must be occupied by F or H:

Officer:	H	L	L
	G	M	K
	F	F/H	F/H
	P	Q	S

Accordingly, answer choice (E) is correct.

Again, note that this hypothetical is sufficient to prove question #10, answer choice (E) correct.

17

Question #12: Global, Cannot Be True. The correct answer choice is (B)

If F and H are assigned to exactly one committee, then that committee is the Policy Committee. Consequently, G would have to be assigned to the other two committees, and then G would be assigned to all three committees. As discussed during the setup and question #8, this is impossible. Hence, answer choice (B) is correct.

17

This is an Advanced Linear: Unbalanced: Overloaded game.

This is a relatively easy game. The first rule can be diagrammed a double-not arrow between Vladimir and Wendy. The second rule limits each person to eating a food exactly once each day, and the third through seventh rules establish what they can eat at each meal.

Because Wendy eats an O for lunch, she cannot eat an O for a snack, and so she must eat the F. Vladimir must then eat the O for a snack. Eliminating O and F from Wendy's options, and O from Vladimir's options results in the following diagram:

B L D S⁴
F H M O P⁵

S:	O	F	(F, O)
D:	___	H/M	(F, H, M, O)
L:	___	O	(F, H, M, O)
B:	P/H	H/P	(H, P, O)
	V ←—┼—→ W		

Question #13: Global, Must Be True. The correct answer choice is (E)

As noted in the setup discussion, because Wendy orders an O for lunch, she only has the option of F for a snack. Accordingly, answer choice (E) is correct.

Question #14: Global, Must Be True. The correct answer choice is (D)

Because Wendy must have F for a snack (as discussed in question #13), Vladimir must have O for a snack. Accordingly, answer choice (D) is correct.

Question #15: Local, Could Be True. The correct answer choice is (D)

The condition in the question stem establishes that both Vladimir and Wendy eat M. Wendy's only opportunity to eat M comes at dinner, and so she must eat M then. This means that Vladimir cannot eat M at dinner (from the first rule), and thus his only opportunity to eat M is at lunch. This then limits some of Vladimir's options at dinner, leading to the following diagram:

```
S:     O            F

D:    F/H           M

L:     M            O

B:    P/H          H/P
       V   ◄——┼——►  W
```

Accordingly, answer choice (D) could be true and is correct.

Question #16: Local, Could Be True. The correct answer choice is (B)

The condition in the question stem forces Wendy to eat H for dinner, and from the second rule we can then infer that Wendy eats P for breakfast. When she eats P for breakfast, Vladimir cannot eat P, and he must eat H, leading to the following diagram:

```
S:     O            F

D:    M/F           H

L:    F/M           O

B:     H            P
       V   ◄——┼——►  W
```

Accordingly, answer choice (B) could be true and is correct.

Question #17: Local, Cannot Be True. The correct answer choice is (B)

If Wendy has P for breakfast, then Vladimir cannot have P for breakfast due to the first rule, and he must have H. Once he has H for breakfast, he cannot have H at any other meal:

```
S:     O            F

D:    M/F          H/M

L:    F/M           O

B:     H            P
       V   ◄——┼——►  W
```

Accordingly, answer choice (B) cannot be true and is correct.

This is an Advanced Linear: Balanced, Identify the Possibilities game.

This is a challenging game made considerably easier by applying the right technique, which, in this case, is to identify each of the possibilities. Some of the "hardest" games on the LSAT are best attacked with this technique, and once the correct technique is applied, the game no longer seems as difficult. An examination of all LSAT games makes it clear that the test makers expect you to have the ability to identify "limited solution set" scenarios when they occur. In this game, there are a large number of rules, and so it is not surprising that there would be some powerful inferences. Let's look at each rule and develop the case for showing the possibilities.

The basic structure of the game from the scenario is as follows:

J K L M N O P R ^{8}

```
4   ___      ___

3   ___      ___

2   ___      ___

1   ___      ___
     X        Y
```

The first rule establishes that J and K are on the same team. Normally this would be a represented as a vertical JK block, but the second and fourth rules establish that K and N are on different teams, and that N is on team Y (along with M). Thus, accounting for the interaction of the first, second, and fourth rules, J and K are on team X, and N and M are on team Y:

```
4   ___          ___

3   ___          ___

2   ___          ___

1   ___          ___
 J K⟶X        Y⟵M N
```

The third rule indicates that R runs in an earlier leg than P:

$$
\begin{array}{c}
P \\
\lor \\
R
\end{array}
$$

From this rule, we can infer that R can never run the fourth leg, and P can never run the first leg:

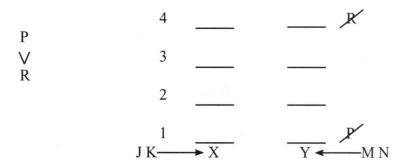

```
          4   ___     ___  R̸
  P
  V       3   ___     ___
  R
          2   ___     ___

          1   ___     ___  P̸
           J K——→X    Y←——M N
```

The fifth rule establishes two more Not Laws, this time for J and M on the third leg:

```
          4   ___     ___  R̸
  P
  V       3   ___     ___  J̸ M̸
  R
          2   ___     ___

          1   ___     ___  P̸
           J K——→X    Y←——M N
```

The sixth rule stipulates that K and L run second. We have already established that K is on team X, so L must be on team Y:

```
          4   ___     ___  R̸
  P
  V       3   ___     ___  J̸ M̸
  R
          2    K       L

          1   ___     ___  P̸
           J K——→X    Y←——M N L
```

The seventh and final rule indicates that O runs fourth:

At this point, most students continue on to the questions. But, there are more inferences to be made, and these inferences come from examining the most restricted open spot on the diagram: the third leg. From the fifth rule, the third leg cannot be run by J or M. But, because of the other rules, we can also eliminate K, L, and O from running third. Thus, J, M, K, L, and O cannot run the third leg, leaving only N, P, and R available to run third. But, from the third rule, R must run an earlier leg than P, which means that both P and R cannot run third simultaneously. By Hurdling the Uncertainty then, we can infer that N must run third. And, from the fourth rule, we know that N is on team Y. Thus, N must run third for team Y, and P or R must run third for team X:

That N must run third for team Y is the key inference of the game, and it destroys questions #21, #22, and #23.

While making the inference that N is third is critical for success in this game, there are additional inferences to be made, namely on the first leg. From the third rule, P can never run first, and from the other inferences and rules K, L, M, and O can also be eliminated from running first. With those five people eliminated, only J, M, and R can run the first leg. As J is on team X and M is on team Y, we can infer that J or R must run first for team X, and M or R must run first for team Y.

In evaluating this setup, three of the people are placed, and every other position has either a dual-option or split-option. Clearly, the game has significant inherent limitations, which suggests that the best approach is to Identify the Possibilities.

There are four possibilities: two when O is on team X, and two when O is on team Y:

Possibility #1: O on Team X, P runs the third leg

When O is on team X and P runs the third leg on team X, then J must run the first leg on team X (that is the only available space on team X for J) and R must run the first leg on team Y, forcing M to run the fourth leg on team Y:

4	O	M
3	P	N
2	K	L
1	J	R
	X	Y

Possibility #2: O on Team X, P runs the fourth leg

When O is on team X and P runs the fourth leg on team Y, then R must run the third leg on team X. J must run the first leg on team X and M must run the first leg on team Y:

4	O	P
3	R	N
2	K	L
1	J	M
	X	Y

Possibility #3: O on Team Y, P runs the third leg

When O is on team Y and P runs the third leg on team X, then M must run the first leg on team Y (that is the only available space on team Y for M). R must then run the first leg on team X, and J must run the fourth leg on team X:

4	J	O
3	P	N
2	K	L
1	R	M
	X	Y

Possibility #4: O on Team Y, P runs the fourth leg

When O is on team Y and P runs the fourth leg on team X, then M must run the first leg on team Y (that is the only available space on team Y for M). R must then run the third leg on team X, and J must run the first leg on team X:

4	P	O
3	R	N
2	K	L
1	J	M
	X	Y

With these four possibilities in hand, the questions can be solved quickly.

Question #18: Global, Must Be True. The correct answer choice is (A)

As shown in Possibilities #1 and #2, when J and O are assigned to the same team, J must run first. Thus, answer choice (A) is correct.

Question #19: Local, Could Be True. The correct answer choice is (D)

R is assigned to team X in Possibilities #2, #3, and #4. In those possibilities she runs first and third, and so answer choice (D) is correct.

Note that even without the possibilities, once you determined that K runs second on team X, and that therefore R could never run second on team X, that would eliminate answer choices (B), (C), and (E), each of which contain the second leg as a possibility.

Question #20: Local, Must Be True. The correct answer choice is (E)

O and R are on the same team only in Possibility #2. In that Possibility, P runs fourth, and so answer choice (E) is correct.

Question #21: Global, Could Be True, Except. The correct answer choice is (C)

As discussed during the setup, N must always run third, and so answer choice (C) cannot be true and is thus correct.

Question #22: Local, Must Be True. The correct answer choice is (C)

As discussed during the setup, N must always run third, and so answer choice (C) is always true regardless of the local condition, and therefore (C) is correct.

Question #23: Global, Could Be True, Except. The correct answer choice is (B)

As discussed during the setup, N must always run third, and so answer choice (B) cannot be true and is thus correct.

Question #24: Local, Must Be True. The correct answer choice is (B)

P and J are on the same team and P runs third only under Possibilities #1 and #3. In both of those possibilities, R runs first (once for team X, and once for team Y), and so answer choice (B) must be true and is correct.

17

POWERSCORE®

18

PREPTEST

DECEMBER 1992 LOGIC GAMES SETUPS

This is a Defined-Fixed, Balanced Grouping game.

This is a very tricky game, and most students set the game up by focusing on the three cities. However, the last rule leads to the key inference of this game. Take a moment to re-examine that rule. Most students do not completely grasp the meaning behind this rule, but *any* rule that addresses the numbers in a game will be important and must be completely understood. If each student visits one of the cities with another student, then the minimum group size is two. With only five students, we can deduce that there are only two groups of students in this game: one group of two students, and another group of three students. These two groups control the game, and they also show that only two of the three of the cities can be visited.

With the two groups established, we can analyze the grouping rules in the game and make inferences.

Because S and P must visit different cities, they must be in different groups. Thus, although we do not know which group S or P is in, they occupy a space in each group. This fact affects the H and R block (who says the makers of the LSAT don't have a sense of humor?), because there is not enough room in the group of two for the HR block. Thus, H and R must be in the group of three, and L must be in the group of two:

H L P R S ^{5}

$$\frac{R}{}$$

$$\frac{H}{} \qquad \frac{L}{}$$

$$\frac{P/S}{3} \qquad \frac{S/P}{2}$$

Adding in a few of the other rules and showing the three cities leads to the final diagram:

H L P R S ^{5}

With this powerful information, we are ready for the questions.

Question #1: Global, Could Be True. The correct answer choice is (C)

Answer choice (A) is incorrect because of the HR block required by the second rule and because L must be in the group of two. The numerical distribution constraints dictate two groups of students, each made up of either two or three students, which proves answer choice (B) to be incorrect. Answer choice (D) is incorrect because L never visits Vancouver, and answer choice (E) is prohibited by the first rule. Thus, answer choice (C) is correct.

Question #2: Local, Could Be True. The correct answer choice is (D)

The new rule provided by this question dictates that S must join H, who is already part of the HR block. Therefore, in this question there is now an HRS block, which means that the other group is made up of L and P. Recognizing the composition of these two groups allows us to rule out answer choices (A), (B), and (C). And Paul is travelling with Lori, who must visit either Montreal or Toronto, so answer choice (E) cannot be correct. Answer choice (D), however, could be true and therefore is the correct answer choice.

Question #3: Local, Must Be True. The correct answer choice is (D)

If S visits Vancouver, then S cannot be in the group of two since L cannot visit Vancouver. Hence, S must visit Vancouver with H and R, and L and P must visit either Montreal or Toronto:

$$
\begin{array}{cc}
\underline{\quad R \quad} & \\
\underline{\quad H \quad} & \underline{\quad L \quad} \\
\underline{\quad S \quad} & \underline{\quad P \quad} \\
V & M/T
\end{array}
$$

This scenario confirms that answer choice (D) is the correct answer choice. Note that this question can be quite challenging if you miss the 3-2 numerical distribution that is at the heart of this game.

Question #4: Global, Not Necessarily True, FTT. The correct answer choice is (A)

For this question, the correct answer choice will be the one that is Not Necessarily True, and the four incorrect answer choices all Must be True.

If P visits Vancouver, S cannot visit Vancouver, but still has the options of visiting either Montreal or Toronto. Since S would not necessarily have to go to Montreal, answer choice (A) is the correct answer choice.

Answer choice (B) is dictated by the fourth and second rules, respectively, so it must be true, and it is therefore incorrect. Answer choice (C) must be true as discussed in the game setup, and therefore answer choice (C) is incorrect. Answer choices (D) and (E) are also proven as true by the discussion of the 3-2 distribution, and therefore both answers are incorrect.

Question #5: Local, Could Be True. The correct answer choice is (C)

If R visits Toronto, then of course she must be joined by H and either S or P. Since L then cannot visit Toronto, from the second rule she must visit Montreal, and she must be joined by either P or S (whoever is not travelling with the HR block).

The rule provided by this question stem therefore creates the following local diagram:

$$
\begin{array}{cc}
 & \underline{\text{P/S}} \\
\underline{\text{S/P}} & \underline{\text{H}} \\
\underline{\text{L}} & \underline{\text{R}} \\
\text{M} & \text{T}
\end{array}
$$

According to this diagram, answer choice (C) is the only choice that could be true.

Question #6: Global, Must Be True. The correct answer choice is (E)

Answer choice (A) is incorrect, because L has the option of travelling to Toronto with either P or S, even if the other block travels to Montreal. Answer choice (B) is incorrect for basically the same reason: Montreal can be visited by the group composed of the HR block and either S or P. The local template created by question #3 disproves answer choices (C) and (D). This leaves answer choice (E), which is the correct answer choice: If anyone is to visit Vancouver, it cannot be L (because of the third rule), so the only way that anyone can visit Vancouver is for the group to be made up of the HR block and either S or P.

This is a Basic Linear: Balanced, Identify the Templates game.

There are six folders in numerical order, so they should be the base of the game. Instead of creating multiple stacks for the courses and for the times, instead simply combine the times and courses and create six unique variables: FM, FN, FO, SM, SN, and SO. In accordance with the first rule, these six variables can then be placed into the six folders, creating a Basic Linear: Balanced game. When the second and third rules are internally diagrammed, we get the following basic structure for the game:

FM FN FO SM SN SO ^{6}

$$\underline{\hspace{1cm}}\ \underline{\hspace{1cm}}\quad\underline{\hspace{1cm}}\ \underline{\hspace{1cm}}\quad\underline{\hspace{1cm}}\ \underline{\hspace{1cm}}$$
$$1\longleftrightarrow2\quad3\longleftrightarrow4\quad5\qquad6$$

However, there is a further inference to be made. If folders 1 and 2 contain the same subject, then there are only two subjects remaining for the four folders (spring and fall of each subject means four course offerings). Because folders 3 and 4 contain different subjects, we can then infer that folders 5 and 6 must also contain different subjects:

FM FN FO SM SN SO ^{6}

$$\underline{\hspace{1cm}}\ \underline{\hspace{1cm}}\quad\underline{\hspace{1cm}}\ \underline{\hspace{1cm}}\quad\underline{\hspace{1cm}}\ \underline{\hspace{1cm}}$$
$$1\longleftrightarrow2\quad3\longleftrightarrow4\quad5\longleftrightarrow6$$

This inference is tested in question #12.

The fourth and fifth rules establish a dual-option for FM and SO on folders 1 and 4, and the sixth rule establishes an SN Not Law on folder 5:

FM FN FO SM SN SO ^{6}

$$\overset{\text{FM/SO}}{\underline{\hspace{1cm}}}\ \underline{\hspace{1cm}}\quad\underline{\hspace{1cm}}\ \overset{\text{SO/FM}}{\underline{\hspace{1cm}}}\quad\underline{\hspace{1cm}}\ \underline{\hspace{1cm}}$$
$$1\longleftrightarrow2\quad3\longleftrightarrow4\quad5\longleftrightarrow6$$
$$\cancel{SN}$$

The second, third, fourth, and fifth rules are so restrictive that they suggest that there are a limited number of solutions to this game. The best approach then, is to create two templates based on the dual-options in folders 1 and 4.

<u>Template #1: FM in folder 1, SO in folder 4</u>

In this template, SM must be in folder 2 according to the second rule. Folder 3 must contain either SN or FN, and because SN cannot be in folder 5 according to the last rule, SN is in folder 3 or 6

Template #1: $\underset{1\longleftrightarrow2}{\underline{\text{FM}\quad\text{SM}}}\quad\underset{3\longleftrightarrow4}{\underline{\text{SN/FN}\quad\text{SO}}}\quad\underset{5\underset{\cancel{\text{SN}}}{\longleftrightarrow}6}{\underline{\qquad\quad/\text{SN}}}$ (SN, FN, FO)

<u>Template #2: FM in folder 4, SO in folder 1</u>

In this template, FO must be in folder 2 according to the second rule. Folder 3 must contain either SN or FN, and because SN cannot be in folder 5 according to the last rule, SN is in folder 3 or 6:

Template #2: $\underset{1\longleftrightarrow2}{\underline{\text{SO}\quad\text{FO}}}\quad\underset{3\longleftrightarrow4}{\underline{\text{SN/FN}\quad\text{FM}}}\quad\underset{5\underset{\cancel{\text{SN}}}{\longleftrightarrow}6}{\underline{\qquad\quad/\text{SN}}}$ (SN, FN, SM)

With these two templates, the game is easy to attack.

Question #7: Global, Could Be True, List. The correct answer choice is (D)

Answer choice (A) is incorrect because, among other reasons, SO must be in folder 1 or 4 according to the fifth rule.

Answer choice (B) is incorrect because FM or SO must be in folder 1 according to the fourth and fifth rules.

Answer choice (C) is incorrect because FM or SO must be in folder 1 according to the fourth and fifth rules.

Answer choice (D) is the correct answer choice, and it is the only answer that provides an order which aligns with one of our two templates (Template #2 above).

Answer choice (E) is incorrect because according to the third rule, folder 3 and folder 4 must have different subjects.

Question #8: Global, Cannot Be True, FTT. The correct answer choice is (A)

Answer choice (A) is the correct answer choice, because, as the templates above reflect, folder 3 must always contain either SN or FN.

18

Question #9: Local, Could Be True. The correct answer choice is (B)

This question stem refers us to Template #2. This immediately eliminates answer choice (A), (C), and (E). It also eliminates answer choice (D) because if SN is not in folder 3 or 6, then it must be in folder 5, a violation of the sixth rule.

Answer choice (B) is possible under the following hypothetical:

$$\underset{1 \longleftrightarrow 2}{\underline{\text{SO} \quad \text{FO}}} \quad \underset{3 \longleftrightarrow 4}{\underline{\text{SN} \quad \text{FM}}} \quad \underset{5 \longleftrightarrow 6}{\underline{\text{FN} \quad \text{SM}}}$$

Thus, answer choice (B) is correct.

Question #10: Global, Could Be True. The correct answer choice is (D)

Under Template #2, it is possible for SO to be in folder 1 and FO to be in folder 2. Thus, answer choice (D) is correct.

Question #11: Local, Must Be True. The correct answer choice is (B)

To respond to this question we should again refer to Template #2. If FO is in folder 2, the other folders whose contents are specifically dictated are folder 1 (SO), and folder 4 (FM). Thus the contents of exactly two of the remaining five folders can be deduced, and the correct answer choice is (B).

Question #12: Global, Must Be True. The correct answer choice is (E)

As mentioned in the game setup, folders 5 and 6 must have different subjects. Hence, answer choice (E) is correct.

Question #13: Global, Could Be True. The correct answer choice is (C)

Answer choice (C) is the correct answer because folder 6 could also contain SM or FO (this is also shown in the hypothetical in question #9). None of the remaining answer choices are allowed by either template.

This is a Mapping—Spatial Relations game.

The five rules in the game produce the following map of the subway connections:

L1: R-T-F-S-U-Q-P-R

L2: T-S

L3: R-U

L4: Q-G-R

L5: Q-T

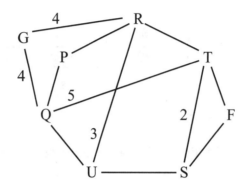

Note that your map of the connections does not have to appear exactly as above. Your map could have R on the bottom and S and U on the top, for example. The only things that must be emulated are the exact connections above.

Note also that the lines connecting each station do not have arrows because travel goes in either direction on a line. Additionally, there is no concern over L3 and L5 "crossing" above as there is no rule prohibiting the lines from crossing (this element is something you must always track in Mapping games).

Intermediate stops are any stops between two points. For example, a traveler going from Urstine to French taking the shortest route on L1 would make an intermediate stop at Semplain.

With the map above, and a clear understanding of how the connections operate, we are ready to attack the questions.

Question #14: Local, Must Be True. The correct answer choice is (C)

Only four stations—T, P, U, and G—can be reached directly from Rincon without any intermediate stops. Thus, answer choice (C) is correct.

Question #15: Local, Must Be True, Minimum. The correct answer choice is (C)

The question stem imposes two criteria: fewest lines and fewest stops. The only route that fits the criteria is G-Q-U-S, which involves 2 intermediate stops and the use of only two: lines, L1 and L4. Although several other routes also contain only two intermediate stops, they involve the use of three lines: G-R-T-S, G-Q-T-S, and G-R-U-S. Thus, since the only route that fits the criteria in the question stem is G-Q-U-S, answer choice (C) is correct.

Question #16: Local, Must Be True, Minimum, List. The correct answer choice is (A)

Given the criteria in the question stem, any of the following routes would suffice for a traveler going from Urstine and Rincon: U-S-T-R, U-Q-G-R, U-Q-P-R, and U-Q-T-R. The last route is reflected in answer choice (A), which is correct.

Question #17: Local, Must Be True, Minimum. The correct answer choice is (C)

Either F-T-Q-G or F-T-R-G satisfies the criteria in the question stem. Thus, the correct answer is two, and answer choice (C) is correct.

Question #18: Local, Must Be True, Minimum. The correct answer choice is (E)

There are three routes that satisfy the criteria in the question stem: S-T-Q-P, S-T-R-P, and S-U-R-P. As R or T or both appears in each of the possible routes, answer choice (E) is correct.

Question #19: Local, Must Be True. The correct answer choice is (A)

The question stem adds the condition that all stations must be connected by two or more lines. Thus, examine the map for the stations currently connected by only one line:

F: connected currently only by line 1

P: connected currently only by line 1

G: connected currently only by line 4

Thus, the correct answer must include all three of the stations above, and consequently answer choice (A) is correct.

This is a Grouping: Partially Defined game.

This is an interesting Grouping game in that movement from one sub-group to another depends on the ability to obtain votes. The game scenario contains a considerable amount of information about the promotion process, including:

> At least one assistant and one associate are promoted each year.

> An assistant is promoted when a majority of both associates and partners votes for promotion.

> An associate is promoted when a majority partners votes for promotion.

> Every eligible voter (partners and associates) votes in each promotion review.

The rules are fairly simple grouping rules, and can be represented as follows:

Part: H R ^{2}
Assoc: O ^{1}
Assis: G J L S T W ^{6}

$$O \longrightarrow \cancel{G}, \cancel{J}, \cancel{T}$$

$$R \longrightarrow \cancel{L}, \cancel{S}$$

$$H \longrightarrow \cancel{J}, \cancel{W}$$

Based on the scenario information and the rules, several inferences can be made:

> 1. J cannot be promoted this year because both O and H will not vote for him.

> 2. O must be promoted this year because he is the only associate.

With this information, we are ready to attack the questions.

Question #20: Global, Could Be True, List. The correct answer choice is (E)

Answer choice (A) is incorrect because J cannot be promoted this year.

Answer choice (B) is incorrect because O must be promoted this year.

Answer choice (C) is incorrect because S cannot be promoted two ranks during one promotion period.

Answer choice (D) is incorrect because at least one assistant must be promoted to associate.

Answer choice (E) is the correct answer.

Question #21: Local, Could Be True, List. The correct answer choice is (D)

The question stem specifies that the associates are under examination. As J cannot receive a majority of votes, answer choice (B) can be eliminated.

As O must be promoted during this year's review, O cannot be on the roster, and thus answer choice (E) can be eliminated.

The remaining incorrect answer choices can be eliminated by examining the votes. O will not vote for G or T (or J, of course), and thus, for G or T to be promoted, G or T would need two votes total from R and H. While the combination of R's and H's votes promotes O, the total vote tally leaves G with one vote and T with no votes. Thus, neither can be promoted, and answer choices (A) and (C) (and (E)) can be eliminated. The correct answer choice is (D).

Question #22: Local, Must Be True, Minimum. The correct answer choice is (B)

The best voting result J can hope for this year is two votes against and one vote for. Since promotion requires a majority vote, to be promoted J needs 2 more "for" votes (to get to a 3-2 majority). Any assistant promoted to associate is a voting member, and thus answer choice (B) is correct.

Question #23: Global, Must Be True. The correct answer choice is (E)

Because there are currently six assistants, and one must be promoted this year, at most there will be five assistants next year. Because at least one assistant must be promoted next year, at most there will be four assistants after next year's review. It follows that answer choice (E) is correct.

Question #24: Global, Must Be True, Minimum. The correct answer choice is (B)

Currently there is one associate, O. O must be promoted to partner this year, and at a minimum one assistant must be promoted, who in a sense "replaces" O. The same situation applies next year, where to minimize the number of associates the one associate would be promoted, but then be replaced by the minimum of one assistant that must be promoted. Thus, the correct answer is one, which is answer choice (B).

18

POWERSCORE®

19 PREPTEST

JUNE 1996 LOGIC GAMES SETUPS

This is a Basic Linear: Balanced game.

Variables: F G H J Q R [5]

$$\quad * $$

F $\longrightarrow$ 1 or 6

$$\frac{F/}{1} \quad \frac{}{2} \quad \frac{}{3} \quad \frac{}{4} \quad \frac{}{5} \quad \frac{/F}{6}$$

J > [Q R]

$$\underset{\cancel{Q}}{\overset{\cancel{R}}{}} \quad \underset{}{\overset{\cancel{R}}{}} \qquad\qquad \underset{}{\overset{\cancel{J}}{}} \quad \underset{\cancel{Q}}{\overset{\cancel{J}}{}}$$

$$G_3 \longrightarrow Q_5$$
$$\cancel{Q}_5 \longrightarrow \cancel{G}_3$$

The great benefit of doing Balanced games is that as you use a variable, that variable is eliminated from the list and can no longer be used; when you fill a space, that space is unavailable to all other variables. In contrast, Unbalanced games have variables that can sometimes be used again, and sometimes a space can contain two or more variables. This tends to make things much more confusing as all of the variables could be used again even if already placed once, and spaces that contain a single variable might still be able to accommodate another.

The first thing that jumps out regarding the rules is the linkage that can be made between the second and third rule. This allows us to make a JQR super rule that yields six Not Laws (if you are unsure why a particular Not Law is given, attempt to place the variable in that space and observe the consequences. This should help you better understand why certain Not Laws appear). Furthermore, since Q appears in both the super rule and the last rule, we can make the following inference:

> If G is inspected on day 3, then Q is inspected on day 5 and R is inspected on day 6. Since R is inspected on day 6, F must be inspected on day 1. This inference leads to the further inference that only two possible scenarios exist when G is inspected on day 3: F-H-G-J-Q-R or F-J-G-H-Q-R.

The other issue to consider is the interaction between F and the Not Laws. If F is inspected first, then the Not Laws shift over one space, and R and Q cannot be inspected second, and R cannot be inspected third. The same logic in reverse can be applied to F in 6.

Question #1: Global, Could Be True, List. The correct answer choice is (B)

This is a Global, Could Be True, List question, so apply the proper technique! Generally, the first rule to apply is one that can be seen easily from a visual perspective. In this case you have the choice of several rules that fit that criterion. Let us start with the rule that states F is inspected on either day 1 or day 6. Applying this rule eliminates answer choice (D). Next, apply the rule that states that Q must be inspected the day before R is inspected. This eliminates answer choice (C). Now apply the rules that states that J is inspected on an earlier day than Q is inspected. This eliminates answer choice (A). Now we are down to answer choices (B) and (E). By applying the last rule about G in 3, we can eliminate answer choice (E), and thus answer choice (B) must be the correct answer.

Question #2: Global, Cannot Be True. The correct answer choice is (E)

This question has been phrased in terms of falsity. Remember, always convert "false" questions into terms of "true." As discussed in Lesson Two, "must be false" is identical to "cannot be true," and so this question simply asks which one of the following cannot be true. In Global Cannot Be True questions, always look to your Not Laws first for an answer since Not Laws reflect which variables have global restrictions. In this case, our initial Not Laws tell us that answer choice (E) must be correct since R can never be inspected on day 2. Remember, Global Cannot Be True questions and Global Must Be True questions lend themselves very well to the use of Not Laws.

Question #3: Global, Cannot Be True. The correct answer choice is (C)

This question is almost the same as #2, except now the focus is specifically on day 5. According to our Not Laws, J cannot be inspected on day 5, and so it must be that answer choice (C) is correct. This is an excellent example of what "attacking the question" means. By using the Not Laws, you should already know what the answer is before looking at the answer choices. Instead of slowly looking at answer choice (A), then (B), and so on, why not immediately look for "J" as one of the choices? This saves time, and more importantly, builds your confidence as you find the answer that you are looking for.

An interesting aside: the worst answer choice for a student to select in this question is answer choice (E). Why? Because from the hypothetical we produced in question #1 we know that R *can* be scheduled for day 5. Even if you cannot figure out which answer was definitely correct in this problem, you could use that hypothetical to kill answer choice (E) and improve your odds of answering correctly. And, although this information is not of very great value on this question, in future games this technique will prove to be very helpful indeed.

Question #4: Global, Could Be True. The correct answer choice is (E)

Since this question focuses specifically on days 3 and 5, again apply the Not Laws from day 3 and day 5. There are none for day 3, but we see that J cannot be inspected on day 5, and so we can kill off answer choice (D), which attempts to place J in day 5. Now, apply linkage to help eliminate more answer choices: Day 3 appears in the question and it also appears in the last rule. Thus, as you should recall, if G is inspected on day 3, then Q must be inspected on day 5. This information is sufficient to eliminate answer choices (A) and (B) since both have G on day 3 but another variable besides Q on day 5. Now we are down to only two remaining answer choices, yet we have only had to do a minimal amount of work. At this point, quickly scan the two remaining answer choices to see if you can identify the correct answer without doing further work. If you cannot, why not use one of the answer choices to help make a hypothetical that will solve the problem? To prove a "Could Be True" answer, all that is needed is one hypothetical that shows that one of the scenarios is possible, or alternately, a hypothetical that shows that one of the scenarios is impossible. Let us try answer choice (C) first. Make the following notation *right beside the problem*:

$$\underline{\quad}\quad\underline{\quad}\quad\underline{H}\quad\underline{\quad}\quad\underline{G}\quad\underline{\quad}$$

Diagramming note: We did not write out the numbers since most people do not need the numbers when they work next to the question. Had this been the main diagram you would most certainly have wanted to write out the number for each space.

As you might see, this scenario presents a problem because there is no room for the QR block. If F is inspected on day 1, there are not two consecutive spaces available for the QR block. If F is inspected on day 6, the only two spaces available for Q and R are days 1 and 2, but that leaves no room for J and so answer choice (C) cannot be correct. By process of elimination this means answer choice (E) must be correct. Notice that we do not need to prove that (E) is possible since we have already eliminated each of the other answer choices. Since the other four are incorrect, answer choice (E) must be correct. Mark it and continue. For those of you wondering if answer choice (E) can fit in a valid solution, here is a hypothetical that fits (E) and fits all of the rules of the game: J-Q-R-G-H-F.

Question #5: Local, Must Be True. The correct answer choice is (D)

The local condition specifies that R is inspected the day before F, which creates this block sequence:

$$J > \boxed{Q\ R\ F}$$

Of course, you should draw out that block sequence right next to the problem. At this point, there are several different ways to proceed with this question. One approach is to check any previous hypothetical to see if it conforms to the requirements in this question. Fortuitously, the only hypothetical we have—from question #1 answer choice (B)—actually conforms to the local condition imposed in this question. Thus, we can use that hypothetical, G-H-J-Q-R-F, to help answer this question. Accordingly, we can eliminate answer choices (C) and (E) since the hypothetical proves that neither *must* be true. Note how the hypothetical partially agrees with answer choices (A), (B), and (D), but it does not prove that they *must* be true.

The other method of attack is to use the linkage involving F. Since F must be in day 1 or day 6, and in this question F is scheduled behind R, we can infer that F must be inspected on day 6. Accordingly, we can make the following hypothetical right next to the problem:

$$\underset{1}{\rule{1.5em}{0.4pt}}\quad \underset{2}{\rule{1.5em}{0.4pt}}\quad \underset{\underset{\cancel{G}}{3}}{\rule{1.5em}{0.4pt}}\quad \underset{4}{\overset{Q}{\rule{1.5em}{0.4pt}}}\quad \underset{5}{\overset{R}{\rule{1.5em}{0.4pt}}}\quad \underset{6}{\overset{F}{\rule{1.5em}{0.4pt}}}$$

Although you may not realize it, this hypothetical solves the problem. If Q, R, and F are already placed, and G cannot be inspected third (that would violate the G3 then Q5 rule), that leaves only H or J to fill day 3. That inference is reflected in the wording of answer choice (D) and thus (D) is correct.

Question #6: Global, Could Be True, List. The correct answer choice is (D)

Note that the question stem asks for a complete and accurate list, and the correct answer must list *all* of the factories that could appear on day 1. So, the correct answer must contain each and every factory that is possible for day 1. As strange as it may sound, the question asks for what must be true about what is possible.

If G and H are to be scheduled as far apart as possible, this would likely place G and H in days 1 and 5 or days 2 and 6 (do not forget that F must be in either day 1 or day 6). Again, there are several ways to approach this question depending on your level of game understanding. At the most advanced level, answer choices (A), (C), and (E) can likely be eliminated since each contains J. If J is inspected on day 1, then F would be inspected on day 6 and G and H would not be as far apart as possible—a violation of the "if" clause in the question. Only F differentiates answer choice (B) from answer choice (D), and since F is a day 1 or day 6 player, it seems likely that answer choice (D) is correct, and in fact it *is* the correct answer. If that type of theoretical analysis makes you a bit nervous, you can always resort to the other form of attack on this question: make a few quick hypotheticals. Here is one that eliminates answer choices (B) and (C): F-G-J-Q-R-H. Another that eliminates answer choice (A) is: G-J-Q-R-H-F. And again, the inclusion of J in answer choice (E) should be a tip-off that answer choice (E) is likely incorrect.

Question #7: Global, Could Be True. The correct answer choice is (C)

The last question in a game is often the most difficult, and that general rule holds true here. Let us take a moment to examine why Law Services so often makes the last question difficult. The key to understanding this phenomenon is to look at it from a psychological perspective. As you near the end of a game, your mind naturally begins to focus on quickly finishing the game at hand and preparing for the next game. At just this point, when you want to go more quickly, Law Services throws in a difficult question. This tends to have the effect of slowing you down considerably, and that usually leads to a degree of frustration. Once you become frustrated, your chances of missing the question increase. And when you go to the next game, you may still be thinking about what happened on the last question, and that can contribute to a poor start on the new game, causing further trouble. In a nutshell, do not forget about the importance of psychology on the test. You must remain positive, focused, and calm throughout each section. If you become upset or frustrated, take a moment to relax and regain your equilibrium.

The local condition in the question stem sets up the following relationship: $J > \boxed{G\ Q\ R}$

This sequential relationship automatically produces several Not Laws:

1	2	3	4	5	6
R̸	R̸	R̸	J̸	J̸	J̸
Q̸	Q̸			G̸	G̸
G̸					Q̸

In addition, the interaction of the last rule and the sequence further establishes that G cannot be inspected on day 3 since it would then be impossible for Q to be inspected on day 5 (in this question if G is inspected on day 3 then R would be inspected on day 5). Also, because of the block produced by the question stem, if G cannot be inspected on day 3, then Q cannot be inspected on day 4 and R cannot be inspected on day 5. Using these inferences and the Not Laws above, we can eliminate answer choices (A), (D), and (E) from consideration. At this point, unless you see what distinguishes answer choice (B) from answer choice (C), the best strategy would probably be to try a quick hypothetical using either answer choice. As it turns out, answer choice (B) is incorrect, since if H is inspected on day 6 the following impossible scenario results:

F	J	G	Q	R	H
1	2	3	4	5	6

As shown above, G is inspected on day 3, but Q is not inspected on day 5—a violation of the last rule. By process of elimination, answer choice (C) is proven correct.

Some students question whether answer choice (C) can be valid since it leads to a solution (F-J-H-G-Q-R) where Q is inspected on day 5 but G is not inspected on day 3. Remember, the conditional rule only activates if G is inspected on day 3. If Q is inspected on day 5, nothing necessarily happens (to think otherwise would be a Mistaken Reversal).

PrepTest 19. June 1996 Game #2: *8. B 9. C 10. A 11. A 12. C*

This is an Advanced Linear: Balanced, Numerical Distribution, Identify the Templates game.

The game scenario creates a five day linear scenario:

L L P P R R S S [8]

$$\overline{\quad}\ \overline{\quad}\ \overline{\quad}\ \overline{\quad}\ \overline{\quad}$$
$$\;\text{M}\quad\text{Tu}\quad\text{W}\quad\text{Th}\quad\text{F}$$

The first rule establishes that the two days of each workshop are consecutive, resulting in four blocks:

| LL | | PP | | RR | | SS |

The second rule establishes that on each of the five days, there is a minimum of one workshop and a maximum of two workshops. This results in an unfixed 2-2-2-1-1 numerical distribution.

The third rule creates a sequencing relationship:

$$\boxed{\text{LL}} > \text{- - - - - - - -}\ \begin{array}{c}\boxed{\text{PP}}\\[4pt]\boxed{\text{RR}}\end{array}$$

While this rule creates several Not Laws, the better decision here is to bypass showing the Not Laws, and use the information in the three rules to Identify the Templates. Based on the position of LL, only two major templates exist:

Template #1: LL on Tuesday-Wednesday:

When LL is in session on Tuesday-Wednesday, Both PP and RR must be in session on Thursday-Friday. SS, the only remaining unplaced workshop, must then be on Monday-Tuesday because Monday must have a workshop in session:

1 possibility:

	S		R	R
S	L	L	P	P
M	Tu	W	Th	F

Template #2: LL on Monday-Tuesday:

When LL is in session on Monday-Tuesday, there are a greater number of possibilities. PP and RR can be in session only on Wednesday, Thursday, and Friday, so no matter what configuration they are in, they will each be in session on Thursday, and their "remainder" will be in session on Wednesday or else on Friday (this is the Overlap Principle at work):

$$
\begin{array}{ccccc}
 & & \text{R/} & \underline{\text{R}} & \text{/R} \\
\underline{\text{L}} & \underline{\text{L}} & \text{P/} & \text{P} & \text{/P} \\
\text{M} & \text{Tu} & \text{W} & \text{Th} & \text{F}
\end{array}
$$

Because Thursday must have a P and an R session, S cannot be in session on Thursday (that would lead to three sessions on Thursday, a violation of the second rule). That also means that S cannot be in session on Friday. Thus, S must be in session on Monday-Tuesday, or Tuesday-Wednesday, leading to two more templates:

Template #2A: LL on Monday-Tuesday, SS on Monday-Tuesday:

When SS is on Monday-Tuesday, then one of P or R must be on Wednesday, and the other must be on Friday in order to conform to the second rule. Both P and R can never both be Wednesday-Thursday because that would leave Friday without a workshop.

2 possibilities:

$$
\begin{array}{ccccc}
\underline{\text{S}} & \underline{\text{S}} & & \underline{\text{R}} & \\
\underline{\text{L}} & \underline{\text{L}} & \text{P/R} & \text{P} & \text{R/P} \\
\text{M} & \text{Tu} & \text{W} & \text{Th} & \text{F}
\end{array}
$$

Template #2B: LL on Monday-Tuesday, SS on Tuesday-Wednesday:

When SS is on Tuesday-Wednesday, P and R could both be on Thursday-Friday, or one could be Wednesday-Thursday and the other could be Thursday-Friday.

3 possibilities:

$$
\begin{array}{ccccc}
 & & \underline{\text{S}} & \underline{\text{R}} & \\
\underline{\text{L}} & \underline{\text{L}} & \text{S} & \text{P} & \underline{} \\
\text{M} & \text{Tu} & \text{W} & \text{Th} & \text{F}
\end{array}
$$

Template #1, Template #2A, and Template #2B capture all six of the possibilities in this game, and with them (or any variation, such as two main templates instead of three), the questions are relatively easy.

Question #8: Global, Could Be True. The correct answer choice is (B)

Answer choice (A) is incorrect because there must be two workshops on Thursday.

Answer choice (B) is the correct answer choice. Friday could have one or two workshops.

Answer choice (C) is incorrect because the earliest R could occur is Wednesday.

Answer choice (D) is incorrect because S can only occur Monday-Wednesday.

Answer choice (E) is incorrect because if R and P are both on Wednesday then no workshop will be scheduled for Friday.

Question #9: Global, Could Be True. The correct answer choice is (C)

Answer choice (A) is incorrect because from the third rule R must be after L.

Answer choice (B) is incorrect because Thursday always has two workshops.

Answer choice (C) is the correct answer choice. This could be true from Template #1.

Answer choice (D) is incorrect because Thursday always has two workshops.

Answer choice (E) is incorrect because from the third rule P must be after L.

Question #10: Local, Must Be True. The correct answer choice is (A)

P can be in session on Wednesday only under Templates #2A and #2B. In both cases, L must be on Monday and Tuesday (L is scheduled before P). Thus, answer choice (A) is the correct answer.

Question #11: Local, Cannot Be True, FTT. The correct answer choice is (A)

If P is the only workshop on Friday, then R must be scheduled for Wednesday and Thursday. This means that L is scheduled on Monday and Tuesday (L is ahead of R), and answer choice (A) cannot be true and is therefore correct.

Question #12: Local, Could Be True. The correct answer choice is (C)

If L is the only workshop on Monday (Template #2B) then S must be on Tuesday and Wednesday. That means that one of either P or R could be scheduled on Wednesday with S, or P and R could both be scheduled for Thursday and Friday. Since it could be true that S is the only workshop scheduled for Wednesday, answer choice (C) is correct.

This is a Grouping: Defined-Fixed, Balanced game.

The game scenario establishes that eight people—three adults and five children—will be assigned to two groups of four people each:

Adults: F G H [3]
Children: V W X Y Z [5]

$$\underline{\quad} \qquad \underline{\quad}$$

$$\underline{\quad} \qquad \underline{\quad}$$

$$\underline{\quad} \qquad \underline{\quad}$$

$$\underline{\quad} \qquad \underline{\quad}$$
$$\;1 \qquad\qquad 2$$

Because there are only two groups, and every variable must be in one of the two groups, the groups form a two-value system, which plays a major role in the game.

The first rule establishes that each boat is assigned at least one adult, so reserve a space in each boat for F, G, and H:

Adults: F G H [3]
Children: V W X Y Z [5]

$$\underline{\quad} \qquad \underline{\quad}$$

$$\underline{\quad} \qquad \underline{\quad}$$

$$\underline{\quad} \qquad \underline{\quad}$$

$$\text{Adult} = \quad \underline{F/G/H} \qquad \underline{F/G/H}$$
$$\qquad\qquad\quad\; 1 \qquad\qquad\;\; 2$$

The second rule is conditional:

$$F_2 \longrightarrow G_2$$

Of course, because the game is a two-value system, when we take the contrapositive, we can convert the negatives into positives by changing the boat number (if G is not in boat 2, then G must be in boat 1, etc):

$$G_1 \longrightarrow F_1$$

Note that this rule (and its contrapositive) does not imply that F and G are always in the same boat. For example, G could be in boat 2 and F could be in boat 1.

The first two rules can be combined to create two inferences. When F is assigned to boat 2, G is assigned to boat 2, and because there must be an adult in each boat, H must then be assigned to boat 1.

$$F_2 \longrightarrow H_1$$

Similarly, using the contrapositive of the second rule, when G is assigned to boat 1, F is assigned to boat 1, and then H must be assigned to boat 2:

$$G_1 \longrightarrow H_2$$

The contrapositive of these last two inferences, again accounting for the two-value system:

$$H_2 \longrightarrow F_1$$
$$H_1 \longrightarrow G_2$$

The third rule is similar to the second:

$$V_1 \longrightarrow W_2$$

As always, make note of the contrapositive in any two-value system game:

$$W_1 \longrightarrow V_2$$

Note that this rule (and its contrapositive) does not imply that V and W are always in different boats. For example, V could be in boat 2 and W could be in boat 2.

The fourth and final rule indicates that X and Z are in different boats. The best diagram for this rule is to place X/Z dual options on the main diagram, while also noting that Y is a random (while H is not directly named, H is covered under the actions of the first rule):

Adults: F G H ^{3}
Children: V W X Y Z ^{5}
           *

	____	____
	____	____
	X/Z	Z/X
Adult =	F/G/H	F/G/H
	1	2

Combining all of the prior information leads to the final setup:

Adults: F G H ^{3}
Children: V W X Y Z ^{5}
           *

$F_2 \longrightarrow G_2$
$G_1 \longrightarrow F_1$

$F_2 \longrightarrow H_1$
$G_1 \longrightarrow H_2$

$H_2 \longrightarrow F_1$
$H_1 \longrightarrow G_2$

$V_1 \longrightarrow W_2$
$W_1 \longrightarrow V_2$

	____	____
	____	____
	X/Z	Z/X
Adult =	F/G/H	F/G/H
	1	2

Question #13: Global, Could Be True, List. The correct answer choice is (C)

Answer choice (A) is incorrect because all three adults are in boat 1, a violation of the first rule.

Answer choice (B) is incorrect because X and Z are both in boat 2, a violation of the fourth rule.

Answer choice (C) is the correct answer choice.

Answer choice (D) is incorrect because from the third rule, when V is assigned to boat 1, W must be assigned to boat 2.

Answer choice (E) is incorrect because from the contrapositive of the second rule, when G is assigned to boat 1, F must be assigned to boat 1.

Question #14: Local, Could Be True. The correct answer choice is (E)

If F is assigned to boat 2, then from the second rule G must be assigned to boat 2, and from the first rule H must be assigned to boat 1:

	boat 1	boat 2
	___	___
		Z/X
	X/Z	G
Adults =	H	F
	1	2

This information eliminates answer choice (B).

The remaining unassigned people are V, W, and Y. Because of the limited number of remaining spaces in boat 2, V and W can never both be in boat 2, and from the third rule, when one of them is assigned to boat 1, the other is assigned to boat 2. Thus, V and W effectively form a rotating dual-option in boats 1 and 2, and the only remaining space for Y is in boat 1:

	boat 1	boat 2
	Y	W/V
	V/W	Z/X
	X/Z	G
Adults =	H	F
	1	2

Thus, answer choice (E) is correct.

Question #15: Local, Could Be True. The correct answer choice is (C)

If three children are assigned to boat 1, then only one adult is assigned to boat 1, and the other two adults are assigned to boat 2. If only adult is assigned to boat 1, then from the contrapositive of rule 2, that adult cannot be G (otherwise F would also have to be assigned to boat 1). Thus, G must be assigned to boat 2. The other two adults—F and H—then rotate in a dual-option:

	boat 1	boat 2
	___	___
		Z/X
	X/Z	H/F
Adults =	F/H	G
	1	2

As in question #14, the remaining unassigned people are V, W, and Y. Because of the limited number of remaining spaces in boat 2, V and W can never both be in boat 2, and from the third rule, when one of them is assigned to boat 1, the other is assigned to boat 2. Thus, V and W effectively form a rotating dual-option in boats 1 and 2, and the only remaining space for Y is in boat 1:

Y	W/V
V/W	Z/X
X/Z	H/F
Adults = F/H	G
1	2

Answer choices (A) and (D) are both incorrect because they reference pairs of variables in dual-options. Answer choices (B) and (E) each contain Y, a person who is known to be in boat 1. Answer choice (C) is the correct answer as shown by the diagram above.

Question #16: Local, Must Be True. The correct answer choice is (A)

As discussed during the setup, when G is assigned to boat 1, from the contrapositive of the second rule F must be assigned to boat 1. When both G and F are assigned to boat 1, H must be assigned to boat 2 per the first rule. Thus, answer choice (A) is correct.

Question #17: Local, Must Be True. The correct answer choice is (B)

If V and W are assigned to the same boat as each other, then in order to comply with the third rule they must be assigned to boat 2. This leaves room for only one adult on boat 2, and so two adults must be assigned to boat 1:

	W
X/Z	V
	Z/X
Adults =	
1	2

Because the second rule stipulates that when F is assigned to boat 2 then G is assigned to boat 2, F cannot be in boat 2 because there is not enough room for G as well. Thus, F must be assigned to boat 1. The remaining two adults—G and H—cannot be determined and they form a dual option. Y, the only unassigned person, then fills in the final spot on boat 1:

	Y	W
	X/Z	V
	G/H	Z/X
Adults =	F	H/G
	1	2

F and Y must be assigned to the same boat, and thus answer choice (B) is correct.

Question #18: Local, Must Be True. The correct answer choice is (A)

If H is assigned to a different boat than Y, the following situation results:

	___	___
	X/Z	Z/X
	H/Y	Y/H
Adults =	___	___
	1	2

The remaining unassigned people are F, G, V, and W, which is an interesting set of four variables remaining because those four are all addressed in the second and third rules. As you might imagine, those rules play a role in determining what occurs.

From the second rule, if F is assigned to boat 2, then G is assigned to boat 2. But, under the condition in this question, that would fill boat 2, forcing V and W into boat 1, a violation of the third rule. Thus, F cannot be in boat 2 and must be in boat 1. Thus, answer choice (A) is correct.

Question #19: Local, Must Be True. The correct answer choice is (B)

The question stem in this condition describes a scenario that is identical to the scenario in question #15. Thus, we can refer back to the diagram in that question. In that scenario, G was assigned to boat 2, and thus answer choice (B) is correct.

This is a Grouping: Defined-Fixed, Balanced game.

This game features nine variables being assigned to three fixed groups of three. Thus, the game is Defined-Fixed and Balanced. Games of this type are usually relatively reasonable, and this game is no exception. However, this game presents a challenge because of the large number of negative grouping rules you must remember.

The basic structure of the game appears as follows:

F G H J K L M N P ⁹

___	___	___
___	___	___
___	___	___
O	R	W

The first two rules create grouping relationships. Given that the game is set up as three groups of three, these rules are best shown as vertical blocks:

> [F / G]   [K / M]

Of course, because each block is comprised of two people, and each panel is made up of only three people, the two blocks cannot be assigned to the same panel, a relationship best shown with a double-not arrow:

> [F / G] ←—|—→ [K / M]

The next three rules create negative grouping relationships. Note that in each rule one of the variables also appeared in one of the first two rules. Thus, the blocks from the first two rules should be tied in, and the only way to efficiently do that is with double-not arrows.

Third and fourth rules combined with the first rule:

> [F / G] ←—|—→ P, H, [K / M]

The fifth rule ties in with the second rule:

$$\boxed{\begin{array}{c}K\\M\end{array}} \longleftarrow\!\!\!\!\mid\!\!\!\!\longrightarrow \;J,\; \boxed{\begin{array}{c}F\\G\end{array}}$$

The sixth rule can be diagrammed initially as:

$$\cancel{P}_O \longrightarrow \cancel{H}_O$$

Of course, in a conditional relationship where both conditions are negative, taking the contrapositive removes both negatives, making the rule easier to work with:

$$H_O \longrightarrow P_O$$

Thus, whenever H is assigned to the Oceans panel, P must also be assigned, meaning that neither block can be assigned to the Oceans panel:

$$H_O \longleftarrow\!\!\!\!\mid\!\!\!\!\longrightarrow \boxed{\begin{array}{c}K\\M\end{array}}_O, \boxed{\begin{array}{c}F\\G\end{array}}_O$$

The information above can be combined to form the final diagram for the game:

F G H J K L M N P [9]

$$\boxed{\begin{array}{c}F\\G\end{array}} \;\overset{*\quad *}{\longleftarrow\!\!\!\!\mid\!\!\!\!\longrightarrow}\; P, H, \boxed{\begin{array}{c}K\\M\end{array}}$$

$$\boxed{\begin{array}{c}K\\M\end{array}} \longleftarrow\!\!\!\!\mid\!\!\!\!\longrightarrow J$$

$$\cancel{P}_O \longrightarrow \cancel{H}_O$$

$$H_O \longrightarrow P_O$$

$$H_O \longleftarrow\!\!\!\!\mid\!\!\!\!\longrightarrow \boxed{\begin{array}{c}K\\M\end{array}}_O, \boxed{\begin{array}{c}F\\G\end{array}}_O$$

___	___	___
___	___	___
___	___	___
O	R	W

Question #20: Global, Could Be True, List. The correct answer choice is (E)

In this List question each of the incorrect answer choices can be eliminated by a simple application of the rules:

Answer choice (A) is incorrect because from the second rule K and M must be assigned to the same panel.

Answer choice (B) is incorrect because from the first rule F and G must be assigned to the same panel.

Answer choice (C) is incorrect because from the last rule if H is assigned to Oceans panel then P must also be assigned to the Oceans panel.

Answer choice (D) is incorrect because from the fifth rule J and K cannot be assigned to the same panel.

Thus, answer choice (E) is proven correct by process of elimination.

Question #21: Local, Must Be True. The correct answer choice is (A)

If M and P are both assigned to the Wetlands panel, from the second rule then K must also be assigned to the Wetlands panel. Since P is not assigned to the Oceans panel, via the last rule H cannot be assigned to the Oceans panel. Therefore, H must be assigned to the Recycling panel:

Accordingly, answer choice (A) is correct.

Question #22: Global, Could Be True. The correct answer choice is (C)

The combination of the rules and inferences allows you to eliminate each of the incorrect answers in this Could Be True problem:

Answer choice (A): F and H can never be assigned to the same panel because from the first rule F and G must be assigned to the same panel, and from the fourth rule G cannot be assigned to the same panel as H.

Answer choice (B): G and P can never be assigned to the same panel because from the first rule F and G must be assigned to the same panel, and from the third rule F cannot be assigned to the same panel as P.

Answer choice (D): F and M can never be assigned to the same panel because each is a part of a different block, and there is not enough room in any of the groups to accommodate both blocks.

Answer choice (E): J and M can never be assigned to the same panel because from the second rule K and M must be assigned to the same panel, and from the fifth rule M cannot be assigned to the same panel as J.

Only the two variables in answer choice (C) can be assigned to the same panel as each other (although that panel cannot be the Oceans panel), and thus answer choice (C) is correct.

Question #23: Local, Could Be True. The correct answer choice is (D)

If K and P are both assigned to the Recycling panel, then from the second rule M must also be assigned to the Recycling panel. Since P is not assigned to the Oceans panel, from the last rule it follows that H cannot be assigned to the Oceans panel. Therefore, H must be assigned to the Wetlands panel. Due to the fourth rule the FG block cannot be assigned to the same panel as H, and so the FG block must be assigned to the Oceans panel:

$$
\begin{array}{cccc}
 & P & & \\
\underline{G} & \underline{K} & \underline{\quad} \\
\underline{F} & \underline{M} & \underline{H} \\
O & R & W \\
\cancel{H} & &
\end{array}
$$

The diagram above eliminates every answer choice except answer choice (D), and thus answer choice (D) is correct.

Question #24: Global, Could Be True, Except. The correct answer choice is (A)

This question asks for what Cannot Be True, and thus we can rely on our inferences. As established in the setup, the two blocks created in the first two rules cannot be assigned to the same panel because there is not enough room for all four variables. Thus, answer choice (A), which contains one variable from each block, presents a pair variables that cannot be assigned to the same panel. Answer choice (A) is therefore correct.

Note that answer choice (B) can be proven possible by referring to the correct answer to question #20.

As an aside, note that all four incorrect answer choices contain one random. Because randoms have no restrictions created by the rules, they can often be paired successfully with other variables. Hence, answers containing a random are not the best starting point for your attack. Answer choice (A), not

---

surprisingly, contains variables involved in two different rules, and the combination of those rules creates the restriction that prevents them from being assigned to the same panel.

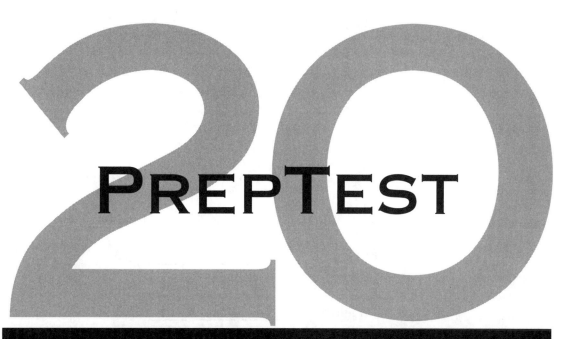

PrepTest 20

October 1996 Logic Games Setups

This is an Advanced Linear: Unbalanced: Underfunded game.

This game is Underfunded because there are only seven variables available to fill nine spaces. Because each traveler can be assigned to only one seat, it follows that two seats will be empty. In order to more gracefully handle these empty spaces, you should create "E" or "X" variables to indicate the two empty spaces (in this case we chose X). This maneuver transforms the game from Unbalanced: Underfunded to Balanced. X is then treated like any other variable:

$$N \; O \; P \; R \; S \; T \; U^7 \; X \; X^9$$

Front row: _____ _____ _____
                   1   2   3

Middle row: _____ _____ _____
                   4   5   6

Last row: _____ _____ _____
                 7   8   9

The first rule is fairly simple, and assigns O to the last row. Consequently, O cannot be in the front or middle row:

Front row: _____ _____ _____ Ø
                   1   2   3

Middle row: _____ _____ _____ Ø
                   4   5   6

Last row: _____ _____ _____
                 7   8   9

The second rule creates a block where P is between R and X:

                             | R P X |
        or
                             | X P R |

When this rule is combined with the first rule, we can infer that this block is never in the last row. More related to this block in a moment.

The third rule is worded in such a way that some students misinterpret the meaning of the rule. Note carefully that the third rule states that R's seat is the *row* behind the row in which N's seat is located. The rule does *not* say that R's seat is the *seat* behind N's seat. Remember, always read closely!

Because the RPX block must be in the row behind N, and O is already in the last row, we can infer that the RPX block will be in the middle row. Consequently, N must be in the front row:

Front row: ___ ___ ___   Ø
                 1   2   3

Middle row: R/X   P   X/R   Ø N̶
                 4   5   6

Last row: ___ ___ ___   N̶
                 7   8   9

At this point, from an abstract standpoint, the first three rules are well represented, and effectively dead from further consideration. The only active rule is the last rule, and you should be expect to be tested multiple times on the application of this rule, which is diagrammed as:

$$\boxed{N/S}$$

$$\boxed{N/U}$$

This last rule produces several Not Laws and inferences:

> Because N must be assigned to the front row, at least one of S and U must be assigned to the last row, and neither S nor U can be assigned seat 2.

> If N is assigned seat 2, then both S and U must be assigned to the last row.

> If S and U is assigned seat 1 or 3, then N must be assigned to the seat at the other end of the row.

The final controlling piece of information is to consider the variables unassigned as of yet: S, T, U, and the other X. These four variables fill the remaining two seats in the front and last rows. Thus, two of these four variables will be assigned to the front row, and the other two will be assigned to the last row.

Combining the information above leads to the final diagram for the game:

NOPRSTU⁷XX⁹
　　　*

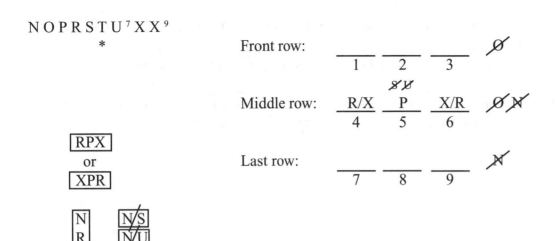

Front row: ___ ___ ___ ~~Ø~~
　　　　　　　 1　 2　 3

Middle row: R/X　P　X/R　~~Ø X~~
　　　　　　　 4　 5　 6

Last row:　 ___ ___ ___ ~~X~~
　　　　　　　 7　 8　 9

RPX
or
XPR

N N/S
R_Row N/U

Question #1: Global, Could Be True, List. The correct answer choice is (A)

This problem can be solved by looking solely at seat 2:

　Answer choice (B) is incorrect because O's seat is in the last row.

　Answer choice (C) is incorrect because, as established in the setup, P's seat is seat 5.

　Answer choice (D) is incorrect because R's seat cannot be in the first row (R must sit in seat 4 or 6).

　Answer choice (E) is incorrect because U cannot be assigned to seat 2.

Accordingly, answer choice (A) is proven correct by process of elimination.

Question #2: Local, Cannot Be True, FTT. The correct answer choice is (A)

If S and U are not assigned seats in the same row, then one of S and U must sit in the front row, and the other must sit in the last row. Because S and U are both involved in the last rule, you should consider the implications of S or U sitting in the first row. As neither S nor U can sit immediately beside N, under the condition of this question stem there is no way for N to sit in seat 2 without violating the last rule. As it cannot be true that N sits in seat 2, answer choice (A) is correct.

Question #3: Local, Could Be True. The correct answer choice is (D)

This question ties in perfectly with question #3. If S and U sit in the same row, from the last rule we can deduce that S and U must sit in the last row (remember, N must sit in the first row and N cannot sit next to either S or U). If S and U sit in the last row, the third seat in that row is occupied by O. As the middle row is occupied by R, P, and X (not necessarily in that order), the front row must be occupied by N, T, and X (again, not necessarily in that order).

From the information above, we know U, S, and O are all seated in the same row, and as they cannot then be next to an empty seat, we can eliminate answer choices (A), (C), and (E).

Answer choice (B) can be eliminated because although R sits in a *row* with an empty seat, P must be in the middle seat, and thus R cannot sit next to the empty seat.

Answer choice (D) is thus correct. T can sit in the front row next to an empty seat (for example, N in seat 1, T in seat 2, and X in seat 3 is one hypothetical that solves this question).

Question #4: Local, Must Be True. The correct answer choice is (A)

In a fortuitous circumstance, this question poses a condition that is met by the hypothetical created in question #3. Thus, we can use that hypothetical to eliminate certain answers such as (B) and (D). However, that said, let us examine this problem as if we did not realize that the hypothetical from question #3 applied to question #4.

If T and X are assigned to the same row (and next to each other), then the other two variables from the S, T, U, X group must be together. Thus, S and U must be in the same row as each other, and we can conclude that S and U must be in the last row (remember, neither can be beside N) and that therefore T and X must be in the front row. Further, from the question stem, T must be seated next to X and another traveler, and so T must be in seat 2. This information is sufficient to prove answer choice (A) correct.

Answer choice (B) is incorrect because if T is assigned to the last row with E, then S and U would be assigned to the first row with N, creating a violation of the last rule.

Answer choice (C) is incorrect because although this could occur in the last row, it does not have to occur. As this is a Must Be True question, this answer is therefore incorrect.

Answer choice (D) is incorrect because O and T must be in different rows, and thus they can never be seated beside each other.

Answer choice (E) is incorrect because although this could occur in the last row, it does not have to occur. As this is a Must Be True question, this answer is therefore incorrect.

Question #5: Local, Must Be True. The correct answer choice is (B)

If O is seated next to X, then from a *row* assignment standpoint the following is known:

Front row: N

Middle row: R, P, X

Last row: O, X

Thus, S, T, and U remain to be assigned to row, and two of those travelers must be assigned to the front row and the other traveler must be assigned to the last row. From the effects of the last rule, we can deduce that both S and U cannot be assigned to the front row. Thus, one of S and U is assigned to the last row, and the remainder of S and U is assigned to the front row, along with T:

Front row: N, T, S/U

Middle row: R, P, X

Last row: O, X, U/S

From the last rule, we know that neither S nor U can be assigned to a seat immediately beside N, and so in the front row T must be assigned to seat 2 (T in the middle seat separates N from the S/U option). Accordingly, answer choice (B) is correct.

This is a Grouping: Defined-Fixed, Unbalanced: Overloaded game.

G L M N P R S W[8]

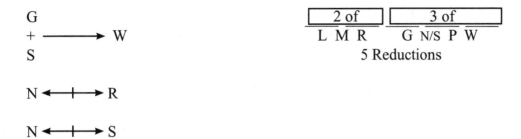

Exactly 2 of L, M, R must be reduced.

The selection of exactly five variables means the game is Defined-Fixed. Since there are eight variables from which to select, the game is Unbalanced: Overloaded.

The second rule bears further analysis. When N is reduced, neither R nor S is reduced, and it can be inferred from the contrapositive that when R or S is reduced, N cannot be reduced. Thus, N and R cannot be reduced together, and N and S cannot be reduced together. Consequently, we have written the rule in two separate parts to fully capture this powerful information.

Because the last rule reserves two of the five spaces, it is the most important one. Any rule that controls the numbers in a game is always important, and this rule is no exception. If two of L, M, and R are reduced, then of the remaining five areas of expenditure—G, N, S, P, and W—exactly three must be reduced. And since N and S cannot be reduced together, the choice is further limited. On the diagram this has been represented with the two blocks. This separation of the variables into two groups is the key to making several powerful inferences:

  1. Because two of the group of L, M, and R must be reduced:

    When L is not reduced, M and R must be reduced.
    When M is not reduced, L and R must be reduced.
    When R is not reduced, L and M must be reduced.

  2. Because three of the group of G, P, W, N/S must be reduced:

    If G is not reduced, then P, W, and N/S must be reduced.
    If P is not reduced, then G, W, and N/S must be reduced.
    If W is not reduced, then G, P, and N/S must be reduced.
        (Later it will be discovered that W must always be reduced so this final
        inference will not be applicable.)

---

3. If G and S are reduced, then W is reduced. Since these three variables fill the reduction allotment of G, N, S, P, and W, it follows that when G and S are reduced, N and P are not reduced:

$$G\,S \longrightarrow W, \cancel{N}, \cancel{P}$$

4. When N is reduced, R and S are not reduced. When R is not reduced, L and M must be reduced. When L and M are reduced, P is not reduced. Thus, when N is reduced, R, S, and P are not reduced. Since there are only eight variables for five slots, when R, S, and P are not reduced, it follows that all five of the remaining variables must be reduced. Thus, when N is reduced, G, L, M, and W must also be reduced.

5. When L is not reduced, M and R must be reduced, and when R is reduced, N is not reduced. Thus, when L is not reduced, N is not reduced. By the same reasoning, when M is not reduced, N is not reduced.

6. When P is reduced, L is not reduced. When L is not reduced, M and R must be reduced. Thus, when P is reduced, M and R must also be reduced. This inference is tested directly on question #8.

Understanding how the two groups work—both separately and together—is clearly a powerful weapon against the questions. In this instance the groups are originated by the final rule, a rule concerning numbers. Always be on the lookout for rules that address the numbers in a game!

Question #6: Global, Could Be True, List. The correct answer choice is (A)

The application of proper List question technique (take a single rule and apply it to all five answer choices consecutively; take another rule and apply it to the remaining answer choices, etc.) eliminates every answer except for answer choice (A). Answer choice (B) is incorrect since both P and L are reduced. Answer choice (C) is incorrect since both N and R are reduced. Answer choice (D) is incorrect since G and S are reduced and W is not reduced. Answer choice (E) is incorrect because all three of L, M, and R are reduced. Consequently, answer choice (A) is correct. Of course, one of the most valuable results of answering a List question correctly is that we now know that the hypothetical G-L-M-N-W is a valid solution to the game.

Question #7: Local, Could Be True, List. The correct answer choice is (E)

Another List question, this time a Local question with the stipulation that W is selected. Do not make the mistake of thinking that because W is reduced that G and S are both reduced! This is a mistaken reversal of the rule. Answer choice (A) is incorrect since two of L, M, and R must be reduced and only M is reduced. Answer choice (B) is incorrect since both N and R are reduced, or alternately, because all three of L, M, and R are reduced. Answer choice (C) is incorrect because both P and L are reduced. Answer choice (D) is incorrect since both N and S are reduced. Consequently, answer choice (E) is correct, and we now know that the hypothetical W-M-P-R-S is a valid solution to the game.

Question #8: Local, Must Be True. The correct answer choice is (B)

As described earlier, when P is reduced, L cannot be reduced. When L is not reduced, M and R must be reduced, and hence answer choice (B) is correct.

Question #9: Local, Could Be True. The correct answer choice is (A)

When L is reduced, P cannot be reduced. Consequently, any answer choice that contains P can be eliminated, and answer choices (B) and (E) can be discarded. When S is reduced, N cannot be reduced and it follows that answer choices (C) and (D) are incorrect. Thus, answer choice (A) is correct.

Question #10: Local, Must Be True. The correct answer choice is (A)

This is one of the key questions of the game. The initial approach taken by most students is to consider the implications of R not being reduced. When R is not reduced, L and M must be reduced, and when L is reduced, P is not reduced. This provides sufficient information to eliminate answer choice (C). At this point the diagram next to the question looks like this:

$$\underline{L} \quad \underline{M} \quad \underline{} \quad \underline{} \quad \underline{}$$
$$\text{5 Reductions}$$
$$\cancel{R} \ \cancel{P}$$

But this leaves four answer choices in contention with no obvious path towards the correct solution. However, there are several approaches to finding the correct answer:

1. Based on our discussion of the reduction of three of the five expenditures G, N, S, P, and W, when P is not reduced then G, W, and N or S must be reduced:

$$\boxed{\underline{L} \quad \underline{M}} \ \boxed{\underline{G} \quad \underline{W} \quad \underline{N/S}}$$
$$\text{5 Reductions}$$

Consequently, only answer choice (A) must be true.

2. Another approach is to make a few hypotheticals based on L and M being selected. The various hypotheticals can then be used to eliminate answer choices.

3. Since making new hypotheticals is useful, checking the hypotheticals created in questions #6 and #7 to see if they apply to question #10 might be even better. Although the W-M-P-R-S hypothetical in question #7 answer choice (E) is inapplicable since R is reduced, the hypothetical in question #6 answer choice (A) meets the criteria in question #10. By applying the G-L-M-N-W solution, we can eliminate answer choices (B), (C), (D), and (E), leaving only answer choice (A).

Remember, always check back to earlier problems to see if you already have enough information to solve the current problem. Of course, only applicable work can be used. Do not forget that you should only use work that you are fully confident is correct. That is why answering List questions correctly is so important!

Question #11: Local, Cannot Be True. The correct answer choice is (C)

When R is reduced, N cannot be reduced. When both M and R are reduced, L cannot be reduced. Answer choice (C), which contains both L and N, is therefore correct.

Question #12: Global, Must Be True. The correct answer choice is (E)

This global question may come as somewhat of a surprise: apparently there is an area of expenditure that is always reduced. Yet this inference did not appear in our initial diagram! To have had this inference would have made the game easier, but it goes to show that there are times where you can miss an inference and still complete the game successfully.

The best way to attack this question is to use previous work. As in question #10, start with the hypotheticals created by questions #6 and #7. G-L-M-N-W, the hypothetical from question #6, shows that P does not have to be reduced, and therefore answer choice (D) can eliminated. W-M-P-R-S, the hypothetical from question #7, shows that G, L, and N do not have to be reduced, and therefore answer choices (A), (B), and (C) can be eliminated. Thus, with little or no work, it can be determined that answer choice (E) is correct. Consider how much faster and easier using this mode of attack is than the alternative of working out several independent solutions.

Abstractly, answer choice (E) is correct because ultimately no valid solution to the game can be created unless that solution contains W. If W is not reduced, then G, P and N must be reduced (see the GSW rule and the group of 3), but when G, P, and N are reduced you cannot reduce R or L (see the second and third rules), and thus the maximum number of reductions that could be made would be four: G, P, N, and M. Because there must be exactly five reductions and eliminating W does not allow for five reductions, it follows that W must be reduced.

One final point must be made about the restriction inherent in the L, M, and R rule. Since only three basic scenarios result under that rule—LM, LR, and MR—one entirely different approach to this game involves creating three templates based on each of those options. Although we feel this approach can be quite effective, its usefulness is dependent on making the inference regarding the three reductions from G, N, S, P, and W. As many students fail to make this inference, the value of the template approach is diminished here.

This is a Pattern game.

The game scenario is careful to stipulate that the strand of beads has only has a single direction, and thus the last bead on a strand is *not* next to the first bead. This is extremely important to understand otherwise you will make false inferences in some of the questions.

The first rule can be diagrammed as follows:

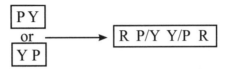

The first rule is quite valuable because it is a "space-eater," meaning that it requires a lot of space to be enacted. When questions ask you to extrapolate out along the strand, this rule should be the first to be examined.

The second rule establishes that the only block that can occur is with the green beads. All other color blocks are prohibited:

The third rule prohibits orange and red beads from being consecutive:

The final rule is easily misinterpreted. The rules states that any *portion* of the strand containing eight consecutive beads must include all colors. Thus, if a strand has 10 beads, then beads 1-8 must contain all colors, beads 2-9 must contain all colors, and beads 3-10 must contain all colors. Understanding this "portional" aspect of the rule is particularly useful on question #17.

Combining all of the above leads to the final setup of the game; note that there is no traditional linear diagram because there is no known number of beads in a strand:

GOPRY [5]

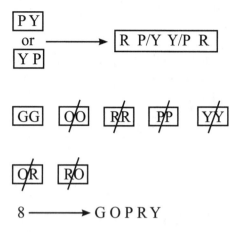

8 ——→ G O P R Y

Question #13: Global, Could Be True, List. The correct answer choice is (C)

In applying the traditional List question approach, remember to apply the rules in the easiest-to-apply and most efficient manner. Thus, in this game, do not start with the last rule—it's too time consuming. Use the middle two rules first, then the first rule, and then the last rule.

Answer choice (A) is incorrect because it violates the third rule.

Answer choice (B) is incorrect because it violates the second rule.

Answer choice (C) is the correct answer.

Answer choice (D) is incorrect because it violates the third rule and the first rule.

Answer choice (E) is incorrect because it violates the fourth rule (there is no O bead).

Question #14: Local, Could Be True, List. The correct answer choice is (D)

The condition in the question stem establishes that O is fourth, and then asks for the beads that could be second and third. When O is fourth, then from the second rule O cannot be third, and from the third rule, R cannot be third:

$$\underline{\quad} \quad \underline{\quad} \quad \underline{\quad} \quad \overset{O}{\underline{\quad}}$$
$$\quad 1 \qquad 2 \qquad 3 \qquad 4$$
$$\qquad\qquad\qquad \cancel{O}$$
$$\qquad\qquad\qquad \cancel{R}$$

This information eliminates answer choices (A) and (B).

Answer choice (C) can be eliminated because it violates the second rule.

Answer choice (D) is the correct answer.

Answer choice (E) can be eliminated because it would violate the first rule: when Y and P are second and third, R would have to be first and fourth.

Question #15: Local, Must Be True. The correct answer choice is (C)

The conditions in the question stem create the following basic diagram:

____	R	G	Y	____	P	R	____
1	2	3	4	5	6	7	8

From the second rule, the first bead cannot be R, the fifth bead cannot be Y or P, and the eighth bead cannot be R. From the third rule, the first bead cannot be O, and the eighth bead cannot be O:

____	R	G	Y	____	P	R	____
1	2	3	4	5	6	7	8
R̸				Y̸			R̸
Ø̸				P̸			Ø̸

At this point, many student move on to the answer choices, but do not forget that the last rule activates when a strand has eight beads, and this question stipulates that this strand has the magic eight beads. Thus, all of the colors must be used in the strand. A glance at the diagram shows that every color except O has been used, so O must appear somewhere among the eight beads. As O cannot be first or eighth, O must be fifth:

____	R	G	Y	O	P	R	____
1	2	3	4	5	6	7	8
R̸				Y̸			R̸
Ø̸				P̸			Ø̸

Accordingly, answer choice (C) is correct.

Question #16: Local, Cannot Be True, List. The correct answer choice is (E)

If the first and second beads are P and Y, then from the first rule the third bead must be R. From the second and third rules, then, the fourth bead cannot be R or O:

P	Y	R	____	____	____
1	2	3	4	5	6
			R̸		
			Ø̸		

If the fourth bead cannot be R, then from the first rule the fifth and six beads cannot be Y and P. Thus, answer choice (E) is correct.

Question #17: Local, Could Be True. The correct answer choice is (E)

The conditions in the question stem produce the following initial diagram:

$$\frac{P}{1} \quad \frac{Y}{2} \quad \frac{\ }{3} \quad \frac{P}{4} \quad \frac{Y}{5} \quad \frac{\ }{6} \quad \frac{\ }{7} \quad \frac{\ }{8} \quad \frac{\ }{9}$$

From the first rule, then, we can infer that the third and sixth beads must be R:

$$\frac{P}{1} \quad \frac{Y}{2} \quad \frac{R}{3} \quad \frac{P}{4} \quad \frac{Y}{5} \quad \frac{R}{6} \quad \frac{\ }{7} \quad \frac{\ }{8} \quad \frac{\ }{9}$$

From the second and third rules, the seventh bead cannot be R or O:

$$\frac{P}{1} \quad \frac{Y}{2} \quad \frac{R}{3} \quad \frac{P}{4} \quad \frac{Y}{5} \quad \frac{R}{6} \quad \frac{\ }{7} \quad \frac{\ }{8} \quad \frac{\ }{9}$$

(with R and O crossed out under bead 7)

The last rule stipulates that all five bead colors must be used in any section of eight beads, and thus far neither G nor O has been used in the first eight beads. Therefore, because the seventh bead cannot be O, it must be G, and the eighth bead must be O:

$$\frac{P}{1} \quad \frac{Y}{2} \quad \frac{R}{3} \quad \frac{P}{4} \quad \frac{Y}{5} \quad \frac{R}{6} \quad \frac{G}{7} \quad \frac{O}{8} \quad \frac{\ }{9}$$

(with R and O crossed out under bead 7)

This information eliminates answer choices (A), (B), and (C). From the third rule, when the eighth bead is O, then the ninth bead cannot be R, which eliminates answer choice (D). Accordingly, answer choice (E) is correct.

Overall, this is a challenging question.

Question #18: Local, Cannot Be True, List. The correct answer choice is (D)

The conditions in the question stem produce the following initial diagram:

R	Y	G	R				
1	2	3	4	5	6	7	8

From the second and third rules, the fifth bead cannot be R or O:

R	Y	G	R				
1	2	3	4	5	6	7	8
				R̸			
				Ø			

At this point, the inference stream appears to stop. So, where should you look to help solve the problem? The key here (as in #16) is to apply the space-eating first rule. If the fifth and sixth beads are P and Y, then the seventh bead will be R. From the third rule the eighth bead cannot be O, which will ultimately cause a violation of the fourth rule because there will be no room for O among the first eight beads. Hence, P and Y cannot be fifth and sixth, and answer choice (D) is correct.

This is a Grouping/Linear Combination game.

There are three variable sets in this game: the songs, the vocalists, and the performance order. The performance order should be chosen as the base, and the other two variable sets stacked on top:

Songs: O P T X Y Z [6]
Vocalists: G H L [3]

Voc: ___ ___ ___ ___ ___ ___

Song: ___ ___ ___ ___ ___ ___
      1   2   3   4   5   6

The first two rules can be combined to make a super sequencing chain:

$$Y >\cdots\cdots\cdots \begin{array}{c} T \\ O > P > Z \end{array}$$

The only song not addressed in the sequence is X, which can be played at any point in the performance order. Thus, because Y must be performed before four other songs, only X or Y can be played first, and Y must be played first or second. We can also draw a number of other Not Laws from the sequence:

Songs: O P T X Y Z [6]
Vocalists: G H L [3]

Voc: ___ ___ ___ ___ ___ ___

Song: X/Y   Y/   ___ ___ ___ T/X/Z
      1   2   3   4   5   6
         Z̶   X̶   X̶   X̶   X̶
         P̶   Z̶   O̶   O̶
                         P̶

Note that with three Not Laws on the sixth performance, we can infer that T, X, or Z performs last.

The third and fourth rules establish the songs that each vocalist can sing:

$$\frac{G}{X\ Y\ Z} \qquad \frac{H}{T\ P\ X} \qquad \frac{L}{O\ P\ X}$$

In examining the songs each vocalist can sing, some notable observations can be made:

Because Y and Z appear only on George's list, Y and Z must be performed by George.

Because T appears only on Helen's list, T must be performed by Helen.

Because O appears only on Leslie's list, O must be performed by Leslie.

Because P appears on Helen's and Leslie's lists, P must be performed by Helen or Leslie.

Because X appears on all three vocalist's lists, X can be performed by any of the vocalists.

The facts above can be shown as subscripts:

$$\frac{G}{X\ Y_G\ Z_G} \qquad \frac{H}{T_H\ P_{H/L}\ X} \qquad \frac{L}{O_L\ P_{H/L}\ X}$$

The subscripts can be attached to the super-sequence created by the first two rules:

$$Y_G > \begin{array}{c} T_H \\ \text{-----------} \\ O_L > P_{H/L} > Z_G \end{array}$$

The final rule indicates that the same vocalists cannot perform both first and last

$$1_V \longleftrightarrow 6_V$$

Also, because the same vocalists cannot perform both first and last and George performs both Y and Z, if Y is performed first, Z is not performed last, and via the contrapositive, if Z is performed last, Y is not performed first:

$$Y_1 \longrightarrow \cancel{Z_6}$$
$$Z_6 \longrightarrow \cancel{X_1}$$

Combining all of this information results in the final diagram for the game:

Songs: O P T X Y Z ^{6}
Vocalists: G H L ^{3}

Voc: __ __ __ __ __ __

Song:	X/Y	Y/				T/X/Z
	1	2	3	4	5	6
		$\cancel{Z}$	$\cancel{Y}$	$\cancel{X}$	$\cancel{X}$	$\cancel{X}$
		$\cancel{P}$	$\cancel{Z}$		$\cancel{O}$	$\cancel{O}$
						$\cancel{P}$

$$\dfrac{G}{X\,Y_G\,Z_G} \quad \dfrac{H}{T_H\,P_{H/L}\,X} \quad \dfrac{L}{O_L\,P_{H/L}\,X}$$

$$Y_G > \overset{T_H}{\underset{O_L > P_{H/L} > Z_G}{\text{- - - - - - - - - - -}}}$$

$$1_V \longleftrightarrow\!\!\!\!| \longrightarrow 6_V$$

$$Y_1 \longrightarrow \cancel{Z_6}$$
$$Z_6 \longrightarrow \cancel{X_1}$$

Question #19: Global, Could Be True. The correct answer choice is (E)

The first rule eliminates answer choice (A), which places T earlier than Y.

The second rule prohibits answer choice (B), which places P later than Z, and answer choice (D), which places O later than P.

This leaves only answer choices (C) and (E). The rule that we have not yet considered is the final one; since G is the only one among the three vocalists who can perform Y, and is also the only one who can perform Z, answer choice (C) can be ruled out, because the order provided by this answer choice would require G to perform both first and last.

This leaves answer choice (E), which is the correct answer choice.

Question #20: Global, Must Be True. The correct answer choice is (C)

The third and fourth rules of this game dictate which vocalists must perform certain songs: as discussed in during the setup and in question #19, G must be the one to perform both Y and Z, because the others are both unable to perform those songs. Similarly, H must be the one to perform T, because neither of the other singers are able to perform that song. Thus, choice (C) is the correct answer choice.

Question #21: Global, Could Be True, List. The correct answer choice is (D)

As discussed during the setup, the Not Laws on the sixth performance dictate that only T, X, or Z could be the last song performed. Hence, answer choice (D) is correct.

Question #22: Local, Must Be True. The correct answer choice is (D)

As discussed during the setup, if X is performed first, then Y must be performed second. Consequently, answer choice (D) is correct.

Question #23: Global, Could Be True, Except, List. The correct answer choice is (B)

Because George must perform both Y and Z, and the same vocalists cannot perform both first and last, Y and Z cannot be performed first and sixth. Thus, answer choice (B) is not an acceptable schedule, and answer choice (B) is correct.

Question #24: Local, Could Be True. The correct answer choice is (C)

If Y is performed first, then according to the inference above, Z cannot be performed sixth. Thus, in this question O cannot be performed fourth because that would force P to be performed fifth and Z to be performed sixth. Therefore, answer choices (A), (B), and (E) can be eliminated because each places O fourth. Additionally, answer choice (B) can be eliminated because O must be performed earlier than Z.

Answer choice (D) can be eliminated since the Y-X-P-Z lineup in the first four performances violates the second rule.

Answer choice (C) is thus correct.

THE POWERSCORE LSAT LOGIC GAMES SETUPS ENCYCLOPEDIA

CONTACTING POWERSCORE

POWERSCORE INTERNATIONAL HEADQUARTERS:

PowerScore Test Preparation
57 Hasell Street
Charleston, SC 29401

Toll-free information number: (800) 545-1750
Website: www.powerscore.com
Email: lsat@powerscore.com

POWERSCORE LSAT PUBLICATIONS INFORMATION:

For information on all PowerScore LSAT publications.

Website: www.powerscore.com/pubs.htm

POWERSCORE FULL-LENGTH LSAT COURSE INFORMATION:

Complete preparation for the LSAT.
Classes available nationwide.

Web: www.powerscore.com/lsat
Request Information: www.powerscore.com/contact.htm

POWERSCORE VIRTUAL LSAT COURSE INFORMATION:

45 hours of online, interactive, real-time preparation for the LSAT.
Classes available worldwide.

Web: www.powerscore.com/lsat/virtual
Request Information: www.powerscore.com/contact.htm

POWERSCORE WEEKEND LSAT COURSE INFORMATION:

Fast and effective LSAT preparation: 16 hour courses, 99th percentile instructors, and real LSAT questions.

Web: www.powerscore.com/lsat/weekend
Request Information: www.powerscore.com/contact.htm

POWERSCORE LSAT TUTORING INFORMATION:

One-on-one meetings with a PowerScore LSAT expert.

Web: www.powerscore.com/lsat/content_tutoring.cfm
Request Information: www.powerscore.com/contact.htm

POWERSCORE LAW SCHOOL ADMISSIONS COUNSELING INFORMATION:

Personalized application and admission assistance.

Web: www.powerscore.com/lsat/content_admissions.cfm
Request Information: www.powerscore.com/contact.htm